Thomas Carlyle

History of Friedrich 2. of Prussia

Called Frederick the Great

Thomas Carlyle

History of Friedrich 2. of Prussia
Called Frederick the Great

ISBN/EAN: 9783741161421

Manufactured in Europe, USA, Canada, Australia, Japa

Cover: Foto ©Thomas Meinert / pixelio.de

Manufactured and distributed by brebook publishing software
(www.brebook.com)

Thomas Carlyle

History of Friedrich 2. of Prussia

EACH VOLUME SOLD SEPARATELY.

COLLECTION
OF
BRITISH AUTHORS

TAUCHNITZ EDITION.

VOL. 700.

FREDERICK THE GREAT BY CARLYLE

VOL. 8.

LEIPZIG: BERNHARD TAUCHNITZ.

PARIS: C. REINWALD & CIE, 15, RUE DES SAINTS PÈRES.

[illegible]CHNITZ EDITION.

Each volume ½ Thlr.

ADAMS: Sacred Allegories 1 v.
[illegible]UILAR: Home Influence 2 v. The [illegible]compense 2 v.
[illegible]lla 1 v. Carr of Carrlyon 2 v. The [illegible]. In that State of Life 1 v.
[illegible]RTH: Windsor Castle 1 v. Saint [illegible] Jack Sheppard (w. portr.) 1 v. The [illegible] Witches 2 v. The Star-Chamber 2 v. [illegible] Flitch of Bacon 1 v. The Spendthrift 1 v. [illegible]ervyn Clitheroe 2 v. Ovingdean Grange 1 v. The Constable of the Tower 1 v. The Lord Mayor of London 2 v. Cardinal Pole 2 v. John Law 2 v. The Spanish Match 2 v. The Constable de Bourbon 2 v. Old Court 2 v. Myddleton Pomfret 2 v. South-Sea Bubble 2 v. Hilary St. Ives 2 v. Talbot Harland 1 v. Tower Hill 1 v.
ALL FOR GREED 1 v. Love the Avenger 2 v.
MISS AUSTEN: Sense and Sensibility 1 v. Mansfield Park 1 v. Pride and Prejudice 1 v. Northanger Abbey, and Persuasion 1 v.
NINA BALATKA 1 v.
REV. R. H. BAYNES: Lyra Anglicana 1 v.
CURRER BELL: Jane Eyre 2 v. Shirley 2 v. Villette 2 v. The Professor 1 v.
E. & A. BELL: Wuthering Heights, and Agnes Grey 2 v.
LADY BLESSINGTON: Meredith 1 v. Strathern 2 v. Femme de Chambre 1 v. Herbert 2 v. Country Quarters (w. portr.) 2 v.
BRADDON: Lady Audley's Secret 2 v. Aurora Floyd 2 v. Eleanor's Victory 2 v. Marchmont's Legacy 2 v. Henry Dunbar 2 v. Doctor's Wife 2 v. Only a Clod 2 v. Sir Jasper's Tenant 2 v. Lady's Mile 2 v. Rupert Godwin 2 v. Dead-Sea Fruit 2 v. Run to Earth 2 v. Fenton's Quest 2 v.
BROOKS: The Silver Cord 3 v. Sooner or Later 3 v.
BROWN: Rab and his Friends 1 v.
TOM BROWN'S School Days 1 v.
BULWER (LORD LYTTON): Pelham (w. portr.) 1 v. Eugene Aram 1 v. Paul Clifford 1 v. Zanoni 1 v. Pompeii 1 v. The Disowned 1 v. Ernest Maltravers 1 v. Alice 1 v. Eva, and the Pilgrims of the Rhine 1 v. Devereux 1 v. Godolphin and Falkland 1 v. [illegible]enzi 1 v. Night and

S. T. COLERIDGE: The Poems 1 v.
WILKIE COLLINS: After Dark 1 v. Hide and Seek 2 v. A Plot in Private Life 1 v. The Dead Secret 2 v. The Woman in White 2 v. Basil 1 v. No Name 3 v. Antonina 2 v. Armadale 3 v. The Moonstone 2 v. Man and Wife 3 v.
FENIMORE COOPER: The Spy (w. portr.) 1 v. The Two Admirals 1 v. Jack O'Lantern 1 v.
THE TWO COSMOS 1 v.
MISS CRAIK: Lost and Won 1 v. Faith Unwin's Ordeal 1 v. Leslie Tyrrell 1 v. Winifred's Wooing 1 v. Mildred 1 v. Esther Hill's Secret 2 v.
MISS CUMMINS: Lamplighter 1 v. Mabel Vaughan 1 v. El Fureidis 1 v. Haunted Hearts 1 v.
DE FOE: Robinson Crusoe 1 v.
CHARLES DICKENS: The Pickwick Club (w. portr.) 2 v. American Notes 1 v. Oliver Twist 1 v. Nicholas Nickleby 2 v. Sketches 1 v. Martin Chuzzlewit 2 v. A Christmas Carol; the Chimes; the Cricket 1 v. Master Humphrey's Clock 3 v. Pictures from Italy 1 v. The Battle of Life; the Haunted Man 1 v. Dombey and Son 3 v. Copperfield 3 v. Bleak House 4 v. A Child's History of England (2 v. 8° 27 Ngr.). Hard Times 1 v. Little Dorrit 4 v. A Tale of two Cities 2 v. Hunted Down; the Uncommercial Traveller 1 v. Great Expectations 2 v. Christmas Stories 1 v. Our Mutual Friend 4 v. Somebody's Luggage; Mrs. Lirriper's Lodgings; Mrs. Lirriper's Legacy 1 v. Doctor Marigold's Prescriptions; Mugby Junction 1 v. No Thoroughfare 1 v. Edwin Drood 2 v.
B. DISRAELI: Coningsby 1 v. Sybil 1 v. Contarini Fleming (w. portr.) 1 v. Alroy 1 v. Tancred 2 v. Venetia 2 v. Vivian Grey 2 v. Henrietta Temple 1 v. Lothair 2 v.
DIXON: Lord Bacon 1 v. The Holy Land 2 v. New America 2 v. Spiritual Wives 2 v. Her Majesty's Tower 4 v.
MISS A. B. EDWARDS: Barbara's History 2 v. Miss Carew 2 v. Hand and Glove 1 v. Half a Million of Money 2 v. Debenham's Vow 2 v.
MRS. EDWARDS: Archie Lovell 2 v. Steven Lawrence 2 v.
ELIOT: Scenes of Clerical Life 2 v. Adam Bede 2 v. The Mill on the Floss 2 v. Silas Marner 1 v. Romola 2 v. Felix Holt 2 v.
THE STORY OF ELIZABETH 1 v. The

COLLECTION

OF

BRITISH AUTHORS.

VOL. 700.

FREDERICK THE GREAT BY THOMAS CARLYLE.

VOL. VIII.

HISTOR'

OF

FRIEDRICH II. O PRUSSIA,

CALLED

FREDERICK TH GREAT.

BY

THOMAS CARI E.

COPYRIGHT EDITION.

VOL. VIII.

LEIPZIG

BERNHARD TAUCHNITZ

1864.

The Right of Translation is reserved.

CONTENTS

OF VOLUME VIII.

BOOK XV.

SECOND SILESIAN WAR, IMPORTANT EPISODE IN THE GENERAL EUROPEAN ONE. 1744-1745.

BOOK XVI.

THE TEN YEARS OF PEACE. 1746-1756.

BOOK XV.

SECOND SILESIAN WAR, IMPORTANT EPISODE IN THE GENERAL EUROPEAN ONE.

15th Aug. 1744—25th Dec. 1745.

CHAPTER I.

PRELIMINARY: HOW THE MOMENT ARRIVED.

Battle being once seen to be inevitable, it was Friedrich's plan not to wait for it, but to give it. Thanks to Friedrich Wilhelm and himself, there is no Army, nor ever was any, in such continual preparation. Military people say, "Some Countries take six months, some twelve, to get in motion for war: but in three weeks Prussia can be across the marches, and upon the throat of its enemy." Which is an immense advantage to little Prussia among its big neighbours. "Some Countries have a longer sword than Prussia; but none can unsheathe it so soon:" — we hope, too, it is moderately sharp, when wielded by a deft hand.

The French, as was intimated, are in great vigour, this Year; thoroughly provoked; and especially since Friedrich sent his Rothenburg among them, have been doing their very utmost. Their main effort is in the Netherlands, at present; — and indeed, as happened, continues all through this War to be. They by no means intend, or ever did, to neglect Teutschland; yet it turns out, they have pretty much done with their fighting there. And next Year, driven or led by accidents of various kinds, they quit it altogether; and turning their whole strength upon the Netherlands and Italy, chiefly on the Netherlands, leave Friedrich, much to his astonishment, with the German War hanging wholly round *his* neck, and take no charge of it farther! In which, to Friedrich's Biographers, there is this inestimable benefit, if far the reverse to Friedrich's self: That we shall soon have done with the French, then; with them and with so much else; and may, in time coming, for most part, leave their huge Sorcerer's Sabbath of a European War to dance itself out, well in the distance, not encumbering us farther, like a circumambient Bedlam, as it has hitherto done. Courage, reader! Let us give, in a glance or two, some notion of the course things took, and what moment it was when Friedrich struck in: — whom alone, or almost alone, we hope to follow thenceforth; "Dismal Swamp" (so gracious was Heaven to us) lying now mostly to rearward, little as we hoped it!

It was mere accident, a series of bad accidents, that led King Louis and his Ministers into gradually forsaking Friedrich. They were the farthest in the world from intending such a thing. Contrariwise, what brain-beating, diplomatic spider-weaving, practical contriving, now and afterwards, for that object; especially now! Rothenburg, Noailles, Belleisle, Cardinal Tencin, have been busy; not less the mistress Châteauroux, who admires Friedrich, being indeed a high-minded unfortunate female, as they say; and has thrown out Amelot, not for stammering alone. They are able, almost high people, this new Châteauroux Ministry, compared with some; and already show results.

Nay, what is most important of all, France has (unconsciously, or by mere help of Noailles and luck) got a real General to her Armies: Comte de Saxe, now Maréchal de Saxe; who will shine very splendent in these Netherland operations, — counter-shone by mere Wades, D'Ahrembergs, Cumberlands, — in this and the Four following Years. Noailles had always recognised Comte de Saxe; had long striven for him, in Official quarters; and here gets the light of him unveiled at last, and set on a high place: loyal Noailles.

This was the Year, this 1744, when Louis XV., urged by his Châteauroux, the high-souled unfortunate female, appeared in person at the head of his troops: "Go, Sire, go, *mon Chou* (and I will accompany); show yourself where a King should be, at the head of your troops; be a second Louis-le-Grand!" Which he did, his Châteauroux and he; actually went to the Netherlands, with baggage-train immeasurable, including not cooks only, but play-actors with their thunder-barrels (off from Paris, May 3d), to the admiration of the Universe.* Took the command, nominal-command, first days of June; and captured in no-time Menin, Ipres, Furnes, and the Fort of Knock, and as much of the Austrian Netherlands as he liked, — that is to say, saw Noailles and Saxe do it; — walking rapidly forward from Siege to Siege, with a most thundering artillery; old Marshal Wade and consorts dismally eating their victuals, and looking on from the distance, unable to attempt the least stroke in opposition. So that the Dutch Barrier, if anybody now cared for it, did go all flat; and the Balance of Power gets kicked out of its sacred pivot: to such purpose have the Dutch been hoisted! Terrible to think of; — had not there, from the opposite quarter, risen a surprising counterpoise; had not there been a Prince Karl, with

* Adelung, IV. 113; Barbier, II. 391, 394; Dulaure, *Hist. de Paris*; &c.

his 70,000, pressing victoriously over the Rhine; which stayed the French in these sacrilegious procedures.

Prince Karl gets across the Rhine (20th June—2d July 1744.)

Prince Karl, some weeks ago, at Heilbronn, joined his Rhine Army, which had gathered thither from the Austrian side, through Baiern, and from the Hither-Austrian or Swabian Winter-quarters; with full intent to be across the Rhine, and home upon Elsass and the Compensation Countries this Summer, under what difficulties soever. Karl, or as some whisper, old Marshal Traun, who is nominally second in command, do make a glorious campaign of it, this Year; — and lift the Cause of Liberty, at one time, to the highest pitch it ever reached. Here, in brief terms, is Prince Karl's Operation on the Rhine, much admired by military men:

"*Stockstadt*, *June 20th*, 1744. Some thirty and odd miles "north of Mannheim, the Rhine, before turning westward at "Mainz, makes one other of its many Islands (of which there "are hundreds since the leap at Schaffhausen): one other, "and I think the biggest of them all; perhaps two miles by "five; which the Germans call *Kuhkopf* (Cowhead), from the "shape it has, — a narrow semi-ellipse; River there splitting "in two, one split (the western) going straight, the other "bending luxuriantly round: so that the *hind*-head or straight "end of the Island lies towards France, and the round end, "or cow-*lips* (so to speak) towards native Teutschland, and "the woody Hills of the Berg-Strasse thereabouts. Stock-"stadt, chief little Town looking over into this Cowhead "Island, lies under the *chin:* understand only farther that "the German branch carries more than two-thirds of the "River; that on the Island itself there is no town, or post of "defence; and that Stockstadt is the place for getting over.

"Coigny and the French, some 40,000, are guarding the River "hereabouts, with lines, with batteries, cordons, the best "they can; Seckendorf, with 20,000 more ('Imperial' Old-"Bavarian Troops, revivified, recruited by French pay), is "in his garrison of Philipsburg, ready to help when needed:" —not moulting now, at Wembdingen, in that dismal manner; new-feathered now into 'Kaiser's Army;' waiting in his Philipsburg to guard the River there. "Coigny's French have "ramparts, ditches, not quite unfurnished, on their own "shore, opposite this Cowhead Island (*Isle de Héron*, as they "call it); looking over to the hind-head, namely: but they "have nothing considerable there; and in the Island itself, "nothing whatever. 'If now Stockstadt were suddenly 'snatched by us,' thinks Karl; — 'if a few pontoons were 'nimbly swung in?'

"June 20th, — Coigny's people all shooting *feu-de-joie*, for "that never enough to be celebrated Capture of Menin and "the Dutch Barrier a fortnight ago, — this is managed to be "done. The active General Bärenklau, active Brigadier "Daun under him, pushes rapidly across into Kuhkopf; "rapidly throws up entrenchments, ramparts, mounts cannon, "digs himself in, — greatly to Coigny's astonishment; whose "people hereabouts, and in all their lines and posts, are busy "shooting *feu-de-joie* for those immortal Dutch victories, at "the moment, and never dreaming of such a thing. Fresh "force floods in, Prince Karl himself arrives next day, in "support of Bärenklau; Coigny (head-quarters at Speyer, "forty miles south) need not attempt dislodging him; but "must stand upon his guard, and prepare for worse. Which "he does with diligence; shifting northward into those Stock-"stadt-Mainz parts; calling Seckendorf across the River, and "otherwise doing his best, — for about ten days more, when "worse, and almost worst, did verily befal him.

"No attempt was made on Bärenklau; nor, beyond the "alarming of the Coigny-Seckendorf people, did anything "occur in Cowhead Island, — unless it were the finis of an "ugly bully and ruffian, who has more than once afflicted us: "which may be worth one word. Colonel Mentzel" (copper-faced Colonel, originally Playactor, "Spy in Persia," and I know not what) "had been at the seizure of Kuhkopf; a pro-"minent man. Whom, on the fifth day after ('June 25th').

"Prince Karl overwhelmed with joy, by handing him a Patent "of Generalcy: 'Just received from Court, my Friend, on "'account of your merits old and late.' — 'Aha,' said Bärenklau, congratulating warmly: 'Dine with me, then, Herr "'General Mentzel, this very day. The Prince himself is to be "'there, Highness of Hessen-Darmstadt, and who not; all are "'impatient to drink your health!' "Mentzel had a glorious "dinner; still more glorious drink, — Prince Karl and the "others, it is said, egging him into much wild bluster and "gasconade, to season their much wine. Eminent swill of "drinking, with the loud course talk supposable, on the part "of Mentzel and consorts did go on, in this manner, all afternoon: in the evening, drunk Mentzel came out for air; went "strutting and staggering about; emerging finally on the "platform of some rampart, face of him huge and red as that "of the foggiest rising Moon; — and stood, looking over into "the Lorraine Country; belching out a storm of oaths, as to "his taking it, as to his doing this and that; and was even "flourishing his sword by way of accompaniment; when, lo, "whistling slightly through the summer air, a rifle-ball from "some sentry on the French side (writers say, it was a French "drummer, grown impatient, and snatching a sentry's piece) "took the brain of him, or the belly of him; and he rushed "down at once, a totally collapsed monster, and mere heap "of dead ruin, never to trouble mankind more." * For which my readers and I are rather thankful. Voltaire, and perhaps other memorable persons, sometimes mention this brute (miraculous to the Plebs and Gazetteers); otherwise eternal oblivion were the best we could do with him. Trenck also, readers will be glad to understand, ends in jail and bedlam by and by.

"Prince Karl had not the least intention of crossing by "this Cowhead Island. Nevertheless he set about two other "Bridges in the neighbourhood, nearer Mainz (few miles "below that City); kept manœuvering his Force, in huge "half-moon, round that quarter, and mysteriously up and "down; alarming Coigny wholly into the Mainz region. For "the space of ten days; and then, stealing off to Schröck, a "little Rhine Village above Philipsburg, many miles away "from Coigny and his vigilances, he —

* *Guerre de Bohême*, III. 165.

"*Night of 30th June — 1st July*, Suddenly shot Pandour "Trenck, followed by Nadasti and 6,000, across at Schröck; "who scattered Seckendorf's poor outposts thereabouts to the "winds; 'built a bridge before morning, and next day an-"'other.' Next day Prince Karl in person appeared; and on "the 3d of July, had his whole Army with its luggages across; "and had seized the Lines of Lauterburg and Weissenburg "(celebrated northern defence of Elsass), — much to Coigny's "amazement; and remained inexpugnable there, with Elsass "open to him, and to Coigny shut, for the present!* Coigny "made bitter wail, accusation, blame of Seckendorf, blame "of men and of things; even tried some fighting, Seckendorf "too doing feats, to recover those Lines of Weissenburg: but "could not do it. And, in fact, blazing to and fro in that "excited rather than luminous condition, could not do any-"thing; except retire into the strong posts of the background; "and send express on express, swifter than the wind if you "can, to a victorious King overturning the Dutch Barrier: "'Help, your Majesty, or we are lost; and France is — what "'shall I say!'"

"Admirable feat of Strategy! What a General, this Prince Karl!" exclaimed mankind, — Cause-of-Liberty mankind with special enthusiasm; and took to writing *Lives* of Prince Karl,** as well as tar-burning and *te-deum*-ing on an extensive scale. For it had sent the Cause of Liberty bounding up again to the top of things, this of crossing the Rhine, in such fashion. And in effect, the Cause of Liberty, and Prince Karl himself, had risen hereby to their acme or culminating point in World-History; not to continue long at such height, little as they dreamt of that, among their tar-burnings. The feat itself, — contrived by Nadasti,

* Adelung, IV. 139-141.

** For instance, *The Life of his Highness Prince Charles of &c., with &c. &c.* (London, 1746); one of the most distracted Blotches ever published under the name of Book; — awakening thoughts of a public dimness very considerable indeed, to which this could offer itself as lamp!

people say, and executed (what was the real difficulty) by Traun, — brought Prince Karl very great renown, this Year; and is praised by Friedrich himself, now and afterwards, as masterly, as Julius Cæsar's method, and the proper way of crossing rivers (when executable) in face of an enemy. And indeed Prince Karl, owing to Traun or not, is highly respectable in the way of Generalship at present; and did in these Five Months, from June onward, really considerable things. At his very acme of Life, as well as of Generalship; which, alas, soon changed, poor man; never to culminate again. He had got, at the beginning of the Year, the high Maria Theresa's one Sister, Archduchess Maria Anna, to Wife;* the crown of long mutual attachment: she safe now at Brussels, diligent Co-Regent, and in a promising family-way; he here walking on victorious: — need any man be happier? No man can be supremely happy long; and this General's strategic felicity and his domestic were fatally cut down almost together. The Cause of Liberty, too, now at the top of its orbit, was — But let us stick by our Excerpting!

"*Dunkirk, 19th July* 1744" (Princess Ulrique's Wedding, just two days ago). "King Louis, on hearing of the Job's-"news from Elsass, instantly suspended his Conquests in "Flanders; detached Noailles, detached this one and that, "double-quick, Division after Division (leaving Saxe, with "45,000, to his own resources, and the fatuities of Marshal "Wade); and, 19th July, himself hastens off from Dunkirk "(leaving much of the luggage, but not the Châteauroux "behind him), to save his Country, poor soul. But could not,

* Age then twenty-five gone: "born 14th September 1718; married to "Prince Karl, 7th January 1744; died, of childbirth, 16th December same "year" (Hormayr, *Œsterreichischer Plutarch.* iv. erstes Bändchen, 54).

"in the least, save it; the reverse rather. August 4th, he "got to Metz, Belleisle's strong Town, about 100 miles from "the actual scene; his detached reinforcements, say 50,000 "men or so, hanging out ahead like flame-clouds, but uncer-"tain how to act;—Noailles being always cunctatious, in "time of crisis, and poor Louis himself nothing of a Cloud-"Compeller;—and then,

"*Metz, August 8th*, The Most Christian King fell ill; danger-"ously, dreadfully, just like to die. Which entirely paralysed "Noailles and Company, or reduced them to mere hysterics, "and excitement of the unluminous kind. And filled France "in general, Paris in particular, with terror, lamentation, "prayers of forty hours; and such a paroxysm of hero-worship "as was never seen for such an object before." *

For the Cause of Liberty here, we consider, was the culminating moment; Elsass, Lorraine, and the Three Bishoprics lying in their quasi-moribund condition; Austrian claims of Compensation ceasing to be visions of the heated brain, and gaining some footing on the Earth as facts. Prince Karl is here actually in Elsass, master of the strong passes; elate in heart, he and his; France, again, as if fallen paralytic, into temporary distraction; offering for resistance nothing hitherto but that universal wailing of mankind, Hero-worship of a thrice-lamentable nature, and the Prayers of Forty-Hours! Most Christian Majesty, now *in extremis*, centre of the basest hubbub that ever was, is dismissing Châteauroux. Noailles, Coigny and Company hang well back upon the Hill regions, and strong posts which are not yet menaced; or fly vaguely, more or less distractedly, hither and thither; not in the least like fighting Karl, much less like beating him. Karl has Germany free at his back (nay it is a German

* Espagnac, II. 12; Adelung, IV. 180; *Fastes de Louis XV*, II. 423; &c. &c.

population round him here); neither haversack nor cartridge-box like to fail: before him are only a Noailles and consorts, flying vaguely about, — and there is in Karl, or under the same cloak with him at present, a talent of manœuvring men, which even Friedrich finds masterly. If old Marshal Wade, at the other end of the line, should chance to awaken and press home on Saxe, and his remnant of French, with right vigour? In fact, there was not, that I can see, for centuries past, not even at the Siege of Lille in Marlborough's time, a more imminent peril for France.

Friedrich decides to intervene.

King Friedrich, on hearing of these Rhenish emergencies and of King Louis's heroic advance to the rescue, perceived that for himself too the moment was come; and hastened to inform heroic Louis, That though the terms of their Bargain were not yet completed, Sweden, Russia and other points being still in a pendent condition, he, Friedrich, — with an eye to success of their Joint Adventure, and to the indispensability of joint action, energy, and the top of one's speed now or never, — would, by the middle of this same August, be on the field with 100,000 men. "An invasion of Bohemia, will not that astonish Prince Karl; and bring him to his Rhine-Bridges again? Over which, if your Most Christian Majesty be active, he will not get, except in a half or wholly ruined state. Follow him close; send the rest of your force to threaten Hanover; sit well on the skirts of Prince Karl. Him as he hurries homeward, ruined or half-ruined, him, or whatever Austrian will fight, I do my best to beat. We may have Bohemia, and a beaten Austria, this very Autumn: see, — and, in one Campaign, there is Peace ready for us!" This is Friedrich's scheme of action; success certain, thinks he, if only there be energy, activity, on your side, as there shall be on mine; — and has sent Count Schmettau, filled with fiery speed and determination, to keep the French full of the like, and concert mutual operations.

"Magnanimous!" exclaim Noailles and the paralysed French Gentlemen (King Louis, I think, now past speech, for Schmettau only came, August 9th): "Most sublime behaviour, on his Prussian Majesty's part!" own they. And truly it is a fine manful indifference (by no means so common as it should be) to all interests, to all considerations, but that of a Joint Enterprise one has engaged in. And truly, furthermore, it was immediate salvation to the paralysed French Gentlemen, in that alarming crisis; though they did not much recognise it afterwards as such; and indeed were conspicuously forgetful of all parts of it, when their own danger was over.

Maria Theresa's feelings may be conceived; George II.'s feelings; and what the Cause of Liberty in general felt, and furiously said and complained, when, — suddenly as a *Deus ex machinâ*, or Supernal Genie in the Minor Theatres, — Friedrich stept in. Precisely in this supreme crisis, 7th August 1744, Friedrich's Minister, Graf von Dohna, at Vienna, has given notice of the Frankfurt Union, and solemn Engagement entered into: "Obliged in honour and conscience; will "and must now step forth to right an injured Kaiser;

"cannot stand these high procedures against an Imperial Majesty chosen by all the Princes of the Reich, "this unheard-of protest that the Kaiser is no Kaiser, "as if all Germany were but Austria and the Queen of "Hungary's. Prussian Majesty has not the least "quarrel of his own with the Queen of Hungary, "stands true, and will stand, by the Treaty of Berlin "and Breslau; — only, with certain other German "Princes, has done what all German Princes and "peoples not Austrian are bound to do, on behalf of "their down-trodden Kaiser, formed a Union of Frankfurt; and will, with armed hand if indispensable, "endeavour to see right done in that matter."*

This is the astonishing fact for the Cause of Liberty; and no clamour and execration will avail anything. This man is prompt, too; does not linger in getting out his sword, when he has talked of it. Prince Karl's Operation is likely to be marred amazingly. If this swift King (comparable to the old Serpent for devices) were to burst forth from his Silesian strengths; tread sharply on the *tail* of Prince Karl's Operation, and bring back the formidably fanged head of *it* out of Alsace, five hundred miles all at once, — there would be a business!

We will now quit the Rhine Operations, which indeed are not now of moment; Friedrich being suddenly the key of events again. I add only, what readers are vaguely aware of, that King Louis did not die; that he lay at death's door for precisely one week (8th-15th August), symptoms mending on the 15th. In the interim, — Grand-Almoner Fitz-James (Uncle of our

* In *Adelung*, iv. 155-6, the Declaration itself (Audience, "7th August 1744;" Dohna off homeward "on the second day after").

Conte di Spinolli) insisting that a certain Cardinal, who had got the Sacraments in hand, should insist; and endless ministerial intrigue being busy, — moribund Louis had, when it came to the Sacramental point, been obliged to dismiss his Châteauroux. Poor Châteauroux; an unfortunate female; yet, one almost thinks, the best man among them: dismissed at Metz here, and like to be mobbed! That was the one issue of King Louis's death-sickness. Sublime sickness; during which all Paris wept aloud, in terror and sorrow, like a child that has lost its mother and sees a mastiff coming; wept sublimely, and did the Prayers of Forty-Hours; and called King Louis *Le Bien-aimé* (The Well-beloved): — merely some obstruction in the royal bowels, it turned out; — a good cathartic, and the Prayers of Forty-Hours, quite reinstated matters. Nay reinstated even Châteauroux, some time after, — "the Devil being well again," and, as the Proverb says, quitting his monastic view. Reinstated Châteauroux: but this time, poor creature, she continued only about a day: — "Sudden fever, from excitement," said the Doctors: "Fever? Poison you mean!" whispered others, and looked for changes in the Ministry. Enough, oh enough! —

Old Marshal Wade did not awaken, though bawled to by his Ligoniers and others, and much shaken about, poor old gentleman. "No artillery to speak of," murmured he; "want baggage-wagons, too!" and lay still. "Here is artillery!" answered the Official people; "With my own money I will buy you baggage-wagons!" answered the high Maria Anna, in her own name and her Prince Karl's, who are Joint-Governors there. Possibly he would have awakened, had they given him time. But time, in War especially, is the thing that is never given. Once Friedrich *had* struck in, the moment was gone by. Poor old Wade! Of him also enough.

CHAPTER II.

FRIEDRICH MARCHES UPON PRAG, CAPTURES PRAG.

It was on Saturday, "early in the morning," 15th August 1744, that Friedrich set out, attended by his two eldest Brothers, Prince of Prussia and Prince Henri, from Potsdam, towards this new Adventure, which proved so famous since. Sudden, swift, to the world's astonishment; — actually on march here, in three Columns (two through Saxony by various routes south-eastward, one from Silesia through Glatz south-westward), to invade Bohemia: rumour says 100,000 strong, fact itself says upwards of 80,000, on their various routes, converging towards Prag.* His Columns, especially his Saxon Columns, are already on the road; he joins one Column, this night, at Wittenberg; and is bent, through Saxony, towards the frontiers of Bohemia, at the utmost military speed he has.

Through Saxony about 60,000 go: he has got the Kaiser's Order to the Government of Saxony, "Our august Ally, requiring on our Imperial business a transit through you;" — and Winterfeld, an excellent soldier and negotiator, has gone forward to present said Order. A Document which flurries the Dresden Officials beyond measure. Their King is in Warsaw; their King, if here, could do little; and indeed has

* *Helden-Geschichte*, II. 1105. Orlich (II. 25, 27) enumerates the various regiments.

been inclining to Maria Theresa this long while. And Winterfeld insists on such despatch; — and not even the Duke of Weissenfels is in Town. Dresden Officials "send off five couriers and thirteen estafettes" to the poor old Duke;* get him at last; and — The march is already taking effect; they may as well consent to it: what can they do but consent! In the uttermost flurry, they had set to fortifying Dresden; all hands driving palisades, picking, delving, making *coupures* (trenches, or sunk barricades) in the streets; — fatally aware that it can avail nothing. Is not this the Kaiser's Order? Prussians, to the amount of 60,000, are across our Frontiers, rapidly speeding on.

"Friedrich's Manifesto, — under the modest Title, '*An-*"'*zeige der Ursachen* (Advertisement of the Causes which have "'induced his Prussian Majesty to send the Romish Kaiser's "'Majesty some Auxiliary Troops),' — had appeared in the "Berlin Newspapers, Thursday 13th, only two days before. "An astonishment to all mankind; which gave rise to endless "misconceptions of Friedrich; but which, supporting itself "on proofs, on punctually excerpted foot-notes, is intrinsically "a modest, quiet Piece; and, what is singular in Manifestoes, "has nothing, or almost nothing, in it that is not, so far as it "goes, a perfect statement of the fact. 'Auxiliary troops, "'that is our essential character. No war with her Hungarian "'Majesty, or with any other, on our own score. But her "'Hungarian Majesty, how has she treated the Romish "'Kaiser, her and our and the Reich's Sovereign Head, and "'to what pass reduced him; refusing him Peace on any "'terms, except those of self-annihilation; denying that he "'is a Kaiser at all;' — and enumerates the various Imperial "injuries, with proof given, quiet foot-notes by way of proof; "and concludes in these words: 'For himself his Majesty re-"'quires nothing. The question here is not of his Majesty's "'own interest at all' (everything his Majesty required, or re-

* *Helden-Geschichte*, II. 1163.

"quires, is by the Treaty of Berlin solemnly his, if the Reich "and its Laws endure): 'and he has taken up arms simply "'and solely in the view of restoring to the Reich its freedom, "'to the Kaiser his Headship of the Reich, and to all Europe "'the Peace which is so desirable.'*

"'Pretences, subterfuges, lies!' exclaimed the Austrian "and Allied Public everywhere, or strove to exclaim; espe-"cially the English Public, which had no difficulty in so "doing; — a Public comfortably blank as to German facts or "non-facts; and finding with amazement only this a very "certain fact, That hereby is their own Pragmatic thunder "checked in mid-volley in a most surprising manner, and the "triumphant Cause of Liberty brought to jeopardy again. "'Perfidious, ambitious, capricious!' exclaimed they: 'a "'Prince without honour, without truth, without constancy;' "— and completed, for themselves, in hot rabid humour, that "English Theory of Friedrich which has prevailed ever since. "Perhaps the most surprising item of which is this latter, very "prominent in those old times, That Friedrich has no 'con-"'stancy,' but follows his 'caprices' and accidental whirls of "impulse: — item which has dropped away in our times, "though the others stand as stable as ever. A monument of "several things! Friedrich's suddenness is an essential part "of what fighting talent he has: if the Public, thrown into "flurry, cannot judge it well, they must even misjudge it: "what help is there?

"That the above were actually Friedrich's reasons for "venturing into this Big Game again, is not now disputable. "And as to the rumour, which rose afterwards (and was "denied, and could only be denied diplomatically to the ear, "if even to the ear), That Friedrich by Secret Article was "'to have for himself the Three Bohemian Circles, Königs-"'grätz, Bunzlau, Leitmeritz, which lie between Schlesien "'and Sachsen,'**—there is not a doubt but Friedrich had so "bargained, 'Very well, if we can get said Circles!' and "would right cheerfully have kept and held them, had the big "game gone in all points completely well (game, To reinstate "the Kaiser *both* in Bohemia and Bavaria) by Friedrich's fine "playing. Not a doubt of all this: — nor of what an ex-

* Given in Seyfarth, *Beylage*, i. 121-136, with date, "August 1744."
** *Helden-Geschichte*, i. 1061; Schöll, ii. 349.

"tremely hypothetic outlook it then and always was; greatly "too weak for enticing such a man."

Friedrich goes in Three Columns. One, on the south or left shore of the Elbe, coming in various branches under Friedrich himself; this alone will touch on Dresden, pass on the south side of Dresden; gather itself about Pirna (in the Saxon Switzerland so-called, a notable locality); thence over the Metal Mountains into Böhmen, by Töplitz, by Lowositz, Leitmeritz, and the Highway called the Pascopol, famous in war. The Second Column, under Leopold the Young Dessauer, goes on the other or north side of the Elbe, at a fair distance; marching through the Lausitz (rendezvous or starting-point was Bautzen in the Lausitz) straight south, to meet the King at Leitmeritz, where the grand Magazine is to be; and thence, still south, straight upon Prag, in conjunction with his Majesty or parallel to him.* These are the Two Saxon Columns. The Third Column, under Schwerin, collects itself in the interior of Silesia; is issuing, by Glatz Country, through the Giant Mountains, *Böhmische Kämme* (Bohemian *Combs*, as they are called, which Tourists know), by the Pass of Braunau,—disturbing the dreams of Rübezahl, if Rübezahl happen to be there. This, say 20,000, will come down upon Prag from the eastern side; and be first on the ground (31st August),—first by one day. In the home parts of Silesia, well eastward of Glatz, there is left another Force of 20,000, which can go across the Austrian Border there, and hang upon the Hills, threatening Olmütz and the Moravian Countries, should need be.

* *Helden-Geschichte*, I. 1081.

And so, in its Three Columns, from west, from north, from east, the march, with a steady swiftness, proceeds. Important especially those Two Saxon Columns from west and north: 60,000 of them, "with a frightful (*entsetzlich*) quantity of big guns coming up the Elbe." Much is coming up the Elbe; indispensable Highway for this Enterprise. Three months' provisions, endless artillery and provender, is on the Elbe; 480 big boats, with immense *Vorspann* (of trace-horses, dreadful swearing, too, as I have heard), will pass through the middle of Dresden: not landing by any means. 'No, be assured of it, ye Dresdeners, all flurried, palisaded, barricaded; no hair of you shall be harmed.' After a day or two, the flurry of Saxony subsided; Prussians, under strict discipline, molest no private person; pay their way; keep well aloof, to south and to north, of Dresden (all but the necessary ammunition-escorts do); — and require of the Official people nothing but what the Law of the Reich authorises to 'Imperial Auxiliaries' in such case. "The Saxons themselves," Friedrich observes, "had some "40,000, but scattered about; King in Warsaw: — "dreadful terror; making *coupures* and *têtes-de-pont;* — "could have made no defence." Had we diligently spent eight days on them! reflects he afterwards. "To "seize Saxony" (and hobble it with ropes, so that at any time you could pin it motionless, and even, if need were, milk the substance out of it), "would not have "detained us eight days."* Which would have been the true plan, had we known what was getting ready there! Certain it is, Friedrich did no mischief, paid for everything; anxious to keep well with Saxony;

* *Œuvres de Frédéric,* III. 53.

hoping always they might join him again, in such a Cause. 'Cause dear to every Patriot German Prince,' urges Friedrich, — though Brühl, and the Polish, once "Moravian," Majesty are of a very different opinion! —

"Maria Theresa, her thoughts at hearing of it may be "imagined: 'The Evil Genius of my House afoot again! My "'high projects on Elsass and Lorraine; Husband for Kaiser, "'Elsass for the Reich and him, Lorraine for myself and him; "'— gone probably to water!' Nevertheless she said (an "Official person heard her say), 'My right is known to "'God; God will protect me, as He has already done.'* And "rose very strong, and magnanimously defiant again; — "perhaps, at the bottom of her heart, almost glad withal that "she would now have a stroke for her dear Silesia again, un-"hindered by Paladin George and his Treaties and notions. "What measures, against this nefarious Prussian outbreak, "hateful to gods and men, are possible, she rapidly takes: in "Bohemia, in Bavaria and her other Countries, that are "threatened or can help. And abates nothing of heart or "hope; — praying withal, immensely, she and her People, "according to the mode they have. Sending for Prince Karl, "we need not say, double-quick, as the very first thing.

"Of Maria Theresa in Hungary, — for she ran to Presburg "again with her woes (August 16th, Diet just assembling "there), — let us say only that Hungary was again chivalrous; "that old Palfy and the general Hungarian Nation answered "in the old tone, — *Vivat Maria; Ad Arma, ad Arma!* with "Tolpatches, Pandours, Warasdins; — and, in short, that "great and small, in infinite 'Insurrection,' have still a stroke "of battle in them *pro Rege Nostro*. Scarcely above a District "or two (as the *Jaszers* and *Kauers*, in their over-cautious way) "making the least difficulty. Much enthusiasm and unanimity "in all the others; here and there a Hungarian gentleman "complaining scornfully that their troops, known as among "the best fighters in Nature, are called irregular troops, — "irregular, forsooth! In one public consultation" (District not important, not very spellable, though doubtless pro-

* *Helden-Geschichte*, II. 1024.

nounceable by natives to it), "a gentleman suggests that, "'Winter is near; should not there be some slight provision of "'tents, of shelter in the frozen sleety Mountains, to our "'gallant fellows bound thither? Upon which another starts "up, 'When our Ancestors came out of Asia-Minor, over the "'Palus Mæotis bound in winter ice; and, sabre in hand, cut "'their way into this fine Country which is still ours, what "'shelter had they? No talk of tents, of barracks or accom- "'modation there; each, wrapt in his sheepskin, found it "'shelter sufficient. Tents!'* and the thing was carried by "acclamation.

"Wide wail in Bohemia that War is coming back. No- "bility all making off, some to Vienna or the intermediate "Towns lying thither-ward, some to their Country-seats; all "out of Prag. Willing mind on the part of the Common "People; which the Government strains every nerve to make "the most of. Here are fasts, processions, Prayers of Forty "Hours; here, as in Vienna and elsewhere. In Vienna was a "Three Days' solemn Fast: the like in Prag, or better; with "procession to the shrine of St. Vitus, — little likely to help, "I should fear. 'Rise, all fencible men,' exclaims the "Government, — 'at least we will ballot, and make you "'rise:' — Militia people enter Prag to the extent of 10,000; "like to avail little, one would fear. General Harsch, with "reinforcement of real soldiers, is despatched from Vienna; "Harsch, one of our ablest soldiers since Khevenhüller died, "gets in still in time; and thus increases the Garrison of re- "gulars to 4,000, with a vigorous Captain to guide it. Old "Count Ogilvy, the same whom Saxe surprised two years ago "in the moonlight, snatching ladders from the gallows, — "Ogilvy is again Commandant; but this time, nominal main- "ly, and with better out-looks, Harsch being under him. In "relays, 3,000 of the Militia men dig and shovel night and "day; repairing, perfecting the ramparts of the place. Then, "as to provisions, endless corn is introduced, — farmers "forced, the unwilling at the bayonet's point, to deliver-in "their corn; much of it in sheaf, so that we have to thrash it "in the market-place, in the streets that are wide: and thus "in Prag is heard the sound of flails, among the Militia drums "and so many other noises. With the great Church-organs

* *Helden-Geschichte*, II. 1030.

"growling; and the bass and treble *Miserere* of the poor "superstitious People rising, to St. Vitus and others. In fact, "it is a general Dance of St. Vitus, — except that of the flails, "and Militia men working at the ramparts, — mostly not "leading anywhither."*

Meanwhile Friedrich's march from west, from north, from east, is flowing on; diligent, swift; punctual to its times, its places; and meets no impediment to speak of. At Tetschen on the Saxon-Bohemian Frontier, — a pleasant Schloss perched on its crags, as Tourists know, where the Elbe sweeps into Saxon-Switzerland and its long stone-labyrinths, — at Tetschen the Austrians had taken post; had tried to block the River, driving piles into it, and tumbling boulders into it, with a view to stop the 480 Prussian Boats. These people needed to be torn out, their piles and they: which was done in two days, the soldier part of it; and occupied the boat-men above a week, before all was clear again. Prosperous, correct to program, all the rest; not needing mention from us; — here are the few sparks from it that dwell in one's memory:

"*August 15th*, 1744, King left Potsdam; joined his First "Column, that night, at Wittenberg. Through Torgau, "Meissen, Freiberg; is at Peterswalde, eastern slope of the "Metal Mountains, August 25th; all the Columns now on "Bohemian ground.

"Friedrich had crossed Elbe by the Bridge of Meissen: on "the southern shore, politely waiting to receive his Majesty, "there stood Feldmarschall the Duke of Weissenfels; to "whom the King gave his hand," no doubt in friendly style, "and talked for above half an hour," — with such success! thinks Friedrich by and by. We have heard of Weissenfels

* "*Letter* from a Citizen of Prag," date, 21st September (in *Helden-Geschichte*, ii. 1108), which gives several curious details.

before; the same poor Weissenfels who was Wilhelmina's Wooer in old time, now on the verge of sixty; an extremely polite but weakish old gentleman; accidentally preserved in History. One of those conspicuous 'Human Clothes-Horses' (phantasmal all but the digestive part), which abound in that Eighteenth Century and others like it; and distress your Historical studies. Poor old soul; now Feldmarschall and Commander-in-Chief here. Has been in Turk and other Wars; with little profit to himself or others. Used to like his glass, they say; is still very poor, though now Duke in reality as well as title (succeeded two egregious Brothers, some years since, who had been spendthrift): he has still one other beating to get in this world, — from Friedrich next year. Died altogether, two years hence; and Wilhelmina heard no more of him.

"At Meissen Bridge, say some, was this Half-hour's Interview; at Pirna, the Bridge of Pirna, others say;* — quite "indifferent to us which. At Pirna, and hither and thither in "Saxon Switzerland, Friedrich certainly was. 'Who ever "'saw such positions, your Majesty?' For Friedrich is "always looking out, were it even from the window of his "carriage, and putting military problems to himself in all "manner of scenery, 'What would a man do, in that kind of "'ground, if attacking, if attacked? with that hill, that brook, "'that bit of bog?' and advises every Officer to be continually "doing the like.** That is the value of picturesque or other "scenery to Friedrich, and their effect on good Prussian Offi- "cers and him.

* * "At Tetschen, Colonel Kahlbutz," diligent Prussian Colonel, "plucks out those 100 Austrians from their rock "nest there; makes them prisoners of war; — which detained "the Leitmeritz branch of us two days. August 28th, junction "at Leitmeritz thereupon. Magazine established there. "Boats coming on presently. Friedrich himself camped at "Lobositz in this part," — Lobositz, or Lowositz, which he will remember one day.

* See Orlich, II. 25; and *Helden-Geschichte*, II. 1166.

** *Military Instructions? Rules for a good Commander of &c.?* — I have, for certain, read this Passage; but the reference is gone again, like a sparrow from the housetop!

"*August 29th*, March to Budin; that is, southward, across "the Eger; arrive within forty miles of Prag. Austrian "Bathyani, summoned hastily out of his Bavarian posts, to "succour in this pressing emergency, has arrived in these "neighbourhoods, — some 12,000 regulars under him, preced-"ed by clouds of hussars, whom Ziethen smites a little, by "way of handsel; — no other Austrian force to speak of here-"abouts; and we are now between Bathyani and Prag.

"*September 1st*, To Mickowitz, near Welwarn, twenty "miles from Prag. September 2d, Camp on the Weissenberg "there."*

And so they are all assembled about Prag, be-girdling the poor City, — third Siege it has stood within these three years (since that moonlight November-night in 1741); — and are only waiting for their heavy artillery to begin battering. The poor inhabitants, in spite of three sieges; the 10,000 raw militia men, mostly of Hungarian breed; the 4,000 regulars, and Harsch and old Ogilvy, are all disposed to do their best. Friedrich is naturally in haste to get hold of Prag. But he finds, on taking survey, that the sword-in-hand method is not now, as in 1741, feasible at all; that the place is in good posture of strength; and will need a hot battering to tear it open. Owing to that accident at Tetschen, the siege-cannon are not yet come up: 'Build your batteries, your Moldau-bridges, your communications, till the cannon come; and beware of Bathyani meddling with your cannon by the road!"

"Bathyani is within twenty miles of us, at Beraun, a com-"pact little Town to south-west; gathering a Magazine there; "and ready for enterprises, — in more force than Friedrich "guesses. 'Drive him out, seize that Magazine of his!' orders

* *Helden-Geschichte*, i. 1080.

"Friedrich (September 5th); and despatches General Hacke "on it, a right man," — at whose wedding we assisted (wedding to an heiress, long since, in Friedrich Wilhelm's time), if anybody now remembered. "And on the morrow there "falls out a pretty little 'Action of Beraun,' about which great "noise was made in the Gazettes *pro* and *contra;* which did "not dislodge Bathyani by any means; but which might "easily have ruined the impetuous Hacke and his 6,000, get"ting into masked batteries, Pandour whirlwinds, charges of "horse 'from front, from rear, and from both flanks,' — had "not he, with masterly promptitude, whirled himself out of it, "snatched instantly what best post there was, and defended "himself inexpugnably there, for six hours, till relief came."* Brilliant little action, well performed on both sides, but leading to nothing; and which shall not concern us farther. Except to say that Bathyani did now, more at his leisure, retire out of harm's way; and begin collecting Magazines at Pilsen far rearward, which may prove useful to Prince Karl, in the route Prince Karl is upon.

Siege-cannon having at last come (September 8th), the batteries are all mounted: — on Wednesday 9th, late at night, the Artillery, "in enormous quantity," opens its dread throat; poor Prag is started from its bed, by torrents of shot, solid and shell, from three different quarters; and makes haste to stand to its guns. From three different quarters; from Bubenetsch northward; from the Upland of St. Lawrence (famed *Weissenberg*, or White-Hill) westward; and from the Ziscaberg eastward (Hill of Zisca, where iron Zisca posted himself on a grand occasion once), — which latter is a broad long Hill, west end of it falling sheer over Prag; and on another point of it, highest point of all, the Praguers have a strong battery and works. The Prag guns otherwise are not too effectual; planted

* *Die bey Beraun vorgefallene Action* (in Seyfarth, *Beylage*, I. 136, 137).

mostly on low ground. By much the best Prag battery is this of the Ziscaberg. And this, after two days' experience had of it, the Prussians determine to take on the morrow.

September 12th, Schwerin, who commands on that side, assaults accordingly; with the due steadfastness and stormfulness; throwing shells and balls by way of prelude. Friedrich, with some group of staff-officers and dignitaries, steps out on the Bubenetsch post, to see how this affair of the Ziscaberg will prosper: the Praguers thereabouts, seeing so many dignitaries, turn cannon on them. 'Disperse, *Ihr Herren*; have a care!" cried Friedrich; not himself much minding, so intent upon the Ziscaberg. And could have skipt indifferently over your cannon-balls ploughing the ground, — had not one fateful ball shattered out the life of poor Prince Wilhelm; a good young Cousin of his, shot down here at his hand. Doubtless a sharp moment for the King. Prince Margraf Wilhelm and a poor young page, there they lie dead; indifferent to the Ziscaberg and all coming wars of mankind. Lamentation, naturally, for this young man, — Brother to the one that fell at Mollwitz, youngest Brother of the Markgraf Karl, who commands in this Bubenetsch redoubt: — But we must lift our eyeglass again; see how Schwerin is prospering. Schwerin, with due steadfastness and stormfulness, after his prelude of bombshells, rushes on double-quick; cannot be withstood; hurls out the Praguers, and seizes their battery; a ruinous loss to them.

Their grand Zisca redoubt is gone, then; and two subsidiary small redoubts behind it withal, which the French had built, and named "the magpie-nests (*nids à pie*);" these also are ours. And we overhang, from our Zisca Hill, the very roofs, as it were; and there is nothing but a long bare curtain now in this quarter, ready to be battered in breach, and soon holed, if needful. It is not needful, — not quite. In the course of three days more, our Bubenetsch battery, of enormous power, has been so diligent, it has set fire to the Water-mill; burns irretrievably the Water-mill, and still worse, the wooden Sluice of the Moldau; so that the river falls to the everywhere wadeable pitch. And Governor Harsch perceives that all this quarter of the Town is open to any comer; — and in fact, that he will have to get away, the best he can.

White flag accordingly (Tuesday 15th): "Free withdrawal, to the Wischerad; won't you?" "By no manner of means!" answers Friedrich. Bids Schwerin from his Ziscaberg make a hole or two in that "curtain" opposite him; and gets ready for storm. Upon which Harsch, next morning, has to beat the chamade, and surrender Prisoner of War. And thus, Wednesday 16th, it is done: a siege of one week, no more, — after all that thrashing of grain, drilling of militia, and other spirited preparation. Harsch could not help it; the Prussian cannonading was so furious.*

Prag has to swear fealty to the Kaiser; and "pay a ransom of 200,000*l*." Drilled militia, regulars, Hungarians, about 16,000, — only that many of the Tolpatches contrived to whisk loose, — are marched prisoners to Glatz and other strong places. Prag City, with plenty of provision in it, is ours. A brilliant beginning of a Campaign; the eyes of all Europe turned

* Orlich, II. 36-39; *Helden-Geschichte*, I. 1062, and II. 1168; *Œuvres de Frédéric*, III. 56; &c. &c.

again, in very various humour, on this young King. If only the French do their duty, and hang well on the skirts of Marshal Traun (or of Prince Karl, the Cloak of Traun), who is hastening hitherward all he can.

CHAPTER III.

FRIEDRICH, DILIGENT IN HIS BOHEMIAN CONQUESTS, UNEXPECTEDLY COMES UPON PRINCE KARL, WITH NO FRENCH ATTENDING HIM.

THIS electrically sudden operation on Prag was considered by astonished mankind, whatever else they might think about it, a decidedly brilliant feat of War: falling like a bolt out of the blue, — like three bolts, suddenly coalescing over Prag, and striking it down. Friedrich himself, though there is nothing of boast audible here or anywhere, was evidently very well satisfied; and thought the aspects good. There is Prince Karl whirling instantly back from his Strasburg Prospects; the general St. Vitus' Dance of Austrian things, rising higher and higher in these home parts: — reasonable hope that "in the course of one Campaign," proud obstinate Austria might feel itself so wrung and screwed as to be glad of Peace with neighbours not wishing War. That was the young King's calculation at this time. And, had France done at all as it promised, — or had the young King himself been considerably wiser than he was, — he had not been disappointed in the way we shall see!

Friedrich admits he did not understand War, at this period. His own scheme now was: To move towards the south-west, there to abolish Bathyani and his Tolpatches, who are busy gathering Magazines for Prince Karl's advent; to seize the said Magazines, which will be very useful to us; then advance straight towards the Passes of the Bohemian Mountains. Towns of Furth, Waldmünchen, unfortunate Town of Cham (burnt by Trenck, where masons are now busy); these stand successive in the grand Pass, through which the highway runs; some hundred miles or so from where we are: march, at one's swiftest, thitherward, Bathyani's Magazines to help; and there await Prince Karl? It was Friedrich's own notion; not a bad one, though not the best. The best, he admits, would have been: To stay pretty much where he was, abolish Bathyani's Tolpatch people, seizing their Magazines, and collecting others; in general, well rooting and fencing himself in Prag, and in the Circles that lie thereabouts upon the Elbe, — bounded to southward by the Sazawa (branch of the Moldau), which runs parallel to the Elbe; — but well refusing to stir much farther at such an advanced season of the year.

That second plan would have been the wisest: — then why not follow it? Too tame a plan for the youthful mind. Besides, we perceive, as indeed is intimated by himself, he dreaded the force of public opinion in France. "Aha, look at your King of Prussia again. Gone to conquer Bohemia: and, except the Three Circles he himself is to have of it, lets Bohemia go to the winds!" This sort of thing, Friedrich admits, he dreaded too much, at that young period; so loud had the criticisms been on him, in the time of the Breslau Treaty: "Out upon your King of Prussia; call you that an honourable Ally!" Undoubtedly, a weakness in the young King; inasmuch, says he, as "every

"General" (and every man, add we) "should look to "the fact, not to the rumour of the fact." Well; but, at least, he will adopt his own other notion; that of making for the Passes of the Bohemian Mountains; to abolish Bathyani at the least, and lock the door upon Prince Karl's advent? That was his own plan; and, though second-best, that also would have done well, had there been no third.

But there was, as we hinted, a third plan, ardently favoured by Belleisle, whose war-talent Friedrich much respected at this time: plan built on Belleisle's reminiscences of the old Tabor-Budweis businesses, and totally inapplicable now. Belleisle said, "Go south-east, not south-west; right towards the Austrian Frontier itself; that will frighten Austria into a fine tremor. Shut up the roads from Austria: Budweis, Neuhaus; seize those two Highroad Towns, and keep them, if you would hold Bohemia; the want of them was our ruin there." Your ruin, yes: but your enemy was not coming from Alsace and the south-west then. He was coming from Austria; and your own home lay on the south-west: it is all different now! Friedrich might well think himself bewitched not to have gone for Cham and Furth, and the Passes of the Böhmer-Wald, according to his own notion. But so it was; he yielded to the big reputation of Belleisle, and to fear of what the world would say of him in France; a weakness which he will perhaps be taught not to repeat. In fact, he is now about to be taught several things; — and will have to pay his school-wages as he goes.

Friedrich, leaving small Garrison in Prag, rushes swiftly up the Moldau Valley, upon the Tabor-Budweis Country; to please his French Friends.

Friedrich made no delay in Prag; in haste at this late time of year. September 17th, on the very morrow of the Siege, the Prussians got in motion southward; on the 19th, Friedrich, from his post to north of the City, defiles through Prag, on march to Kunraditz, — first stage on that questionable Expedition up the Moldau Valley, right bank; towards Tabor, Budweis, Neuhaus; to threaten Austria, and please Belleisle and the French.

Prag is left under General Einsiedel with a small garrison of 5,000; — Einsiedel, a steady elderly gentleman, favourite of Friedrich Wilhelm's, has brief order, or outline of order to be filled up by his own good sense. Posadowsky follows the march, with as many meal-wagons as possible, — draught-cattle in very ineffectual condition. Our main Magazine is at Leitmeritz (should have been brought on to Prag, thinks Friedrich); Commissariat very ill-managed in comparison to what it ought to be, — to what it shall be, if we ever live to make another Campaign. Heavy artillery is left in Prag (another fault); and from each regiment, one of its baggage-wagons.* "We rest a "day here at Kunraditz: 21st September, get to the "Sazawa River; — 22d, to Bistritz (rest a day); — "26th, to Miltschin; and 27th, to Tabor:" — But the Diary would be tedious.

* *Helden-Geschichte*, I. 1083; Orlich, II. 41 et sqq.; *Frédéric*, III. 59; &c.

Friedrich goes in two Columns; one along the great road towards Tabor, under Schwerin this, and Friedrich mainly with him; the other to the right, along the River's bank, under Leopold, Young Dessauer, which has to go by wild country roads, or now and then roads of its own making; and much needs the pioneer (a difficult march in the shortening days). Posadowsky follows with the proviant, drawn by cattle of the horse and ox species, daily falling down starved: great swearing there too, I doubt not! General Nassau is vanguard, and stretches forward successfully at a much lighter pace.

There are two Rivers, considerable branches of the Moldau, coming from eastward; which, and first of them the Sazawa, concern us here. After mounting the southern Uplands from Prag for a day or two, you then begin to drop again, into the hollow of a River called Sazawa, important in Bohemian Wars. It is of winding course, the first considerable branch of the Moldau, rising in Teutschbrod Country, seventy or eighty miles to east of us: in regard to Sazawa, there is, at present, no difficulty about crossing, the Country being all ours. After the Sazawa, mount again, long miles, day after day, through intricate stony desolation, rocks, bogs, untrimmed woods, you will get to Tabor, which is the crown of that rough moor country: from Prag to Tabor is some sixty miles. After Tabor the course of those brown mountain-brooks is all towards the Luschnitz, the next considerable branch of the Moldau; branch still longer and more winding than the Sazawa; Budweis stands on this branch; and there you are out of the stony moors and in a rich champaign, comfortable to man and horse, were you but once there, after plodding through the desolations. But from that Sazawa to the Luschnitz, mounting and falling in such fashion, there must be six-score miles or thereby. Plod along; and keep a sharp eye upon the whirling clouds of Pandours, for those too have got across upon us, — added to the other tempests of Autumn.

On the ninth day of their march, the Prussians begin to descry on the horizon ahead the steeples and chimney-tops of Tabor, on its high scarped rock, or "Hill of Zisca," — for it was Zisca and his Hussites that built themselves this Bit of Inexpugnability, and named it Tabor from their Bibles, — in those waste mountain regions. On the tenth day (27th Sept.), the Prussians without difficulty took Tabor; walls being ruined, garrison small. We lie at Tabor till the 30th, last day of September. Thence, 2d October, part of us to Moldau Tein leftwards; where cross the Moldau by a Bridge, — 'Bridge' one has heard of, in old Broglio times; — cross there, with intent (easily successful) to snatch that 'Castle of Frauenberg,' darling of Broglio, for which he fought his Pharsalia of a Sahay to no purpose!

Both Columns got united at Tabor; and paused for a day or two, to rest, and gather up their draggled skirts there. The Expedition does not improve in promise, as we advance in it; the march one of the most untowardly; and Posadowsky comes up with only half of his provision-carts, — half of his cattle having fallen down of bad weather, hill-roads, and starvation; what could he do? That is an ominous circumstance, not the less.

Three things are against the Prussians on this March; two of them accidental things. *First*, there is, at this late season too, the intrinsic nature of the Country; which Friedrich with emphasis describes as boggy, stony, precipitous; a waste, hungry, and altogether barren Country, — too emphatically so described. But then *secondly*, what might have been otherwise, the Population, worked upon by Austrian officials, all fly from the sight of us; nothing but fireless deserted hamlets; and the corn, if they ever had any, all thrashed and hidden. No amount of money can purchace any service from them. Poor dark creatures; not loving Austria much, but loving some others even less, it would appear. Of bigoted Papist Creed, for one thing; that is a great point. We do not meddle with their worship more or less; but we are Heretics, and they hate us as the Night. Which is a dreadful difficulty you always have in Bohemia: nowhere but in the Circle of Königsgratz, where there are Hussites (far to the rear of us at this time), will you find it otherwise. This is difficulty second.

Then, *thirdly*, what much aggravates it, — we neglected to abolish Bathyani! And here are Bathyani's Pandours come across the Moldau on us. Plenty of Pandours; — to whom '10,000 fresh Hungarians,' of a new Insurrection which has been got up there, are daily speeding forward to add themselves: — such a swarm of hornets, as darkens the very daylight for you. Vain to scourge them down, to burn them off by blaze of gunpowder: they fly fast; but are straightway back again. They lurk in these bushy wildernesses, scraggy woods: no foraging possible, unless whole regiments are sent out to do it; you cannot get a letter safely carried for them. They are an unspeakable contemptible grief to the earnest leader of men. — Let us proceed, however; it will serve nothing to complain. Let us hope the French sit well on the skirts of Prince Karl: these sorrowful labours may all turn to good, in that case.

Friedrich pushes on from Tabor; shoots partly (as we have seen) across the Moldau, to the left bank as well; captures romantic Frauenberg on its high rock, where Broglio got into such a fluster once. We could push to Pisek, too, and make a 'Bivouac of Pisek,' if we lost our wits! Nassau is in Budweis, in Neuhaus; and proper garrisons are gone thither: nothing wanting on our side of the business. But these Pandours, these 10,000 Insurrection Hungarians, with their Trencks spurring them! A continual unblessed swarm of hornets, these; which shut out the very light of day from us. Too literally, the light of day: we can get no free messaging from part to part of our own Army even.

"As many as six Orderlies have been despatched to an "outlying General; and not one of them could get "through to him. They have snapt up three Letter-"bags destined for the King himself. For four weeks "he is absolutely shut out from the rest of Europe;" knows not in the least what the Kaiser, or the Most Christian or any other King, is doing; or whether the French are sitting well on Prince Karl's skirts, or not attempting that at all. This also is a thing to be amended, a thing you had to learn, your Majesty? An Army absolutely shut out from news, from letters, messages to or fro, and groping its way in darkness, owing to these circumambient thunder-clouds of Tolpatches, is not a well-situated Army! And, alas, when at last the Letterbag did get through, and — But let us not anticipate!

At Tabor there arose two opinions; which, in spite of the King's presence, was a new difficulty. South from Tabor a day's march, the Highway splits; left-hand goes to Neuhaus, direct way for Vienna; right-hand, or straight-forward rather, goes to Budweis, bearing upon Linz: which of these two? Nassau has already seized Budweis; and it is a habitable champaign country in comparison. Neuhaus, farther from the Moldau and its uses, but more imminent on Austria, would be easy to seize; and would frighten the Enemy more. Leopold the Young Dessauer is for Budweis; rapid Schwerin, a hardy outspoken man, is emphatic for the other place as Head-quarter. So emphatic are both that the two Generals quarrel there; and Friedrich needs his authority to keep them from outbreaks, from open incompatibility henceforth, which would be destructive to the service. For the rest, Friedrich seizes both places; sends a detachment to Neuhaus as well; but holds by Budweis and the Moldau region with his main Army; which was not quite gratifying to the hardy Schwerin. On the opposite or left bank, holding Frauenberg, the renowned Hill-fortress there, we make inroads at discretion: but the country is woody, favourable to Pandours; and the right bank is our chief scene of action. How we are to maintain ourselves in this country? To winter in these towns between the Sazawa and the Luschnitz? Unless the French sit well on Prince Karl's skirts, it will not be possible.

The French are little grateful for the Pleasure done them at such ruinous Expense.

French sitting well on Prince Karl's skirts? They are not molesting Prince Karl in the smallest; never tried such a thing; — are turned away to the Brisgau, to the Upper Rhine country; gone to besiege Freyburg there, and seize Towns about the Lake of Constance, as if there were no Friedrich in the game! It must be owned the French do liberally pay off old scores against Friedrich, — if, except in their own imagination, they had old scores against him. No man ever delivered them from a more imminent peril; and they, the rope once cut that was strangling them, magnificently forget who cut it; and celebrate only their own distinguished conduct during and after the operation. To a degree truly wonderful.

It was moonlight, clear as day that night, 23d August, when Prince Karl had to recross the Rhine, close in their neighbourhood;* — and instead of harassing Prince Karl 'to half or to whole ruin,' as the bargain was, their distinguished conduct consisted in going quietly to their beds (old Maréchal de Noailles even calling back some of his too forward subalterns), and joyfully leaving Prince Karl, then and afterwards, to cross the Rhine, and march for Böhmen at his own perfect convenience.

'Seckendorf will sit on Karl's skirts,' they said: 'too late for *us*, this season; next season, you shall 'see!' Such was their theory, after Louis got that cathartic, and rose from bed. Schmettau, with his importunities, which at last irritated everybody, could make nothing more of it. 'Let the King of France crown his glories by the Siege of Freyburg, the conquest of Brisgau: — for behoof of the poor Kaiser, don't you observe? Hither Austria is the Kaiser's; — and furthermore, were Freyburg gone, there will be no invading of Elsass again' (which is another privately very interesting point)!

And there, at Freyburg, the Most Christian King now is, and his Army up to the knees in mud, conquering Hither Austria; besieging Freyburg, with much difficulty owing to the wet, — besieging there with what energy; a spectacle to the world! And has, for the present, but one wife, no mistress either! With rapturous eyes France looks on; with admiration too big for words. Voltaire, I have heard, made pilgrimage to Freyburg, with rhymed Panegyric in his pocket; saw those miraculous operations of a Most Christian King miraculously awakened; and had the honour to present said Panegyric; and be seen, for the first time, by the royal eyes, — which did not seem to relish him

* *Guerre de Bohême*, iii. 196.

much.* Since the first days of October, Freyburg had been under constant assault; "amid rains, amid frosts; a siege long and murderous" (to the besieging party); —and was not got till November 5th; not quite entirely, the Citadels of it, till November 25th; Majesty gone home to Paris, to illuminations and triumphal arches, in the interim.** It had been a difficult and bloody conquest to him, this of Freyburg and the Brisgau Country; and I never heard that either the Kaiser or he got sensible advantage by it, — though Prince Karl, on the present occasion, might be said to get a great deal.

"Seckendorf will do your Prince Karl," they had cried always: "Seckendorf and his Prussian Majesty! Are not we conquering Hither Austria here, for the Kaiser's behoof?" Seckendorf they did officially appoint to pursue; appoint or allow; — and laid all the blame on Seckendorf; who perhaps deserved his share of it. Very certain it is, Seckendorf did little or nothing to Prince Karl; marched "leisurely behind him through the Ober-Pfalz," — skirting Baireuth Country, Karl and he, to Wilhelmina's grief;*** — "leisurely behind him at a distance of four days," knew better than meddle with Prince Karl. So that Prince Karl, "in twenty-one marches," disturbed only by the elements and bad roads, reached Waldmünchen, 25th September, in the Furth-Cham Country;† and was heard to exclaim: "We are let off for the fright, then (*Nous voilà*

* The Panegyric (*Epître au Roi devant Fribourg*) is in *Œuvres de Voltaire*, XVII. 184.

** Adelung, IV. 266; Barbier, II. 414 (13th November, &c.), for the illuminations, grand in the extreme, in spite of wild rains and winds.

*** Her Letters (*Œuvres de Frédéric*, XXVII. i. 133, &c.).

† Ranke, III. 187.

"*quittes pour la peur*)!" — Seckendorf, finding nothing to live upon in Ober-Pfalz, could not attend Prince Karl farther; but turned leftwards home to Bavaria; made a kind of Second "Reconquest of Bavaria" (on exactly the same terms as the First, Austrian occupants being all called off to assist in Böhmen again); — concerning which, here is an Excerpt:

"Seckendorf, following at his leisure, and joined by the "Hessians and Pfalzers, so as now to exceed 30,000, leaves "Prince Karl and the rest of the enterprise to do as it can; "and applies himself, for his own share, as the needfullest "thing, to getting hold of Bavaria again, that his poor Kaiser "may have where to lay his head, and pay old servants their "wages. Dreadfully exclaimed against, the old gentleman, "especially by the French co-managers: 'Why did not the "'old traitor stick in the rear of Prince Karl, in the difficult "'passes, and drive him prone, — while we went besieging "'Freyburg, and poaching about, trying for a bit of the "'Brisgau while chance served!' A traitor beyond doubt; "probably bought with money down, thinks Valori. But, "after all, what could Seckendorf do? He is now of weight "for Bärenklau and Bavaria, not for much more. He does "sweep Bärenklau and his Austrians from Bavaria, clear out "(in the course of this October), all but Ingolstadt and two or "three strong towns, — Passau especially, 'which can be "'blockaded, and afterwards besieged if needful.' For the "rest, he is dreadfully ill off for provisions, incapable of the "least attempt on Passau (as Friedrich urged, on hearing of "him again); and will have to canton himself in home quar-"ters, and live by his shifts till Spring.

"The noise of French censure rises loud, against not "themselves, but against Seckendorf: — Friedrich, before "that Tolpatch eclipse of Correspondence" (when three of his Letterbags were seized, and he fell quite dark), "had too well "foreboded, and contemptuously expressed his astonishment "at the blame *both* were well earning: Passau, said he, cannot "you go at least upon Passau; which might alarm the enemy "a little, and drag him homewards? 'Adieu, my dear Secken-

"'dorf, your Officer will tell you how we did the Siege of "'Prag. You and your French are wetted hens (*poules* "'*mouillées*),' — cowering about like drenched hens in a day "of set rain. 'As I hear nothing of either of you, I must try "'to get out of this business without your help,' — otherwise it will be ill for me indeed!* "Which latter expression "alarmed the French, and set them upon writing and bust- "ling, but not upon doing anything."

"Prince Karl had crossed the Rhine unmolested, in the "clearest moonlight, August 23d-24th; Seckendorf was not "wholly got to Heilbronn, September 8th: a pretty way be- "hind Prince Karl! The 6,000 Hessians, formerly in English "pay, indignant Landgraf Wilhelm" (who never could forgive that Machiavellian conduct of Carteret at Hanau, never till he found out what it really was) "has, this year, put into "French pay. And they have now joined Seckendorf;** "Prince Friedrich" (Britannic Majesty's Son-in-law), "not "good fat Uncle George, commanding them henceforth: — "with extreme *lack* of profit to Prince Friedrich, to the "Hessians, and to the French, as will appear in time. These "6,000, and certain thousands of Pfalzers likewise in French "pay, are now with Seckendorf, and have raised him to above "30,000; — it is the one fruit King Friedrich has got by that "'Union of Frankfurt,' and by all his long prospective "haggling, and struggling for a 'Union of German Princes "'in general.' Two pears, after that long shaking of the "tree; both pears rotten, or indeed falling into Seckendorf, "who is a basket of such quality! 'Seckendorf, increased in "'this munificent manner, can he still do nothing?' cry the "French: 'the old traitor!' — 'I have no magazines,' said "Seckendorf, 'nothing to live upon, to shoot with; no "'money!' And it is a mutual crescendo between the 'per- "'fidious Seckendorf' and them; without work done. In the "Nürnberg Country, some Hussars of his picked up Lord "Holderness, an English Ambassador making for Venice by "that bad route. 'Prisoner, are not you?' But they did not

* Excerpted Fragment of a Letter from Friedrich, — (exact date not given, date of *Excerpt* is, Donauwörth Country, 23d September 1744), — which the French Agent in Seckendorf's Army had a reading of (*Campagnes de Coigny*, iv. 165-167; ib. 216-219: cited in Adelung, iv. 225).

** Espagnac, II. 13; Buchholz, II. 123.

"use him ill; on consideration, the Heads of Imperial Departments gave him a Pass, and he continued his Venetian Journey (result of it zero) without farther molestation that I heard of.*

"These French-Seckendorf cunctations, recriminations, and drenched-hen procedures, are an endless sorrow to poor Kaiser Karl; who at length can stand it no longer; but resolves, since at least Bavaria, though moneyless and in ruins, is his, he will in person go thither; confident that there will be victual and equipment discoverable for self and Army, were he there. Remonstrances avail not: 'Ask me to die with honour, ask me not to lie rotting here;'** — and quits Frankfurt, and the Reich's-Diet and its babble, 17th October 1744 (small sorrow, were it for the last time), — and enters his München in the course of a week.*** München is transported with joy to see the Legitimate Sovereign again; and blazes into illuminations, — forgetful who caused its past wretchedness, hoping only all wretchedness is now ended. Let ruined huts, and Cham and the burnt Towns, rebuild themselves; the wasted hedges make up their gaps again: here is the King come home! Here, sure enough, is an unfortunate Kaiser of the Holy Romish Reich, who can once more hope to pay his milk-scores, being a loved Kurfürst of Bavaria at least. Very dear to the hearts of these poor people; — and to their purses, interests and skins, has not he in another sense been dear? What a price the ambitions and cracked fantasms of that weak brain have cost the seemingly innocent population! Population harried, hungered down, dragged off to perish in Italian Wars; a Country burnt, tribulated, torn to ruin, under the harrow of Fate and ruffian Trenck and Company. Britannic George, rather a dear morsel too, has come much cheaper hitherto. England is not yet burnt; nothing burning there, — except the dull fire of deliriums; Natural Stupidities all set flaming, which (whatever it may *be* in the way of loss) is not felt as a loss, but rather as a comfort for the time being; — and in fact there are only, say, a forty or fifty thousand armed Englishmen rotted down, and scarcely a Hundred

* Adelung, IV. 222. ** Ibid. IV. 241.

*** 17th October 1744, leaves Frankfurt; arrives in München, 23d (Adelung, IV. 241-244).

"Millions of money yet spent. Nothing to speak of, in the "Cause of Human Liberty. Why Populations suffer for their "guilty Kings? My friend, it is the Populations too that are "guilty in having such Kings. Reverence, sacred Respect "for Human Worth, sacred Abhorrence of Human Unworth, "have you considered what it means? These poor Popula-"tions have it not, or for long generations have had it less and "less. Hence, by degrees, this sort of 'Kings' to them, and "enormous consequences following!"

Karl VII. got back to München, 23d October 1743; and the tarbarrels being once burnt, and indispensable sortings effected, he went to the field along with Seckendorf, to encourage his men under Seckendorf, and urge the French by all considerations to come on. And really did what he could, poor man. But the cordage of his life had been so strained and torn, he was not now good for much; alas, it had been but little he was ever good for. A couple of dear Kurfürsts, his Father and he; have stood these Bavarian Countries very high, since the Battle of Blenheim and downwards!

CHAPTER IV.

FRIEDRICH REDUCED TO STRAITS; CANNOT MAINTAIN HIS MOLDAU CONQUESTS AGAINST PRINCE KARL.

ONE may fancy what were Friedrich's reflections when he heard that Prince Karl had, prosperously and unmolested, got across, by those Passes from the Ober-Pfalz, into Böhmen and the Circle of Pilsen, into junction with Bathyani and his magazines;* heard, moreover, that the Saxons, 20,000 strong, under Weissenfels, crossing the Metal Mountains, coming on by Eger and Karlsbad regions, were about uniting with him (bound by Treaty to assist the Hungarian Majesty when invaded); — and heard finally, what confirms everything, that the said Prince Karl in person (making for Budweis, "just seen his advanced guard," said rumour under mistake) was but few miles off. Few miles off, on the other side of the Moldau; — of unknown strength, hidden in the circumambient clouds of Pandours.

Suppressing all the rages and natural reflections but those needful for the moment, Friedrich (October 4th, by Moldau-Tein) dashes across the Moldau, to seek Prince Karl at the place indicated, and at once smite him down if possible; — that will be a remedy for all things. Prince Karl is not there, nor was; the indication had been false; Friedrich searches about, for four

* "At Mirotitz, October 2d' (Ranke, III. 194); Orlich, II. 49.

days, to no purpose. Prince Karl, he then learns for certain, has crossed the Moldau farther down, farther northward, between Prag and us. Means to cut us off from Prag, then, which is our fountain of life in these circumstances? That is his intention: — "Old Traun, who is with him, understands his trade!" thinks Friedrich. Traun, or the Prince, is diligently forming magazines, all the Country carrying to him, in the Town of Beneschau, hither side of the Sazawa, some seventy miles north of us, an important Town where roads meet: — unless we can get hold of Beneschau, it will be ill with us here! Across the River again, at any rate; and let us hasten thither. That is an affair which must be looked to; and speed is necessary!

October 8th. After four days' search ending in this manner, Friedrich swiftly crosses towards Tabor again, to Bechin (over on the Luschnitz, one march), there to collect himself for Beneschau and the other intricacies. Towards Tabor again; by his Bridge of Moldau-Tein; — clouds of Pandour people, larger clouds than usual, hanging round; hidden by the woods till Friedrich is gone. Friedrich being gone, there occurs the *Affair of Moldau-Tein*, much talked of in Prussian Books. Of which, in extreme condensation, this is the essence:

"*October 9th.* Friedrich once off to Bechin, the Pandour "clouds gather on his rearguard next day at Tein Bridge here, "to the number of about 10,000" (rumour counts 14,000); "and "with desperate intent, and more regularity than usual, attack "the Tein-Bridge Party, which consists of perhaps 2,000 gre-"nadiers and hussars, the whole under Ziethen's charge, — "obliged to wait for a cargo of Breadwagons here. 'Defend "your Bridge, with cannon, with case-shot:' that is what the "grenadiers do. The Pandour cloud, with horrid lances cut in "it, draws back out of this; then plunges at the River itself, "which can be ridden above or below; rides it, furious, by the "thousand: 'Off with your infantry; quit the Bridge!' cries

"Ziethen to his Captain there: 'Retire you, Parthian-like; "thrice-steady,' orders Ziethen: "It is to be hoped our hussars "can deal with this mad-doggery!" And they do it; cutting "in with iron discipline, with fierceness not undrilled; a wedge "of iron hussars, with ditto grenadiers continually wheeling, "like so many reapers steady among wind-tossed grain; and "gradually give the Pandours enough. Seven hours of it, in "all: 'of their sixty cartridges the grenadiers had fired fifty-"four,' when it ended, about 7 P.M. The coming bread-wagons, "getting word, had to cast their loaves into the River (sad to "think of); and make for Bechin at their swiftest. But the "rearguard got off with its guns, in this victorious manner: "thanks to Major-General Ziethen, Colonel Reusch and the "others concerned.*

"Ziethen handsels his Major-Generalcy in this fine way:** "a man who has had promotion, and also has had none, and "may again come to have none; — and is able to do either way. "Never mind, my excellent tacit friend! Ziethen is five-and-"forty gone; has a face which is beautiful to me, though one "of the coarsest. Face thrice-honest, intricately ploughed "with thoughts which are well kept silent (the thoughts, "indeed, being themselves mostly inarticulate; thoughts "of a simple-hearted, much-enduring, hot-tempered son of "iron and oatmeal); — decidedly rather likeable, with its "lazily hanging under-lip, and respectable bearskin cylinder "atop."

Friedrich tries to have Battle from Prince Karl, in the Moldau Countries; cannot, owing to the Skill of Prince Karl or of old Feldmarschall Traun; — has to retire behind the Sazawa, and ultimately behind the Elbe, with much Labour in Vain.

October 14th-18th: Retreat from Bechin-Tabor Country to Beneschau. * * "These Pandours give us trouble enough; no "Magazine here, no living to be had in this Country beside "them. Unfortunate Colonel Jahnus went out from Tabor

* *Feldzüge der Preussen*, I. 268; Orlich, II. 55.

** Patent given him "3d October 1744," only a week ago, "and ordered to be dated eight months back" (Rödenbeck, I. 109).

"lately, to look after requisitioned grains: infinite Pandours set "upon him" (Mühlhausen is the memorable place); "Jahnus "was obstinate (too obstinate thinks Friedrich), and perished "on the ground, he and 200 of his.* Nay, next, a swarm of "them came to Tabor itself, Nadasti at their head; to try "whether Tabor, with its small garrison, could not be esca-"laded, and perhaps Prince Henri, who lies sick there, be "taken? Tabor taught them another lesson; sent them home "with heads broken; — which Friedrich thinks was an ex-"tremely suitable thing. But so it stands: Here by the "thousand and the ten thousand they hang round us; and "Prince Karl — It is of all things necessary we get hold of "that Beneschau, and the Magazine he is gathering there!

"Rapidity is indispensable, — and yet how quit Tabor? "We have detachments out at Neuhaus, at Budweis, and in "Tabor 300 men in hospital, whom there are no means of "carrying. To leave them to the Tolpatches? Friedrich "confesses he was weak on this occasion; he could not leave "these 300 men, as was his clear duty, in this extremity of "War. He ordered-in his Neuhaus Detachment; not yet any "of the others. He despatched Schwerin towards Beneschau "with all his speed; Schwerin was lucky enough to take "Beneschau and its provender, — a most blessed fortune, — "and fences himself there. Hearing which, Friedrich, having "now got the Neuhaus Detachment in hand, orders the other "Three, the Budweis, the Tabor here, and the Frauenberg "across the River, to maintain themselves; and then, leaving "those southern regions to their chance, hastens towards "Beneschau and Schwerin; encamps (October 18th) near "Beneschau, — 'Camp of Konopischt,' unattackable Camp, "celebrated in the Prussian Books; — and there, for eight "days, still on the south side of Sazawa, tries every shift to "mend the bad posture of affairs in that Luschnitz-Sazawa "Country. His Three Garrisons (3,000 men in them, besides "the 300 sick) he now sees will not be able to maintain them-"selves; and he sends in succession 'eight messengers,' not "one messenger of whom could get through, to bid them come "away. His own hope now is for a Battle with Prince Karl; "which might remedy all things."**

* *Œuvres de Frédéric*, III. 61.
** *Œuvres de Frédéric*, III. 62-64.

That is Friedrich's wish; but it is by no means Traun's, who sees that hunger and wet weather will of themselves suffice for Friedrich. There ensues accordingly, for three weeks to come, in that confused Country, a series of swift shufflings, checkings, and manœuverings between these two, which is gratifying and instructive to the strategic mind, but cannot be inflicted upon common readers. Two considerable chess-players, an old and a young; their chess-board a bushy, rocky, marshy parallelogram, running fifty miles straight east from Prag, and twenty or fewer south, of which Prag is the north-west angle, and Beneschau, or the impregnable Konopischt the south-east: the reader must conceive it; and how Traun will not fight Friedrich, yet makes him skip hither and thither, chiefly by threatening his victuals. Friedrich's main magazine is now at Pardubitz, the extreme north-east angle of the parallelogram. Parallelogram has one river in it, with the innumerable rocks and brooks and quagmires, the river Sazawa; and on the north side, where are Kuttenberg, Czaslau, Chotusitz, places again become important in this business, it is bounded by another river, the Elbe. Intricate manœuvering there is here, for three weeks following: "old Traun an admirable man!" thinks Friedrich, who ever after recognised Traun as his Schoolmaster in the art of War. We mark here and there a date, and leave it to readers.

"*Radicz, October 21st-22d.* At Radicz, a march to south-
"west of us, and on our side of the Moldau, the Saxons, under
"Weissenfels, 20,000 effective, join Prince Karl; which raises
"his force to 69,514 men, some 10,000 more than Friedrich is

"master of.* Prospect of wintering between the Luschnitz "and the Sazawa there is now little; unless they will fight us, "and be beaten. Friedrich, from his inaccessible Camp of "Konopischt, manœuvres, reconnoitres, in all directions, to "produce this result; but to no purpose. An Austrian Detach-"ment did come, to look after Beneschau and the Magazines "there; but rapidly drew back again, finding Konopischt on "their road, and how matters were. Friedrich will guard the "door of this Sazawa-Elbe tract of Country; hope of the Sazawa-"Luschnitz tract has, in few days, fallen extinct. Here is "news come to Konopischt: our Three poor Garrisons, Bud-"weis, Tabor, Frauenberg, already all lost; guns and men, "after defence to the last cartridge, — in Frauenberg their "water was cut off, it was eight-and-forty hours of thirst at "Frauenberg: — one way or other, they are all Three gone; "eight couriers galloping with message, 'Come away,' were "all picked up by the Pandours; so they stood, and were lost. "'Three thousand fighting men gone, for the weak chance of "'saving three hundred who were in hospital!' thinks Fried-"rich: War is not a school of the weak pities. For the chance "of ten, you lose a hundred and the ten too. Sazawa-Elbe "tract of country, let us vigilantly keep the door of that!

"*Saturday, October 24th*, Friedrich out reconnoitering from "Konopischt, discovers of a certainty that the whole Austrian-"Saxon force is now advancing towards Beneschau, and will, "this night, encamp at Marschowitz, to south-west, only one "march from us! On the instant Friedrich hurries back; gets "his Army on march thitherward, though the late October sun "is now past noon; off instantly; a stroke yonder will perhaps "be the cure of all. Such roads we had, says Friedrich, as "never Army travelled before: long after nightfall, we arrive "near the Austrian camp, bivouac as we can till daylight re-"turn. At the first streak of day, Friedrich and his chief "generals are on the heights with their spyglasses: Austrian "Army sure enough; and there they have altered their pos-"ture over night (for Traun too has been awake); they lie now "opposite our *right* flank; 'on a scarped height, at the foot of "'which, through swamps and quagmires, runs a muddy "'stream.' Unattackable on this side: their right flank and "foot are safe enough. Creep round and see their left: —

* Orlich, II. 66.

"Nothing but copses, swampy intricacies! We may shoulder "arms again, and go back to Konopischt: no fight here!* "Speaking of defensive Campaigns, says Friedrich didactically, years afterwards, 'If such situations are to answer the "'purpose intended, the front and flanks must be equally "'strong, but the rear entirely open. Such, for instance, are "'those heights which have an extensive front, and whose "'flanks are covered by morasses: — as was Prince Karl's "'Camp at Marschowitz in the year 1744, with its front covered "'by a stream, and the wings by deep hollows; or that which "'we ourselves then occupied at Konopischt,' — as you well "remember.**

"*October 26th—November 1st.* The Sazawa-Luschnitz tract "of Country is quite lost, then; lost with damages: the question now is, Can we keep the Sazawa-Elbe tract? For about "three weeks more, Friedrich struggles for that object; "cannot compass that either. Want of horse provender is "very great: — country entirely eaten, say the peasants, and "not a truss remaining. October 26th, Friedrich has to cross "the Sazawa; we must quit the door of that tract (hunger "driving us), and fight for the interior in detail. Traun gets "to Beneschau in that cheap way; and now, in behalf of "Traun, the peasants find forage enough, being zealous for "Queen and creed. Pandours spread themselves all over this "Sazawa-Elbe country; endanger our subsistences, make our "lives miserable. It is the old story: Friedrich, famine and "mud and misery of Pandours compelling, has to retire northward, Elbe-ward, inch by inch: whither the Austrians follow "at a safe distance, and, in spite of all manœuvering, cannot "be got to fight.

"Brave General Nassau, who much distinguishes himself "in these businesses, has (though Friedrich does not yet know "it) dexterously seized Kolin, westward in those Elbe parts, — "ground that will be notable in years coming. Important "little feat of Nassau's; of which anon. On the other hand, "our Magazine at Pardubitz, eastward on the Elbe, is not out "of danger: Pandours and regulars 2,000 and odd, 'sixty of "'the Pandour kind disguised as peasants leading haycarts,' "made an attempt there lately; but were detected by the

* *Œuvres de Frédéric,* III. 63, 64; Orlich, II. 69.

** *Military Instructions* (above cited), p. 44.

"vigilant Colonel, and blown to pieces, in the nick of time, "some of them actually within the gate.* Nay, a body of "Austrian regulars were in full march for Kolin lately, "intending to get hold of the Elbe itself at that point (midway "between Prag and Pardubitz): but the prompt General "Nassau, as we remarked, had struck in before them; and "now holds Kolin; — though, for several days, Friedrich could "not tell what had become of Nassau, owing to the swarms of "Pandours.

"Friedrich, standing with his back to Prag, which is fifty "miles from him, and rather in need of his support than able "to give him any; and drawing his meal from the uncertain "distance, with Pandours hovering round, — is in difficult "case. While old Traun is kept luminous as midday; the "circumambient atmosphere of Pandours is tenebrific to "Friedrich, keeps him in perpetual midnight. He has to read "his position as with flashes of lightning, for most part. A "heavy-laden, sorely exasperated man; and must keep his "haggard miseries strictly secret; which I believe he does. "Were Valori here, it is very possible he might find the coun-"tenance *farouche* again; eyes gloomy, on damp November "mornings! Schwerin, in a huff, has gone home: Since your "Majesty is pleased to prefer his young Durchlaucht of An-"halt's advice, what can an elderly servant (not without rheu-"matisms) do other? — 'Well!' answers Friedrich, not with "eyes cheered by the phenomenon. The Elbe-Sazawa tract, "even this looks as if it would be hard to keep. A world very "dark for Friedrich, enveloped so by the ill chances and the "Pandours. But what help?

"From the French Camp far away, there comes, dated "17th October (third week of their Siege of Freyburg), by "way of help to Friedrich, magnanimous promise: 'So soon "'as this Siege is done, which will be speedily, though it is "'difficult, we propose to send fifty battalions and a hundred "'squadrons,' — say only 60,000 horse and foot (not a hoof or toe of which ever got that length, on actually trying it), — 'towards Westphalia, to bring the Elector of Köln to reason' (poor Kaiser's lanky Brother, who cannot stand the French procedures, and has lately sold himself, that is sold his troops, to England), 'and keep the King of England and the Dutch

* *Œuvres de Frédéric*, III. 65.

in check,' — by way of solacement to your Majesty. Will you indeed, you magnanimous Allies? — This was picked up by the Pandours; and I know not but Friedrich was spared the useless pain of reading it.*

"*November 1st-9th: Friedrich loses Sazawa-Elbe Country* "*too.* On the first day of November, here is a lightning-flash "which reveals strange things to Friedrich. Traun's late "manœuverings, which have been so enigmatic, to right and "to left, upon Prag and other points, issue now in an attempt "towards Pardubitz; which reveals to Friedrich the intention "Traun has formed, of forcing him to choose one of those two "places, and let go the other. Formidable, fatal, thinks "Friedrich; and yet admirable on the part of Traun: 'a "'design beautiful and worthy of admiration.' If we stay "near Prag, what becomes of our Communication with Silesia; "what becomes of Silesia itself? If we go towards Pardubitz, "Prag and Böhmen are lost! What to do? 'Despatch rein-"'forcement to Pardubitz; thanks to Nassau, the Kolin-"'Pardubitz road is ours!' That is done, Pardubitz saved "for the moment. Could we now get to Kuttenberg before "the old Marshal, his design were overset altogether. Alas, "we cannot march at once, have to wait a day for the bread. "Forward, nevertheless; and again forward, and again; three "heavy marches in November weather: let us make a fourth "forced march, start tomorrow before dawn, — Kuttenberg "above all things! In vain; tomorrow, 4th November, there "is such a fog, dark as London itself, from six in the morning "onwards, no starting till noon: and then impossible, with all "our efforts, to reach Kuttenberg. We have to halt an eight "miles short of it, in front of Kolin; and pitch tents there. "On the morrow, 5th November, Traun is found encamped, "unattackable, between us and our object; sits there, at his "ease in a friendly Country, with Pandour whirlpools flowing "out and in; an irreducible case to Friedrich. November "5th, and for three days more, Friedrich, to no purpose, tries "his utmost; — finds he will have to give up the Elbe-Sazawa "region, like the others. Monday, November 9th, Friedrich "gathers himself at Kolin; crosses the Elbe by Kolin Bridge, "that day. Point after point of the game going against "him."

* Orlich, II. 73.

Kolin was, of course, attacked, that Monday evening, so soon as the main Army crossed: but, so soon as the Army left, General Nassau had taken his measures; and, with his great guns and his small, handled the Pandours in a way that pleased us.* Thursday night following, they came back, with regular grenadiers to support; under cloud of night, in great force, ruffian Trenck at the head of them: a frightful phenomenon to weak nerves. But this also Nassau treated in such a fiery fashion that it vanished without return; three hundred dead left on the ground, and ruffian Trenck riding off with his own crown broken, — beautiful indigo face streaking itself into *gingham*-pattern, for the moment!

Except Pardubitz, where also the due battalions are left, Friedrich now holds no post south of the Elbe in this quarter; Elbe-Sazawa Tract is gone like the others, to all appearance. And we must now say, Silesia or Prag? Prince Leopold, Council-of-War being held on the matter, is for keeping hold of Prag: "Pity to lose all the excellent siege-artillery we brought thither," says he. True, too true; an ill-managed business that of Prag! thinks Friedrich sadly to himself: but what is Prag and artillery, compared to Silesia? Parthian retreat into Silesia; and let Prag and the artillery go: that, to Friedrich, is clearly the sure course. Or perhaps the fatal alternative will not actually arrive? So long as Pardubitz and Kolin hold; and we have the Elbe for barrier? Truth is, Prince Karl has himself written to Court that, having now pushed his Enemy fairly over the Elbe, and Winter being come with its sleets and slushes, ruinous to

* *Œuvres de Frédéric*, III. 68.

troops that have been so marched about, the Campaign ought to end; — nay, his own young Wife is in perilous interesting circumstances, and the poor Prince wishes to be home. To which, however, it is again understood, Maria Theresa has emphatically answered, "No, — finish first!"

November 9th-19th: We defend the Elbe River. Friedrich has posted himself on the north shore of the Elbe, from Pardubitz to the other side of Kolin; means to defend that side of the River, where go the Silesian roads. At Bohdenetz, short way across from Pardubitz, he himself is; Prince Leopold is near Kolin: thirty miles of river-bank to dispute. The controversy lasts ten days; ends in *Elbe-Teinitz*, a celebrated "passage," in Books and otherwise. Friedrich is in shaggy, intricate country; no want of dingles, woods and quagmires; now and then pleasant places too, — here is Kladrup for example, where our Father came three hundred miles to dine with the Kaiser once. The grooms and colts are all off at present; Father and Kaiser are off; and much is changed since then. Grim tussle of War now; sleety winter, and the Giant Mountains in the distance getting on their white hoods! Friedrich doubtless has his thoughts as he rides up and down, in sight of Kladrup, among other places, settling many things; but what his thoughts were, he is careful not to say except where necessary. Much is to be looked after, in this River controversy of thirty miles. Detachments lie, at intervals, all the way; and mounted sentries, a sentry every five miles, patrol the River-bank; vigilant, we hope, as lynxes. Nothing can cross but alarm will be given, and by degrees the whole Prussian force be upon it. This is the Circle of Königgrätz, this that now lies to rear; and happily there are a few Hussites in it, not utterly indisposed to do a little spying for us, and bring a glimmering of intelligence, now and then.

It is now the second week that Friedrich has lain so, with his mounted patrols in motion, with his Hussite spies; guarding Argus-like this thirty miles of River; and the Austrians attempt nothing, or nothing with effect. If the Austrians go home to their winter-quarters, he hopes to issue from Kolin again before Spring, and to sweep the Elbe-Sazawa Tract clear of them, after all. Maria Theresa having answered No, it is likely the Austrians will try to get across: Be vigilant, therefore, ye mounted sentries. Or will they perhaps make an attempt on Prag? Einsiedel, who has no garrison of the least adequacy, apprises us, That "in all the villages round Prag, people are busy making ladders," — what can that mean? Friedrich has learned, by intercepted letters, that something great is to be done on Wednesday 18th: he sends Rothenburg with reinforcement to Einsiedel, lest a scalade of Prag should be on the cards. Rothenburg is right welcome in the lines of Prag, though with reinforcement still ineffectual; but it is not Prag that is meant, nor is Wednesday the day. Through Wednesday, Friedrich, all eye and ear, could observe nothing: much marching to and fro on the Austrian side of the River; but apparently it comes to nothing? The mounted patrols had better be vigilant, however.

On the morrow, 5 A.M., what is this that is going on? Audible booming of cannon, of musketry and battle, echoing through the woods, penetrates to Friedrich's quarters at Bohdenetz in the Pardubitz region: Attack upon Kolin, Nassau defending himself there? Out swift scouts, and see! Many scouts gallop out; but none comes back. Friedrich, for hours, has to remain uncertain; can only hope Nassau will defend himself. Boom, go the distant volleyings; no scout comes back. And it is not Nassau or Kolin; it is something worse: very glorious for Prussian valour, but ruinous to this Campaign.

The Austrians, at two o'clock this morning, Austrians and Saxons, came in great force, in dead silence, to the south brink of the River, opposite a place called Teinitz (Elbe-Teinitz), ten miles east of Kolin; that was the fruit of their marching yesterday. They sat there forbidden to speak, to smoke tobacco or do anything but breathe, till all was ready; till pontoons, cannons had come up, and some gleam of dawn had broken. At the first gleam of dawn, as they are shoving down their pontoon boats, there comes a "*Wer-da*, Who goes?" from our Prussian patrol across the River. Receiving no answer, he fires; and is himself shot down. One Wedell, Wedell and Ziethen, who keep watch in this part, start instantly at sound of these shots; and make a dreadful day of it for these invasive Saxon and Austrian multitudes. Naturally, too, they send off scouts, galloping for more help, to the right and to the left. But that avails not. Wild doggery of Pandours, it would seem, have already swum or waded the River, above Teinitz and below: — "Want of vigilance!" barks Friedrich impatiently: but such a doggery is difficult to watch with effect. At any rate, to the right and to the left, the woods are already beset with Pandours; every scout sent out is killed: and to east or to west there comes no news but an echoing of musketry, a boom of distant cannon.* Saxon-Austrian battalions, four or five, with unlimited artillery going, *versus* Wedell's one battalion, with musketry and Ziethen's hussars: it is fearful odds. The Prussians stand to it like heroes; doggedly, for four hours, continue the dispute, — till it is fairly desperate; "two bridges of the enemy's now finished;" — whereupon they manœuvre off, with Parthian or Prussian countenance, into the woods, safe, towards Kolin; "despatching definite news to Friedrich, which does arrive "about 11 A.M., and sets him at once on new measures."

This is a great feat in the Prussian military annals; for which, sad as the news was, Wedell got the name of Leonidas attached to him by Friedrich himself. And indeed it is a gallant passage of war; "Forcing of the Elbe at Teinitz;" of which I could give two Narratives, one from the Prussian, and one from the Saxon side;** didactic, admonitory to the military mind, nay to the civic reader that has sympathy with heroisms, with work done manfully, and terror and danger and difficulty well trampled under foot. Leonidas Wedell has an admirable silence, too; and Ziethen's lazily-hanging under-lip is in its old attitude again, now that the spasm is over. "*Was thuts?* They are across, without a doubt. We would have helped it, and could not. Steady!" —

* Orlich, II. 82-85.

** Seyfarth, *Beylage*, I 595-98; *Helden-Geschichte*, II. 1175-81.

Friedrich's Retreat; especially Einsiedel's from Prag.

Seeing, then, that they are fairly over, Friedrich, with a creditable veracity of mind, sees also that the game is done; and, that same night, he begins manœuvring towards Silesia, lest far more be lost by continuing the play. One column, under Leopold the Young Dessauer, goes through Glatz, takes the Magazine of Pardubitz along with it; — good to go in several columns, the enemy will less know which to chase. Friedrich, with another column, will wait for Nassau about Königsgrätz, then go by the more westerly road, through Nachod and the Pass of Braunau. Nassau, who is to get across from Kolin, and join us northwards, has due rendezvous appointed him in the Königsgrätz region. Einsiedel, in Prag, is to spike his guns, since he cannot carry them; blow up his bastions, and the like; and get away with all discretion and all diligence, — north-westward first, to Leitmeritz, where our magazines are; there to leave his heavier goods, and make eastward towards Friedland, and across the "Silesian Combs," by what Passes he can. Will have a difficult operation; but must stand to it. And speed; steady, simultaneous, regular, unresting velocity; that is the word for all.

And so it is done, — though with difficulty, on the part of poor Einsiedel for one. It was Thursday 19th November, when the Austrians got across the Elbe: on Monday 23d, the Prussian rendezvousings are completed; and Friedrich's column, and the Glatz one under Leopold, are both on march; infinite baggage-wagons groaning orderly along ('sick-wagons well ahead,' and the like precautions and arrangements), on both these highways for Silesia: and before the week ends, Thursday 26th, even Einsiedel is under way. Let us give something of poor Einsiedel, whose disasters made considerable noise in the world, that Winter and afterwards.

"The two main columns were not much molested; that "which went by Glatz, under Leopold, was not pursued at "all. On the rear of Friedrich's own column, going towards "Braunau, all the way to Nachod or beyond, there hung the "usual doggery of Pandours, which required whipping off "from time to time; but in the defiles and difficult places due "precaution was taken, and they did little real damage. "Truchsess von Waldburg" (our old friend of the Spartan feat near Austerlitz in the *Moravian-Foray* time, whom we have known in London society as Prussian Envoy in bygone years) "was in one of the divisions of this column; and one "day, at a village where there was a little river to cross "(river Mietau, Königsgrätz branch of the Elbe), got pro-"voked injudiciously into fighting with a body of these "people. Intent not on whipping them merely, but on whip-"ping them to death, Truchsess had already lost some forty "men, and the business with such crowds of them was getting "hot; when, all at once a loud squeaking of pigs was heard "in the village," — apprehensive swineherd hastily penning his pigs belike, and some pig refractory; — "at sound of "which, the Pandour multitude suddenly pauses, quits fight-"ing, and, struck by a new enthusiasm, rushes wholly into "the village; leaving Truchsess, in a tragi-comic humour, "victorious, but half ashamed of himself.* In the beginning "of December, Friedrich's column reached home, by Braunau "through the Mountains, the same way part of it had come in "August; not quite so brilliant in equipment now as then.

"It was upon Einsiedel's poor Garrison, leaving Prag in "such haste, that the real stress of the retreat fell; its diffi-"culties great indeed, and its losses great. Einsiedel did "what was possible; but all things are not possible on a

* *Œuvres de Frédéric*, III. 73.

"week's warning. He spiked great guns, shook endless "hundredweights of powder, and 10,000 stand of arms, into "the River; he requisitioned horses, oxen, without number; "put mines under the bastions, almost none of which went off "with effect. He kept Prag accurately shut, the Praguers "accurately in the dark; took his measures prudently; and "laboured night and day. One measure I note of him: "stringent Proclamation to the inhabitants of Prag, 'Pro-"'vision yourselves for three months; nothing but starvation "'ahead otherwise.' Alas, we are to stand a fourth siege, "then? say the Praguers. But where are provisions to be "had? At such and such places; from the Royal Magazines "only, if you bring a certificate and ready money! Whereby "Einsiedel got delivered of his meal-magazine, for one thing. "But his difficulties otherwise were immense.

"On the Thursday morning, 26th November 1744, he "marched. His wagons had begun the night before; and "went all night, rumbling continuous (Anonymous of Prag* "hearing them well), through the Karl-thor, north-west gate "of Prag, across the Moldau Bridge. All night across that "bridge, — Leitmeritz road, great road to the north-west: — "followed finally by the march of horse and foot. But news "had already fled abroad. Five hundred Pandours were in "the City, backed by the Butchers' lads and other riotous "*Gesindel*, before the rearguard got away. Sad tugging and "wriggling in consequence, much firing from windows, and "uproarious chaos; — so that Rothenburg had at last to "remount a couple of guns, and blow it off with case-shot. "A drilled Prussian rearguard struggling, with stern com-"posure, through a real bit of burning chaos. With effect, "though not without difficulty. Here is the scene on the "Moldau Bridge, and past that high Hradschin** mass of "buildings; all Prag, not the Hradschin only, struggling to "give us fatal farewell if it durst. River is covered with "Pandours firing out of boats; Bridge encumbered to im-"passability by forsaken wagons, the drivers of which had "cut traces and run; shot comes overhead from the Hradschin

* Second "*Letter* from a Citizen &c." (date, 27th November, see suprà, p. 24), in *Helden-Geschichte*, II. 1181-88.

** Old Palace of the Bohemian Kings (pronounce *Radsheen*); one of the steepest Royal Sites in the world.

"on our left, much shot, infinite tumult all round, thorough-"fare impossible for two-wheeled vehicle, or men in rank. "'Halt!' cries Colonel Brandes, who has charge of the thing; "divides them in three: 'First one party, deal with these "'river-boats, that Pandour doggery; second party, pull "'these stray wagons to right and left, making the way clear; "'third party, drag our own wagons forward, shoulder to shaft, "'and yoke them out of shot-range; — you, Captain Carlo-"'witz,' and calls twenty volunteers to go with Carlowitz, and "drag their own cannon, 'step you forward, keep the gate of "'that Hradschin till we all pass!' In this manner, rapid, "hard of stroke, clear-headed and with stern regularity, "drilled talent gets the burning Nessus'-shirt wriggled off; "and tramps successfully forth with its baggages. About "eleven A.M., this rearguard of Brandes's did; should have "been at seven, — right well that it could be at all.

"Einsiedel, after this, got tolerably well to Leitmeritz; "left his heavy baggage there; then turned at an acute angle "right eastward, towards the Silesian Combs, as ordered: "still a good seventy miles to do, and the weather getting "snowy and the days towards their shortest. Worse still; "old Weissenfels, now in Prag with his Saxons, is aware that "Einsiedel, before ending, will touch on a wild high-lying "corner of the Lausitz which is Saxon Country; and thither-"ward Weissenfels has despatched Chevalier de Saxe (in "plenty of time, November 29th), with horse and foot, to "waylay Einsiedel, and block the entrance of the Silesian "Mountains for him. Whereupon, in the latter end of his "long march, and almost within sight of home, ensues the "hardest brush of all for Einsiedel. And, in the desolation "of that rugged Hill country of the Lausitz, '*Hochwald* "'(Upper Wold),' twenty or more miles from Bohemian Fried-"land, from his entrance on the Mountain Barrier and Silesian "Combs, there are scenes — which gave rise to a Court-"Martial before long. For unexpectedly, on the winter after-"noon (December 9th), Einsiedel, struggling among the "snows and pathless Hills, comes upon Chevalier de Saxe "and his Saxon Detachment, — entrenched with trees, snow-"redoubts, and a hollow bog dividing us; plainly unas-"sailable; — and stands there, without covering, without "'food, fire, or salt,' says one Eye-witness, 'for the space of "'fourteen hours.' Gazing gloomily into it, exchanging a "few shots, uncertain what more to do; the much-dubitating "Einsiedel. 'At which the men were so disgusted and en-"'raged, they deserted' (the foreign part of them, I fancy) "'in groups at a time,' says the above Eye-witness. Not to "think what became of the equipments, baggage-wagons, "sick-wagons: — too evident Einsiedel's loss, in all kinds, "was very considerable. Nassau, despatched by Leopold "out of Glatz, from the other side of the Combs, is marching "to help Einsiedel; — who knows, at this moment, where or "whitherward? For the peasants are all against us; our "very guides desert, and become spies. 'Push to the left, "'over the Hochwald top, must not we?' thinks Einsiedel: "'that is Lausitz, a Saxon Country; and Saxony, though the "'Saxons stand entrenched here, with the knife at our throat, "'are not at war with us, oh no, only allies of Her Majesty of "'Hungary, and neutral otherwise!' And here, it is too "clear, the Chevalier de Saxe stands entrenched behind his "trees and snow; and it is the fourteenth hour, men deserting "by the hundred, without fire and without salt; and Nassau "is coming, — God knows by what road!

"Einsiedel pushes to the left, the Hochwald way; finds, "in the Hochwald too, a Saxon Commandant waiting him, "with arms strictly shouldered. 'And we cannot pass through "'this moor skirt of Lausitz, say you, then?' 'Unarmed, "'yes; your muskets can come in wagons after you,' replies "the Saxon Commandant of Lausitz. 'Thousand thanks, "'Herr Commandant; but we will not give you all that "'trouble,' answer Einsiedel and his Prussians; 'and march "'on, overwhelming him with politenesses,' says Friedrich; — "the approach of Nassau, above all, being a stringent civility. "Of course, despatch is very requisite to Einsiedel; the "Chevalier, with his force, being still within hail. The Prus-"sians march all night, with pitch-links flaring, — nights (I "think) of the 13th-15th December 1744, up among the high-"lands there, rugged buttresses of the Silesian Combs: a "sight enough to astonish Rübezahl, if he happened to be "out! As good chance would have it, Nassau and Einsiedel, "by preconcert, partly by lucky guess of their own, were "hurrying by the same road: three heaven-rending cheers "(December 16th) when we get sight of Nassau; and find "that here is land! December 16th, we are across, — by "Rückersdorf, not far from Friedland (Böhmisch Friedland, "not the Silesian town of that name, once Wallenstein's); — "and rejoice now to look back on labour done."*

These were intricate strange scenes, much talked of at the time: Rothenburg, ugly Walrave, Hacke, and other known figures, concerned in them. Scenes in which Friedrich is not well informed; who much blames Einsiedel, as he is apt to do the unsuccessful. Accounts exist, both from the Prussian and from the Saxon side, decipherable with industry; not now worth deciphering to English readers. Only that final scene of the pitch-links, the night before meeting with Nassau, dwells voluntarily in one's memory. And is the farewell of Einsiedel withal. Friedrich blames him to the last: though a Court-Martial had sat on his case, some months after, and honourably acquitted him. Good solid, silent Einsiedel; — and in some months more, he went to a still higher court, got still stricter justice: I do not hear expressly that it was the winter marches, or strain of mind; but he died in 1745; and that flare of pitch-links in Rübezahl's country is the last scene of him to us, — and the end of Friedrich's unfortunate First Expedition in the Second Silesian War.

"Foiled, ultimately then, on every point; a totally ill-ordered game on our part! Evidently we, for our part, have been altogether in the wrong, in various essential particulars. Amendment, that and no other, is the word now. Let us take the scathe and the scorn candidly home to us; — and try to prepare for doing better. The world will crow over us. Well,

* *Helden-Geschichte*, II. 1181-90, 1191-94; *Feldzüge*, I. 276-80.

the world knows little about it; the world, if it did know, would be partly in the right!" — Wise is he who, when beaten, learns the reasons of it, and alters these. This wisdom, it must be owned, is Friedrich's; and much distinguishes him among generals and men. Veracity of mind, as I say, loyal eyesight superior to sophistries; noble incapacity of self-delusion, the root of all good qualities in man. His epilogue to this Campaign is remarkable; — too long for quoting here, except the first word of it and the last:

"No general committed more faults than did the "King in this Campaign. * * The conduct of M. "de Traun is a model of perfection, which every soldier "that loves his business ought to study, and try to "imitate, if he have the talent. The King has him-"self admitted that he regarded this Campaign as his "school in the Art of War, and M. de Traun as his "teacher." But what shall we say? "Bad is often "better for Princes than good; — and instead of in-"toxicating them with presumption, renders them cir-"cumspect and modest."* Let us still hope! —

* *Œuvres*, III. 76, 77.

———

CHAPTER V.

FRIEDRICH, UNDER DIFFICULTIES, PREPARES FOR A NEW CAMPAIGN.

To the Court of Vienna, especially to the Hungarian Majesty, this wonderful reconquest of Bohemia, without battle fought, — or any cause assignable but Traun's excellent manœuvering and Friedrich's imprudences and trust in the French, — was a thing of heavenly miracle; blessed omen that Providence had vouchsafed to her prayers the recovery of Silesia itself. All the world was crowing over Friedrich: but her Majesty of Hungary's views had risen to a clearly higher pitch of exultation and triumphant hope, terrestrial and celestial, than any other living person's. "Silesia back again," that was now the hope and resolution of her Majesty's high heart: "My wicked neighbour shall be driven out, and smart dear for the ill he has done; Heaven so wills it!" "Very little uplifts the Austrians," says Valori; which is true, under such a Queen; "and yet "there is nothing that can crush them altogether down," adds he.

No sooner is Bohemia cleared of Friedrich, than Maria, winter as it is, orders that there be, through the Giant-Mountains, vigorous assault upon Silesia. Highland snows and ices, what are these to Pandour people, who, at their first entrance on the scene of History, "crossed the Palus-Mæotis itself" (Father of

Quagmires, so to speak) "in a frozen state," and were sufficiently accommodated each in his own dirty sheepskin? "Prosecute the King of Prussia," ordered she; "take your winter-quarters in Silesia;" — and Traun, in spite of the advanced season, and prior labours and hardships, had to try, from the south-western Bohemian side, what he could do; while a new Insurrection, coming through the Jablunka, spread itself over the south-east and east. Seriously invasive multitudes; which were an unpleasant surprise to Friedrich; and did, as we shall see, require to be smitten back again, and re-smitten; — making a very troublesome winter to the Prussians and themselves; but by no means getting winter-quarters, as they once hoped.

In a like sense, Maria Theresa had already (December 2d) sent forth her Manifesto or Patent, solemnly apprising her ever-faithful Silesian Populations, "That the Treaty of Breslau, not by her fault, is broken; palpably a Treaty no longer. That they, accordingly, are absolved from all oaths and allegiance to the King of Prussia; and shall hold themselves in readiness to swear anew to her Majesty, which will be a great comfort to such faithful creatures; suffering, as her Majesty explains to them that they have done, under Prussian tyranny for these two years past. Immediate dead-lift effort there shall be; that is certain; and 'the Almighty God assisting, who does not leave 'such injustices unpunished, We have the fixed Christian hope, Omnipotence blessing our arms, of almost 'immediately (*ehestens*) delivering you from this temporary Bondage (*bisherigen Joch*).' You can pray, in the mean while, for the success of her Majesty's arms;

good fighting, aided by prayer, in a Cause clearly Heaven's, will now, to appearance bring matters swiftly round again, to the astonishment and confusion of bad men."*

These are her Majesty's views; intensely true, I doubt not, to her devout heart. Robinson and the English seem not to be enthusiastic in that direction; as indeed how can they? They would fain be tender of Silesia, which they have guaranteed; fain, now and afterwards, restrain her Majesty from driving at such a pace down hill: but the declivity is so encouraging, her Majesty is not to be restrained, and goes faster and faster for the time being. And indeed, under less devout forms, the general impression, among Pragmatic people, Saxon, Austrian, British even, was, That Friedrich had pretty much ruined himself, and deserved to do so; that this of his being mere "Auxiliary" to a Kaiser in distress was an untenable pretext, now justly fallen bankrupt upon him. The evident fact, That he had by his "Frankfurt Union," and struggles about "union," *re*opened the door for French tribulations and rough-ridings in the Reich, was universally distasteful; all chance of a "general union of German Princes, in aid of their Kaiser," was extinct for the present.

Friedrich's rapidity had served him ill with the Public, in this as in some other instances! Friedrich, contemplating his situation, not self-delusively, but with the candour of real remorse, was by no means yet aware how very bad it was. For six months coming, partly as existing facts better disclosed themselves,

* In *Helden-Geschichte*, II. 1194-1198; Ib. 1201-1206, is Friedrich's Answer, "19th December 1744."

as France, Saxony and others showed what spirit they were of; partly as new sinister events and facts arrived one after the other, — his outlook continued to darken and darken, till it had become very dark indeed. There is perennially the great comfort, immense if you can manage it, of making front against misfortune; of looking it frankly in the face, and doing with a resolution, hour by hour, your own utmost against it. Friedrich never lacked that comfort; and was not heard complaining. But from December 13th, 1744, when he hastened home to Berlin, under such aspects, till June 4th, 1745, when aspects suddenly changed, are probably the worst six months Friedrich had yet had in the world. During which, his affairs all threatening to break down about him, he himself, behoving to stand firm if the worst was not to realise itself, had to draw largely on what silent courage, or private inexpugnability of mind, was in him, — a larger instalment of that royal quality (as I compute) than the Fates had ever hitherto demanded of him. Ever hitherto; though perhaps nothing like the largest of all, which they had upon their Books for him, at a farther stage! As will be seen. For he was greatly drawn upon in that way, in his time. And he paid always; no man in his Century so well; few men, in any Century, better. As perhaps readers may be led to guess or acknowledge, on surveying and considering. To see, and sympathetically recognise, cannot be expected of modern readers, in the present great distance, and changed conditions of men and things.

Friedrich, after despatching Nassau to cut out Einsiedel, had delivered the Silesian Army to the Old Dessauer, who is to command in chief during Winter;

and had then hastened to Berlin, — many things there urgently requiring his presence; preparations, reparations, not to speak of diplomacies, and what was the heaviest item of all, new finance for the coming exertions. In Schweidnitz, on Leopold's appearance, there had been an interview, due consultings, orderings; which done, Friedrich at once took the road; and was at Berlin, Monday December 14th, — precisely in the time while Nassau and Einsiedel were marching with torch-lights in Rübezahl's Country, and near ending their difficult enterprise better or worse.

Friedrich, fastening eagerly on Home business, is astonished and provoked to learn that the Austrians, not content with pushing him out of Böhmen, are themselves pushing into Schlesien, — so Old Leopold reports, with increasing emphasis day by day; to whom Friedrich sends impatient order: Hurl them out again, gather what force you need, ten thousand, or were it twenty or thirty thousand, and be immediate about it; "I will "as soon be pitched (*herausgeschmissen*) out of the Mark "of Brandenburg as out of Schlesien:" no delay, I tell you! And as the Old Dessauer still explains that the ten or fifteen thousand he needs are actually assembling, and cannot be got on march quite in a moment, Friedrich dashes away his incipient Berlin Operations; will go himself and do it. Haggle no more, you tedious Old Dessauer:

Berlin, "*19th December*" 1744. — "On the 21st" (Monday, one week after my arriving), "I leave Berlin, and mean to be "at Neisse on the 24th at latest. Your Serenity will in the "interim make out the Order-of-Battle" (which is also Order-of-March) "for what regiments are come in. For I will, on "the 25th, without delay, cross the Neisse, and attack those "people, cost what it may, — to chase them out of Schlesien "and Glatz, and follow them so far as possible. Your Serenity "will therefore take your measures, and provide everything, "so far as in this short time you can, that the project may be "executable the moment I arrive."*

And rushed off accordingly, in a somewhat flamy humour; but at Schweidnitz, where the Old Dessauer met him again, became convinced that the matter was weightier than he thought; not one of Tolpatchery alone, but had Traun himself in it. Upon which Friedrich candidly drew bridle; hastened back, and, with a loss of four days, was at his Potsdam Affairs again. To which he stuck henceforth, ardently, and I think rather with increase of gloom, though without spurt of impatience farther, for three months to come. Before his return, — nay, had he known, it was the night before he went away, — a strange little thing had happened in the opposite or Western parts: surprising accident to Maréchal de Belleisle; which now lies waiting his immediate consideration. But let us finish Silesia first.

Old Dessauer repels the Silesian Invasion (Winter 1744-5).

"This Silesian Affair includes due inroad of Pandours; or "indeed two inroads, south-west and south-east; and in the "south-west, or Traun quarter, regulars are the main element "of it. Traun, 20,000 strong, *plus* stormy enough Pandour "*accompaniment*, is by this time through into Glatz; in three "columns; — is master of all Glatz, except the Rock-Fortress "itself; and has spread himself, right and left, along the "Neisse River, and from the south-west northwards, in a skil"ful and dangerous manner. In concert with whom, far to "the east, are Pandour whirlwinds on their own footing "(brand-new 'Insurrection' of them, got thus far), starting

* Friedrich to the Old Dessauer (*Orlich*, ii. 356).

"from Olmütz and Brünn; scouring that eastern country, as "far as Namslau northward" (a place we were at the taking of, in old Brieg times); "much more, infesting the Mountains "of the South. A rather serious thing; with Traun for "general manager of it."

With Traun, we say: Poor Prince Karl is off, weeks ago; on the saddest of errands. His beautiful young Wife, — Hungarian Majesty's one Sister, Vice-Regents of the Netherlands he and she, conspicuous among the bright couples of the world, — she had a bad lying-in (child still-born), while those grand Moldau Operations went on; has been ill, poor lady, ever since; and, at Brussels, on December 16th, she herself lies dead, Prince Karl weeping over her and the days that will not return. Prince Karl's felicities, private and public, had been at their zenith lately, which was very high indeed; but go on declining from this day. Never more the Happiest of Husbands (did not wed again at all); still less the Greatest of Captains, equal or superior to Cæsar in the Gazetteer judgment, with distracted *Eulogies*, *Biographies*, and such-like, filling the air: before long, a War-Captain of quite moderate renown; which we shall see sink gradually into no renown at all, and even (unjustly) into *minus* quantities, before all end. A mad world, my masters! —

"Between Traun on the south-west hand, and his Pan-"dours on the south-east, the small Prussian posts have all "been driven in upon Troppau-Jägerndorf region; more and "more narrowed there; — and, in fine (two days before this "new Interview of Leopold and the impatient King at "Schweidnitz), have had to quit the Troppau-Jägerndorf "position; to quit the Hills altogether, and are now in full "march towards Brieg. Of which march I should say "nothing, were it not that Marwitz, Father of Wilhelmina's "giggling Marwitzes, commanded; — and came by his death "in the course of it; though our Wilhelmina is not now there, "pen in hand, to tell us what the effects at Baireuth were. "Marwitz had been left for dead on the Field of Mollwitz; "lay so all night, but was nursed to some kind of strength "again by those giggling young women; and came back to "Schlesien, to posts of chief trust, for the last year or two, — "was guarding the Mountains, and even invading Mähren, "during the late Campaign; — but saw himself reduced "latterly to Jägerndorf and Troppau; and had even to retreat "out of these. And in the whirlpool of hurries thereupon, — "how is not very clear; by apoplexy, say some; by accidental "pistol from a servant of his own; in actual skirmish with "Pandours, — too certainly, one way or the other, on December 23d (just during that second Interview at Schweidnitz), "brave old Marwitz did suddenly sink dead, and is ended.* "Even so, ye poor giggling creatures, and your loud weeping "will not mend it at all!

"Friedrich, looking candidly into these phenomena, could "not but see that, what with Tolpatcheries, what with Traun's "20,000 regulars, and the whole Army at their back, his "Silesian Border is girt in by a very considerable inroad of "Austrians, — huge Chain of them, in horse-shoe form, 300 "miles long, pressing in; from beyond Glatz and Landshut, "round by the southern Mountains, and up eastward again as "far as Namslau, nothing but war whirlwinds in regular or "irregular form, in the centre of them Traun; — and that the "Old Dessauer really must have time to gird himself for dealing with Traun and them.

"It was not till January 9th that Old Leopold, 25,000 "strong, equipped to his mind, which was a difficult matter, "crossed the Neisse River; and marched direct upon Traun, "with Ziethen charging ahead. Actually marched; after "which the main wrestle was done in a week. January 16th, "Old Leopold got to Jägerndorf; found the actual Traun "concentrated at Jägerndorf; and drew up, to be ready for "assault tomorrow morning, — had not Traun, candidly "computing, judged it better to glide wholly away in the "night-time, diligently towards Mähren, breaking the bridges "behind him. And so, in effect, to give up the Silesian Invasion for this time. After which, though there remained a "good deal of rough tusselling with Pandour details, and "some rugged exploits of fight, there is, — except that of "Lehwald in clearing of Glatz, — nothing farther that we "can afford to speak of. Lehwald's exploit, Lehwald *versus* "Wallis (same Wallis who defended Glogau long since), "which came to be talked of, and got name and date, 'Action

* *Helden Geschichte*, II. 1201.

"'of Habelschwert, February 14th,' something almost like a "pitched fight on the small scale, is to the following effect:

"*Plomnitz, near Habelschwert, 14th February* 1745. Old "General Lehwald, marching in the hollow ground near "Habelschwert (hollow of the young Neisse River, twenty "miles south of Glatz), with intent to cut that Country free; "the Enemy, whom he is in search of, appears in great force, "—posted on the uphill ground ahead, half-frozen difficult "stream in front of them, cannon on flank, Pandour multitude "in woods; all things betokening inexpugnability on the "part of the Enemy. So that Lehwald has to take his "measures; study well where the vital point is, the *root* of that "extensive Austrian junglery, and cut in upon the same. By "considerable fire of effort, the uphill ground, half-frozen "stream, sylvan Pandours, cannon-batteries, and what in-"expugnabilities there may be, are subdued; Austrian wide "junglery, the root of it slit asunder, rolls homeward simul-"taneously, not too fast: nay it halted and re-ranked itself "twice over, finding woods and quaggy runlets to its mind; "but was always slit out again, disrooted, and finally tum-"bled home, having had enough. 'Wenzel Wallis,' Fried-"rich asserts with due scorn, 'was all this while in a Chapel; "'praying ardently,' to St. Vitus, or one knows not whom; "'without effect; till they shouted to him, ""Beaten, Sir! Off, "'or you are lost!"" upon which he sprang to saddle, and "'spurred with both heels *(piqua des deux)*.'* That was the "feat of Lehwald, clearing the Glatz Country with one good "cut: a skilful Captain; now getting decidedly oldish, close "on sixty; whom we shall meet again a dozen years hence, "still in harness.

"The old Serene Highness himself, face the colour of "gunpowder, and bluer in the winter frost, went rushing far "and wide in an open vehicle, which he called his 'cart;' "pushing out detachments, supervising everything; wheeling "hither and thither as needful; sweeping out the Pandour "world, and keeping it out: not much of fighting needed, but "'a great deal of marching' (murmurs Friedrich), 'which in "'winter is as bad, and wears down the force of the battalions.' Of all which we give no detail: sufficient to fancy, "in this

* *Œuvres de Frédéric*, III. 79, 80.

"manner, the Old Dessauer flapping his wide military wings "in the faces of the Pandour hordes, with here and there a "hard twitch from beak or claws; tolerably keeping down "the Pandour interest all Winter. His sons, Leopold and "Dietrich, were under him, occasionally beside him; the "Junior Leopold so worn down with feverish gout he could "hardly sit on horseback at all, while old Papa went tearing "about in his cart at that rate." *

There was, on the 21st of February, *Te-deum* sung in the Churches of Berlin "for the Deliverance of Silesia from Invasion." Not that, even yet, the Pandours would be quite quiet, or allow Old Leopold to quit his cart; far from it. And they returned in such increased and tempestuous state, as will again require mention, with the earliest Spring: — precursors to a second, far more serious and deadly "Invasion of Silesia;" for which it hangs yet on the balance whether there will be a *Te-deum* or a *Miserere* to sing!

Hungarian Majesty, disappointed of Silesia, — which, it seems, is not to be had "all at once (*ehestens*)," in the form of miracle, — makes amends by a rush upon Seckendorf and Bavaria; attacks Seckendorf furiously ("Bathyani pressing up the Donau Valley, "with Browne on one hand, and Bärenklau on the "other") in mid-winter; and makes a terrible hand of him; reducing his "Reconquest of Bavaria" to nothing again, nay to less. Of which in due time.

* *Unternehmung in Ober-Schlesien, unter dem Fürsten Leopold* von *Anhalt-Dessau, im Januar und Februar* 1745 (Seyfarth, *Beyträge*, I. 141-152); Stenzel, IV. 232; &c.

The French fully intend to behave better next Season to Friedrich and their German Allies; — but are prevented by various Accidents (November 1744 — April 1745; April — August 1745).

It is not divine miracle, Friedrich knows well, that has lost him his late Bohemian Conquests without battle fought: it was rash choosing of a plan inexecutable without French coöperation, — culpable blindness to the chance that France would break its promises, and not coöperate. Had your Majesty forgotten the Joint-Stock Principle, then? His Majesty has sorrowful cause to remember it, from this time, on a still larger scale!

Reflections, indignant or exculpatory, on the conduct of the French in this Business are useless to Friedrich, and to us. The performance, on their part, has been nearly the worst; — though their intentions, while the Austrian Dragon had them by the throat, were doubtless enthusiastically good! But, the big Austrian Dragon being jerked away from Elsass, by Friedrich's treading on his tail, 500 miles off, they were charmed, quite into new enthusiasm, to be rid of said Dragon: and, instead of chasing *him* according to bargain, took to destroying his *Den*, that he might be harmless thenceforth. Freyburg is a captured Town, to the joy and glory of admiring France; and Friedrich's Campaign has gone the road we see! The Freyburg Illuminations having burnt out, there might rise, in the triumphant mind, some thought of Friedrich again, — perhaps almost of a remorseful nature? Certain it is, the French intentions are now again magnanimous, more so than ever; coupled now with some attempts at fulfilment, too; which obliges us to mention them here. They were still a matter of important hope to Friedrich; hope which did not quite go out till August coming. Though, alas, it did then go out, in gusts of indignation on Friedrich's part! And as the whole of these magnanimous French intentions, latter like former, again came to zero, we are interested only in rendering them conceivable to readers for Friedrich's sake, — with the more brevity, the better for everybody. Two grand French Attempts there were; listen, on the threshold, a little:

* * "It is certain the French intend gloriously; regard-"less of expense. They are dismantling Freyburg, to render "it harmless henceforth. But, withal, in answer to the poor "Kaiser's shrieks, they have sent Ségur" (our old Linz friend), "with 12,000, to assist Seckendorf; 'the bravest troops in the "'world,'" — who did bravely take one beating (at Pfaffenhofen, as will be seen), and go home again. "They have "Coigny guarding those fine Brisgau Conquests. And are "furthermore diplomatising diligently, not to say truculently, "in the Rhine Countries; bullying poor little fat Kur-Trier, "lean Kur-Köln, and others, 'To join the Frankfurt Union' "(not one of whom would, under menace), — though 'it is "'the clear duty of all Reich's-Princes with a Kaiser under "'oppression:' — and have marched Maillebois, directly "after Freyburg, into the Middle-Rhine Countries, to Köln "Country, to Mainz Country, and to and fro, in support of "said compulsory diplomacies; — but without the least effect."

To the "Middle-Rhine Countries," observe, and under Maillebois, then under Conti, little matter under whom: only let readers recollect the name of it; — for it is the *First* of the French Attempts to do something of a joint-stock nature; something for self *and* Allies, instead of for self only. It caused great alarm in those months, to Britannic George and others; and brought out poor Duc d'Ahremberg with portions (no English included) of the poor Pragmatic Army, to go marching about in the winter-slushes, instead of resting in bed,* — and is indeed a very loud business in the old Gazettes and books, till August coming. Business which almost broke poor D'Ahremberg's heart, he says, "till once I got out of it" (was *turned* out, in fact): Business of Pragmatic Army, under D'Ahremberg, *versus* Middle-Rhine Army under Maillebois, under Conti; Business now wholly of Zero *versus* Zero to us, — except for a few dates and reflex glimmerings upon King Friedrich. Result otherwise — We shall see the result!

"Attempt *Second* was still more important to Friedrich; "being directed upon the Kaiser and Bavaria. Belleisle is to "go thither and take survey; Belleisle thither first: you may "judge if the intention is sincere! Valori is quite eloquent "upon it. Directly after Freyburg, says he, Séchelles, that "first of Commissaries, was sent to München. Séchelles "cleared up the chaos of Accounts; which King Louis then "instantly paid. 'Your Imperial Majesty shall have Maga- "'zines also,' said Louis, regardless of expense; 'and your "'Army, with auxiliaries (Ségur and 25,000 of them French), "'shall be raised to 60,000.' Belleisle then came: 'We will "'have Ingolstadt, the first thing, in Spring.' Alas, Belleisle "had his Accident in the Harz; and all went aback, from "that time."** Aback, too indisputably, all! — 'And Belleisle's Accident?' Patience, readers.

"The truth is, Attempt *Second*, and chief, broke down at "once" (Bathyani beating it to pieces, as will be seen), — "the ruins of it painfully reacting on Attempt *First;* which "had the like fate some months later; — and there was no "*Third* made. And in fact from the date of that latter down- "break, August, or end of July, 1745" (and quite especially from 'September 13th,' by which time several irrevocable things had happened, which we shall hear of), "the French "withdrew altogether out of German entanglements; and "concentrated themselves upon the Netherlands, there to de- "molish his Britannic Majesty, as the likelier enterprise. "This was a course to which, ever since the Exit of Broglio "and the Oriflamme, they had been more and more tending "and inclining, 'Nothing for us but loss on loss, to be had in "'Germany!' and so they at last frankly gave up that bad

* Adelung, IV. 276, 490 ("Dec. 1744 — June 1745"). ** Valori, I. 223-8.

"Country. They fought well in the Netherlands, with great "splendour of success, under Saxe *versus* Cumberland and "Company. They did also some successful work in Italy; — "and left Friedrich to bear the brunt in Germany; too glad if "he or another were there to take Germany off their hand! "Friedrich's feelings on his arriving at this consummation, "and during his gradual advance towards it, which was "pretty steady all along from those first 'drenched-hen "'(*poules mouillées*)' procedures, were amply known to Ex-"cellency Valori, and may be conceived by readers," — who are slightly interested in the dates of them at farthest. And now for the Belleisle Accident, with these faint preliminary lights.

Strange Accident to Maréchal de Belleisle in the Harz Mountains (20th December 1744).

Siege of Freyburg being completed, and the River and most other things (except always the bastions, which we blow up) being let into their old channels there, Maréchal de Belleisle, who is to have a chief management henceforth, — the Most Christian King recognising him again as his ablest man in war or peace, — sets forth on a long tour of supervision, of diplomacy, and general arrangement, to prepare matters for the next Campaign. Need enough of a Belleisle: what a business *we* have made of it, since Friedrich trod on the serpent's tail for us! Nothing but our own Freyburg to show for ourselves; elsewhere, mere downrush of every thing whitherward it liked; — and King Friedrich got into such a humour! Friedrich must be put in tune again; something real and good to be agreed on at Berlin: let that be the last thing, crown of the whole. The first thing is, look into Bavaria a little; and how the Kaiser, poor gentleman, in want of all requisites but goodwill, can be put into something of fighting posture.

"In the end of November, Maréchal Duc de Belleisle, with "his Brother the Chevalier (now properly the *Count*, there "having been promotions), and a great retinue more, alights "at München; holds council with the poor Kaiser for certain "days: — Money wanted; many things wanted; and all "things, we need not doubt, much fallen out of square. "'Those Seckendorf troops in their winter-quarters,' say our "French Inspectors and Ségur people, as usual, 'Do but "'look on it, your Excellency! Scattered, along the valleys, "'into the very edge of Austria; Austria will swallow them, "'the first thing, next year; they will never rendezvous again "'except in the Austrian prisons. Surely, Monseigneur, only "'a man ignorant of war, or with treasonous intention,' — (or "ill off for victuals), — 'could post troops in that way? "'Seckendorf is not ignorant of war!' say they.* For, in fact, "suspicion runs high; and there is no end to the accusations "just and unjust; and Seckendorf is as ill treated as any of us "could wish. Poor old soul. Probably nobody in all the "Earth, but his old Wife in the Schloss of Altenburg, has "any pity for him, — if even she, which I hope. He has "fought and diplomatised and intrigued in many countries, "very much; and in his old days is hard bested. Monseigneur, "whose part is rather that of Jove the Cloud-compeller, is "studious to be himself noiseless amid this noise; and makes "no alteration in the Seckendorf troops; but it is certain he "meant to do it, thinks Valori."

And indeed Seckendorf, tired of the Bavarian bed-of-roses, had privately fixed with himself to quit the same; — and does so, inexorable to the very Kaiser, on New-Year arriving.** Succeeded by Thörring (our old friend, *Drum Thörring*), if that be an improvement. Maréchal de Belleisle has still a long journey ahead, and infinitely harder problems than these, — assuagement of the King of Prussia, for example. Let us follow his remarkable steps.

"*Wednesday*, *9th December* 1744, the Maréchal leaves "München, northwards through Öttingen and the Bamberg-

* Valori, i. 206. ** *Seckendorf's Leben*, p. 865.

"Anspach regions towards Cassel; — journey of some three "hundred and fifty miles: with a great retinue of his own; "with an escort of two hundred horse from the Kaiser; these "latter to prevent any outfall or insult in the Ingolstadt "quarter, where the Austrians have a garrison, not at all "very tightly blocked by the Seckendorf people thereabouts. "No insult or outfall occurring, the Maréchal dismisses his "escort at Öttingen; fares forward in his twenty coaches "and fourgons, some score or so of vehicles: — mere neutral "Imperial Countries henceforth, where the Kaiser's Agent, "as Maréchal de Belleisle can style himself, and Titular "Prince of the German Empire withal, has only to pay his "way. By Donauwörth, by Öttingen; over the Donau ac-"clivities, then down the pleasant Valley of the Mayn.*

"*Sunday, 13th December*, Maréchal Belleisle arrives at "Hanau" (where we have seen Conferences held before now, and Carteret, Prince Karl and great George our King very busy), "there to confer with Marshals Coigny, Maillebois, "and other high men, Commanders in those Rhine parts. "Who all come accordingly, except Maréchal Maillebois, "who is sorry that he absolutely cannot; but will surely do "himself the honour as Monseigneur returns." As Monseigneur returns! "And so, on Monday 14th, Monseigneur "starts for Cassel; say a hundred miles, right north; where "we shall meet Prince Wilhelm of Hessen-Cassel, a zealous "Ally; inform him how his Troops, under Seckendorf, are "posted" (at Vilshofen yonder; hiding how perilous their post is, or promising alterations); "perhaps rest a day or "two, consulting as to the common weal: How the King of "Prussia takes our treatment of him? How to smooth the "King of Prussia, and turn him to harmony again? We are "approaching the true nodus of our business, difficulty of "difficulties; and Wilhelm, the wise Landgraf, may afford "a hint or two. Thus travels magnanimous Belleisle in twenty "vehicles, a man loaded with weighty matters, in these deep "Winter months; suffering dreadfully from rheumatic neural-"gic ailments, a Doctor one of his needfullest equipments; "and has the hardest problem yet ahead of him.

"Prince Wilhelm's consultations are happily lost alto-

* See *Review of the Case of Marshal Belleisle* (or Abstract of it, *Gentleman's Magazine*, 1745, pp. 366-373); &c. &c.

"gether; buried from sight forever, to the last hint, — all "except as to what road for Berlin would be the best from "Cassel. By Leipzig, through low-lying country, is the "great Highway, advisable in winter; but it runs a hundred "and thirty miles to right, before ever starting northward; "such a roundabout. Not to say that the Saxons are allies of "Austria, — if there be anything in that. Enemies, they, to "the Most Christian King: though surely, again, we are on "Kaiser's business, nay we are titular 'Prince of the Reich,' "for that matter, such the Kaiser's grace to us? Well; it is "better perhaps to *avoid* the Saxon Territory. And, of course, "the Hanoverian much more; through which lies the other "Great Road! 'Go by the Harz,' advises Landgraf Wilhelm: "'a rugged Hill Country; but it is your hypotenuse towards "'Berlin; passes at once, or nearly so, from Cassel Territory "'into Prussian: a rugged road, but a shorter and safer.' "That is the road Belleisle resolves upon. Twenty carriages; "his Brother the Chevalier and himself occupy one; and "always the courier rides before, ordering forty post-horses "to be ready harnessed.

"*Sunday, 20th December* 1744. In this way they have "climbed the eastern shin of the Harz Range, where the Harz "is capable of wheel-carriages; and hope now to descend, "this night, to Halberstadt; and thence rapidly by level "roads to Berlin. It is sinking towards dark; the courier is "forward to Elbingerode, ordering forty horses to be out. "Roughish uphill road; winter in the sky and earth, winter "vapours and tumbling wind-gusts: westward, in torn storm-"cloak, the Brocken, with its witch-dances; highland Goslar, "and ghost of Henry the Fowler, on the other side of it. A "multifarious wizard Country, much overhung by goblin re-"miniscences, witch-dances, sorcerers' sabbaths, and the "like, — if a rheumatic gentleman cared to look on it, in the "cold twilight. Brrh! Waste chasmy uplands, now-choked "torrents; wild people, gloomy firs! Here at last, by one's "watch 5 P.M., is Elbingerode, uncomfortable little Town; "and it is to be hoped the forty post-horses are ready.

"Behold, while the forty post-horses are getting ready, a "thing takes place, most unexpected; — which made the "name of Elbingerode famous for eight months to come. Of "which let us hastily give the bare facts, Fancy making of "them what she can. Was Monseigneur aware that this El- "bingerode, with a patch of territory round it, is Hanoverian "ground; one of those distracted patches or ragged outskirts "frequent in the German map? Prussia is not yet, and Hes- "sen-Cassel has ceased to be. Undoubtedly Hanoverian! "Apparently the Landgraf and Monseigneur had not thought "of that. But Münchhausen of Hanover, spies informing him, "had. The Bailiff (Vogt, *Advocatus*) has gathered twenty "*Jäger*" (official Gamekeepers) "with their guns, and a select "idle Sunday population of the place with or without guns: "the Vogt steps forward, and inquires for Monseigneur's "passport. 'No passport, no need of any!' — 'Pardon!' and "signifies to Monseigneur, on the part of George Elector of "Hanover, King of Great Britain, France and Ireland, that "Monseigneur is arrested!

"Monseigneur, with compressed or incompressible feel- "ings, indignantly complies, — what could he else, un- "fortunate rheumatic gentleman? — and is plucked away in "such sudden manner, he for one, out of that big German "game of his raising. The twenty vehicles are dragged dif- "ferent roads; towards Scharzfels, Osterode, or I know not "where, — handiest roads to Hanover; — and Monseigneur "himself has travelling treatment which might be complained "of, did not one disdain complaint: 'my Brother parted "'from me, nay my Doctor, and my Interpreter;'" — not even speech possible to me.* That was the Belleisle Accident in the Harz. Sunday Evening, 20th December 1744.

"Afflicted indignant Valori, soon enough apprised, runs "to Friedrich with the news, — greets Friedrich with it just "alighting from that Silesian run of his own. Friedrich, not "without several other things to think of, is naturally sorry "at such news; sorry for his own sake even; but not over- "much. Friedrich refuses 'to despatch a party of horse,' and "cut out Maréchal de Belleisle. 'That will never do, *mon* "'*cher!*' — and even gets into *froides plaisanteries:* 'Perhaps "'the Maréchal did it himself? Tallard, prisoner after "Blenheim, made *Peace*, you know, in England?' — and

* Letter of Belleisle next morning, "Neuhof, 21st December, 9 a.m." in *Valori*, I. 204), to Münchhausen at Hanover, — by no possibility "to Valori," as the distracted French Editor has given it!

"the like; which grieved the soul of Valori, and convinced "him of Friedrich's inhumanity, in a crying case.

"Belleisle is lugged on to Hanover; his case not doubtful "to Münchhausen, or the English Ministry, — though it "raised great argument, 'Was the capture fair, was it "'unfair? Is he entitled to exchange by cartel, or not "'entitled?' and produced, in the next eight months, much "angry animated pamphleteering and negotiation. For we "hear by and by, he is to be forwarded to Stade, on the Ham-"burg sea-coast, where English Seventy-fours are waiting "for him; his case still undecided; — and in effect it was not "till after eight months that he got dismissal. 'Lodged hand-"'somely in Windsor Palace,' in the interim; free on his "parole, people of rank very civil to him, though the Ga-"zetteers were sometimes ill-tongued, — had he understood "their *patois*, or concerned himself about such things.*

"It was a current notion among contemporary mankind, "this of Friedrich, that Belleisle's capture might be a mere "collusion, meant to bring about a Peace in that Tallard "fashion, — wide of the truth as such a notion is, far as any "Peace was from following. To Britannic George and his "Hanoverians it had merely seemed, Here was a chief War-"Captain and Diplomatist among the French; the pivot of "all these world-wide movements, as Valori defines him; "which pivot, a chance offering, it were well to twitch from "its socket, and see what would follow. Perhaps nothing "will follow; next to nothing? A world, all waltzing in "mad war, is not to be stopped by acting on any pivot; your "waltzing world will find new pivots, or do without any, and "perhaps only waltz the more madly for wanting the prin-"cipal one."

* "*Tuesday, 18th February*" (1st March 1745), "Marshal Belleisle landed "at Harwich; lay at Greenwich Palace, having crossed Thames at the Isle "of Dogs: next morning, about 10, set out, in a coach-and-six, Colonel "Douglas and two troops of horse escorting; arrived, 3 p.m., — by Cam-"berwell, Clapham, Wandsworth, over Kingston and Staines Bridges, — "at Windsor Castle, and the apartments ready for him." (*Gentleman's Magazine*, 1745, p. 107.) Was let go, 13th (24th) August, again with great pomp and civilities (ib. p. 448). See *Adelung*, iv. 299, 346; v. 83, 84.

This withdrawal of Belleisle, the one Frenchman respected by Friedrich, or much interested for his own sake in things German, is reckoned a main cause why the French Alliance turned out so ill for Friedrich; and why French effort took more and more a Netherlands direction thenceforth, and these new French magnanimities on Friedrich's behalf issued in futility again. Probably they never could have issued in very much: but it is certain that, from this point, they also do become zero; and that Friedrich, from his French alliance, reaped from first to last nothing at all, except a great deal of obloquy from German neighbours, and from the French side endless tròuble, anger, and disappointment in every particular. Which might be a joy (though not unmixed) to Britannic Majesty and the subtle fowlers who had ginned this fine Belleisle bird in its flight over the Harz Range? Though again, had they passively let him wing his way, and he had *got* "to be Commander and Manager," as was in agitation, — he, Belleisle and in Germany, instead of Maréchal de Saxe with the Netherlands as chief scene, — what an advantage might that have been to them!

The Kaiser Karl VII. gets secured from Oppressions, in a tragic Way. Friedrich proposes Peace, but to no purpose.

A still sadder cross for Friedrich, in the current of foreign Accidents and Diplomacies, was the next that befel; exactly a month later, — at München, 20th January 1745. Hardly was Belleisle's back turned, when her Hungarian Majesty, by her Bathyani and Company, broke furiously in upon the poor Kaiser and his

Seckendorf-Ségur defences. Belleisle had not reached the Harz, when all was going topsy-turvy there again, and the Donau-Valley fast falling back into Austrian hands. Nor is that the worst, or nearly so.

"*München*, *20th January* 1745. This day poor Kaiser "Karl laid down his earthly burden here, and at length gave "all his enemies the slip. He had been ill of gout, for some "time; a man of much malady always, with no want of "vexations and apprehensions. Too likely the Austrians will "drive him out of München again; then nothing but furnished "lodgings, and the French to depend upon. He had been "much chagrined by some Election, just done, in the "Chapter of Salzburg.* The Archbishop there, — it was "Firmian, he of the *Salzburg Emigration*, memorable to "readers, — had died, some while ago. And now, in flat "contradiction to Imperial customs, prerogatives, these "people had admitted an Austrian Garrison; and then, in "the teeth of our express precept, had elected an Austrian "to their benefice: what can one account it but an insult as "well as an injury? And the neuralgic maladies press sore, "and the gouty twinges; and Belleisle is seized, perhaps "with important papers of ours; and the Seckendorf-Ségur "detachments were ill placed; nay here are the Austrians "already on the throat of them, in mid-winter! It is said, "a babbling valet, or lord-in-waiting, happened to talk of "some skirmish that had fallen out (called a battle, in the "valet rumour), and how ill the French and Bavarians had "fared in it, owing to their ill behaviour. And this, add "they, proved to be the ounce-weight too much for the so "heavy-laden back.

"The Kaiser took to bed, not much complaining; patient, "mild, though the saddest of all mortals; and, in a day or "two, died. Adieu, adieu, ye loved faithful ones; pity me, "and pray for me! He gave his Wife, poor little fat devout "creature, and his poor Children (eldest lad, his Heir, only "seventeen), a tender blessing; solemnly exhorted them, "To eschew ambition, and be warned by his example; — to

* Adelung, IV. 249, 276, 313.

"make their peace with Austria; and never, like him, try "*com' è duro calle*, and what the charity of Christian Kings "amounts to. This counsel, it is thought, the Empress "Dowager zealously accedes to, and will impress upon her "Son. That is the Austrian and Cause-of-Liberty account; "King Friedrich, from the other side, has heard a directly "opposite one. How the Kaiser, at the point of death, "exhorted his son, 'Never forget the services which the King "'of France and the King of Prussia have done us, and do "'not repay them with ingratitude.'* The reader can choose "which he will, or reject both into the region of the un-"certain. 'Karl Albert's pious and affectionate demeanour "'drew tears from all eyes,' say the bystanders: 'the manner "'in which he took leave of his Empress would have melted "'a heart of stone.' He was in his forty-eighth year; he had "been, of all men in his generation, the most conspicuously "unhappy."

What a downrush of confusion there ensued on this event, not to Bavaria alone, but to all the world, and to King Friedrich more than another, no reader can now take the pains of conceiving. The "Frankfort Union," then, has gone to air! Here is now no "Kaiser to be delivered from oppression:" here is a new Kaiser to be elected, — "Grand-Duke Franz the man," cry the Pragmatic Potentates with exultation, "no Belleisle to disturb!" — and questions arise innumerable thereupon. Will France go into electioneering again? The new Kur-Baiern, only seventeen, poor child, cannot be set up as candidate. What will France do with *him*; what he with France? Whom can the French try as Candidate against the Grand-Duke? Kur-Sachsen, the Polish Majesty again? Belleisle himself must have paused uncertain over such a welter, — and probably

* *Œuvres de Frédéric*, III. 92; — and see (*per contra*) in Adelung, IV. 314 *n*; in Coxe, &c.

have done, like the others, little or nothing in it, but left it to collapse by natural gravitation.

Hungarian Majesty checked her Bavarian Armaments a little: "If perhaps this young Kur-Baiern will detach himself from France, and on submissive terms come over to us?" Whereupon, at München, and in the cognate quarters, such wriggling, dubitating and diplomatising, as seldom was, — French, Anti-French (Seckendorf busiest of all), straining every nerve in that way, and for almost three months, nothing coming of it, — till Hungarian Majesty sent her Bärenklaus and Bathyanis upon them again; and these rapidly solved the question, in what way we shall see!

Friedrich has still his hopes of Bavaria, so grandiloquent are the French in regard to it; who but would hope? The French diplomatise to all lengths in München, promising seas and mountains; but they perform little; in an effectual manner, nothing. Bavarian "Army raised to 60,000," counts in fact little above half that number; with no General to it but an imaginary one; Ségur's actual French contingent, instead of 25,000, is perhaps 12,000; — and so of other things. Add to all which, Seckendorf is there, not now as War-General, but as extra-official "Adviser;" busier than ever, — "scandalous old traitor!" say the French; — and Friedrich may justly fear that Bavaria will go, by collapse, a bad road for him.

Friedrich, a week or two after the Kaiser's death, seeing Bavarian and French things in such a hypothetic state, instructs his Ambassador at London to declare his, Friedrich's, perfect readiness and wish for Peace: "Old Treaty of Breslau and Berlin made indubitable to me; the rest of the quarrel has, by decease of the Kaiser, gone to air." To which the Britannic Majesty, rather elated at this time, as all Pragmatic people are, answers somewhat in a careless way, "Well, if the others like it!" and promises that he will propose it in the proper quarter. So that henceforth there is always a hope of Peace through England; as well as contrariwise, especially till Bavaria settle itself (in April next), a hope of great assistance from the French. Here are potentialities and counter-potentialities, which make the Bavarian Intricacy very agitating to the young King, while it lasts. And indeed his world is one huge imbroglio of Potentialities and Diplomatic Intricacies, agitating to behold. Concerning which we have again to remark how these huge Spectres of Diplomacy, now filling Friedrich's world, came mostly in result to Nothing; — shaping themselves wholly, for or against, in exact proportion, direct or inverse, to the actual Quantity of Battle and effective Performance that happened to be found in Friedrich himself. Diplomatic Spectralities, wide Fatamorganas of hope, and hideous big Bugbears blotting out the sun: of these, few men ever had more than Friedrich at this time. And he is careful, none carefuller, not to neglect his Diplomacies at any time; though he knows, better than most, that good fighting of his own is what alone can determine the value of these contingent and aërial quantities, — mere Lapland witchcraft the greater part of them.

A second grand Intricacy and difficulty, still more enigmatic, and pressing the tighter by its close neighbourhood, was that with the Saxons. "Are the Saxons enemies; are they friends? Neutrals, at lowest; bound by Treaty to lend Austria troops; but to lend for defence merely, not for offence! Could not one, by good methods, make friends with his Polish Majesty?" Friedrich was far from suspecting the rages that lurked in the Polish Majesty, and least of all owing to what. Owing to that old *Moravian-Foray* business; and to his, Friedrich's, behaviour to the Saxons in it; excellent Saxons, who had behaved so beautifully to Friedrich! That is the sad fact, however. Stupid Polish Majesty has his natural envies, jealousies, of a Brandenburg waxing over his head at this rate. But it appears, the Moravian Foray entered for a great deal into the account, and was the final overwhelming item. Brühl, by much descanting on that famous Expedition, — with such candid Eye-witnesses to appeal to, such corroborative Staff-officers and appliances, powerful on the idle heart and weak brain of a Polish Majesty, — has brought it so far. Fixed indignation, for intolerable usage, especially in that Moravian-Foray time: fixed; not very malignant, but altogether obstinate (as, I am told, that of the pacific sheep species usually is); which carried Brühl and his Polish Majesty to extraordinary heights and depths in years coming! But that will deserve a section to itself by and by.

A third difficulty, privately more stringent than any, is that of Finance. The expenses of the late Bohemian Expedition, "Friedrich's Army costing 75,000*l*. a month," have been excessive. For our next Campaign, if it is to be done in the way essential, there are, by rigorous arithmetic, "900,000*l*." needed. A frugal Prussia raises no new taxes; pays its Wars from "the Treasure," from the Fund saved beforehand for emergencies of that kind; Fund which is running low, threatening to be at the lees if such drain on it continue. To fight with effect being the one sure hope, and salve for all sores, it is not in the Army, in the Fortresses, the Fighting Equipments, that there shall be any flaw left! Friedrich's budget is a sore problem upon him; needing endless shift and ingenuity, now and onwards, through this War:—already, during these months, in the Berlin Schloss, a great deal of those massive Friedrich-Wilhelm plate Sumptuosities, especially that unparalleled Music-Balcony up stairs, all silver, has been, under Fredersdorf's management, quietly taken away; "carried over, in the night-time, to the Mint."*

And, in fact, no modern reader, not deeper in that distressing story of the Austrian Succession-War than readers are again like to be, can imagine to himself the difficulties of Friedrich at this time, as they already lay disclosed, and kept gradually disclosing themselves, for months coming; nor will ever know what perspicacity, patience of scanning, sharpness of discernment, dexterity of management, were required at Friedrich's hands; — and under what imminency of peril, too; victorious deliverance, or ruin and annihilation, wavering fearfully in the balance for him, more than once, or rather all along. But it is certain the deeper one goes into that hideous Medea's Cauldron of stupidities, once so flamy, now fallen extinct, the more is one sensible of Friedrich's difficulties; and of the talent for all kinds of Captaincy, — by no means in the Field only, or perhaps even chiefly, — that was now required of him. Candid readers shall accept these hints,

* Orlich, II. 126-128.

and do their best: — Friedrich himself made not the least complaint of men's then misunderstanding him; still less will he now! We, keeping henceforth the Diplomacies, the vaporous Foreshadows, and general Dance of Unclean Spirits with their intrigues and spectralities, well underground, so far as possible, will stick to what comes up as practical Performance on Friedrich's part, and try to give intelligible account of that.

Valori says, he is greatly changed, and for the better, by these late reverses of fortune. All the world notices it, says Valori. No longer that brief infallibility of manner; that lofty light air, that politely disdainful view of Valori and mankind: he has now need of men. Complains of nothing, is cheerful, quizzical; — ardently busy to "grind out the notches," as our proverb is; has a mild humane aspect, something of modesty, almost of piety in him. Help me, thou Supreme Power, Maker of men, if my purposes are manlike! Though one does not go upon the Prayers of Forty Hours, or apply through St. Vitus and such channels, there may be something of authentic petition to Heaven in the thoughts of that young man. He is grown very amiable; the handsomest young bit of Royalty now going. He must fight well next Summer, or it will go hard with him!

CHAPTER VI.

VALORI GOES ON AN ELECTIONEERING MISSION TO DRESDEN.

Some time in January, a new Frenchman, a "Chevalier de Courten," if the name is known to anybody, was here at Berlin; consulting, settling about mutual interests and operations. Since Belleisle is snatched from us, it is necessary some Courten should come; and produce what he has got: little of settlement, I should fear, of definite program that will hold water; in regard to War operations chiefly a magazine of clouds.* For the rest, the Bavarian question; and very specially, Who the new Emperor is to be? "King of Poland, thinks your Majesty?" — "By all means," answers Friedrich, "if you can! Detach him from Austria; that will be well!" Which was reckoned magnanimous, at least public-spirited, in Friedrich; considering what Saxony's behaviour to him had already been. "By all means, his Polish Majesty for Kaiser; do our utmost, Excellencies Valori, Courten and Company!" answers Friedrich, — and for his own part, I observe, is intensely busy upon Army matters, looking after the main chance.

And so Valori is to go to Dresden, and manage this cloud or cobwebbery department of the thing; namely, persuade his Polish Majesty to stand for the

* Specimens of it, in Ranke, III. 219.

Kaisership: "Baiern, Pfalz, Köln, Brandenburg, there are four votes, Sire; your own is five: sure of carrying it, your Polish Majesty; backed by the Most Christian King, and his Allies and resources!" And Polish Majesty does, for his own share, very much desire to be Kaiser. But none of us yet knows how he is tied up by Austrian, Anti-Friedrich, Anti-French considerations; and can only "accept if it is offered me:" thrice willing to accept, if it will fall into my mouth; which, on those terms, it has so little chance of doing! — Saxony and its mysterious affairs and intentions having been, to Friedrich, a riddle and trouble and astonishment, during all this Campaign, readers ought to know the fact well; — and no reader could stand the details of such a fact. Here, in condensed form, are some scraps of Excerpt; which enable us to go with Valori on this Dresden Mission, and look for ourselves:

1°. *Friedrich's position towards Saxony.*

* * "By known Treaty, the Polish Majesty is bound to "assist the Hungarian with 12,000 men, 'whenever invaded "'in her own dominions.' Polish Majesty had 20,000 in the "field for that object lately, — part of them, 8,000 of them, "hired by Britannic subsidy, as he alleges. The question now "is, Will Saxony assist Austria in invading Silesia, with or "without Britannic subsidy? Friedrich hopes that this is "impossible! Friedrich is deeply unaware of the humour "he has raised against himself in the Saxon Court-circles; "how the Polish Majesty regards that Moravian Foray; with "what a perfect hatred little Brühl regards him, Friedrich; "and to what pitch of humour, owing to those Moravian-"Foray starvings, marchings about, and inhuman treatment "of the poor Saxon Army, not to mention other offences and "afflictive considerations, Brühl has raised the simple Polish "Majesty against Friedrich. These things, as they gradually "unfolded themselves to Friedrich, were very surprising.

"And proved very disadvantageous at the present juncture "and for a long time afterwards. To Friedrich disadvantageous and surprising; and to Saxony, in the end, "ruinous; poor Saxony having got its back broken by them, "and never stood up in the world since! Ruined by this "wretched little Brühl; and reduced, from the first place in "Northern Teutschland, to a second or third, or no real place "at all."

2°. *There is a "Union of Warsaw"* (8th January 1745); *and still more specially a "Treaty of Warsaw"* (8th January — 18th May 1745).

"January 8th, 1745, before the Old Dessauer got ranked "in Schlesien against Traun, there had concluded itself at "Warsaw, by way of counterpoise to the 'Frankfurt Union,' "a 'Union of Warsaw,' called also 'Quadruple Alliance of "'Warsaw;' the parties to which were Polish Majesty, Hungarian ditto, Prime-Movers, and the two Sea-Powers as "Purseholders; stipulating, to the effect: 'We Four will "'hold together in affairs of the Reich, *versus* that dangerous "'Frankfurt Union; we will' — do a variety of salutary "things; and as one practical thing, "There shall be, this "'Season, 30,000 Saxons conjoined to the Austrian Force, for "'which we Sea-Powers will furnish subsidy.' — This was the "one practical point stipulated, January 8th; and farther "than this the Sea-Powers did not go, now or afterwards, in "that affair.

"But there was then proposed by the Polish and Hungarian Majesties, in the form of Secret Articles, an ulterior "Project; with which the Sea-Powers, expressing mere disbelief and even abhorrence of it, refused to have any concern "now or henceforth. Polish Majesty, in hopes it would have "been better taken, had given his 30,000 soldiers at a rate of "subsidy miraculously low, only 150,000*l.* for the whole: but "the Sea-Powers were inexorable, perhaps almost repented "of their 150,000*l.*; and would hear nothing farther of secret "Articles and delirious Projects.

"So that the 'Union of Warsaw' had to retire to its pigeon-hole, content with producing those 30,000 Saxons for the immediate occasion; and there had to be concocted between "the Polish and Hungarian Majesties themselves what is "now, in the modern Pamphlets, called a '*Treaty* of Warsaw,' "— much different from the innocent '*Union* of Warsaw;' "though it is merely the specifying and fixing down of what "had been shadowed out as secret codicils in said 'Union,' "when the Sea-Power parties obstinately recoiled. Treaty "of Warsaw let us continue to call it; though its actual birth-"place was Leipzig (in the profoundest secrecy, 18th May "1745), above four months after it had tried to be born at "Warsaw, and failed as aforesaid. Warsaw Union is not "worth speaking of; but this other is a Treaty highly remark-"able to the reader, — and to Friedrich was almost infinitely "so, when he came to get wind of it long after.

"Treaty which, though it proved abortional, and never "came to fulfilment in any part of it, is at this day one of the "remarkablest bits of sheepskin extant in the world. It was "signed, 18th May 1745;* and had cost a great deal of pain-"ful contriving, capable still of new altering and retouching, "to hit mutual views: Treaty not only for reconquering Silesia "(which to the Two Majesties, though it did not to the Sea-"Powers, seems infallible, in Friedrich's now ruined circum-"stances), but for cutting down that bad Neighbour to some-"thing like the dimensions proper for a Brandenburg Vassal; "— in fact, quite the old 'Detestable Project' of Spring 1741, "only more elaborated into detail (in which Britannic George "knows better than to meddle!) — Saxony to have share of "the parings, when we get them. 'What share?' asked "Saxony, and long keeps asking. 'A road to Warsaw; strip "'of Country carrying us from the end of the Lausitz, which "'is ours, into Poland, which we trust will continue ours, "'would be very handy! Duchy of Glogau; some small "'paring of Silesia, won't your Majesty?' 'Of my Silesia not "'one handbreadth,' answered the Queen impatiently (though "she did at last concede some outlying handbreadths, famed "old 'Circle of Schwiebus,' if I recollect); and they have had "to think of other equivalent parings for Saxony's behoof "(Magdeburg, Halberstadt, Saale-Circle, or one knows not "what); and have had, and will have, their adoes to get it "fixed. Excellent bearskin to be slit into straps; only the "bear is still on his feet! — Polish Majesty and Hungarian,

* Schöll, ii. 350.

"Polish with especial vigour, Brühl quite restless upon it, are, "— little as Valori or any mortal could dream of it, — en- "gaged in this partition of the bearskin, when Valori arrives. "Of their innocent Union of Warsaw, there was, from the "first, no secret made; but the Document now called '*Treaty* "of Warsaw' needs to lie secret and thrice-secret; and it was "not till 1756 that Friedrich, having unearthed it by in- "dustries of his own, and studied it with great intensity for "some years, made it known to the world."*

Treaties, vaporous Foreshadows of Events, have oftenest something of the ghost in them; and are importune to human nature, longing for the Events themselves; all the more if they have proved abortional Treaties, and become doubly ghost-like or ghastly. Nevertheless the reader is to note well this Treaty of Warsaw, as important to Friedrich and him; and indeed it is perhaps the remarkablest Treaty, abortional or realised, which got to parchment in that Century. For though it proved abortional, and no part of it, now or afterwards, could be executed, and even the subsidy and 30,000 Saxons (stipulated in the "*Union* of Warsaw") became crow's meat in a manner, — this preternatural "Treaty of Warsaw," trodden down never so much by the heel of Destiny, and by the weight of new Treaties, superseding it or presupposing its impossibility or inconceivability, would by no means die (such the humour of Brühl, of the Two Majesties and others); but lay alive under the ashes, carefully tended, for Ten or Twenty Years to come; — and had got all Europe kindled again, for destruction of that bad Neighbour, before it would itself consent to go out! And did succeed in getting Saxony's back broken, if not the bad Neighbour's, — in answer to the humour of little Brühl; unfortunate Saxony to possess such a Brühl!

In those beautiful Saxon-Austrian developments of the Treaty of Warsaw, Czarina Elizabeth, bobbing about in that unlovely whirl-pool of intrigues, amours, devotions, and strong liquor, which her History is, took (ask not for what reason) a lively part: — and already in this Spring 1745, they hope she could, by "a gift of two millions for her pleasures" (gift so easy to you Sea-Powers), be stirred up to anger

* Adelung, v. 308, 397; Ranke, III. 231 (who, for some reason of his own dates "3d May" instead of 18*th*).

against Friedrich. And she did, in effect, from this time, hover about in a manner questionable to Friedrich; though not yet in anger, but only with the wish to be important, and to make herself felt in Foreign affairs. Whether the Sea-Powers gave her that trifle of pocket-money ("for her pleasures"), I never knew; but it is certain they spent, first and last, very large amounts that way, upon her and hers; especially the English did, with what result may be considered questionable.

As for Graf von Brühl, most rising man of Saxony, once a page; now by industry King August III.'s first favourite and factotum; the fact that he cordially hates Friedrich is too evident; but the why is not known to me. Except indeed, That no man, — especially no man with three hundred and sixty-five fashionable suits of clothes usually about him, different suit each day of the year, — can be comfortable in the evident contempt of another man. Other man of sarcastic bantering turn, too; tongue sharp as needles; whose sayings many birds of the air are busy to carry about. Year after year, Brühl (doubtless with help enough that way, if there had needed such) hates him more and more; as the too jovial Czarina herself comes to do, wounded by things that birds have carried. And now we will go with Valori, — seeing better into some things than Valori yet can.

3°. *Valori's Account of his Mission* (in compressed form).*

"Valori" (I could guess about the 10th of February, but there is no date at all) "was despatched to Dresden with that fine project, Polish Majesty for Kaiser: is authorised to offer "60,000 men, with money corresponding, and no end of "brilliant outlooks; — must keep back his offers, however, if "he find the people indisposed. Which he did, to an extreme "degree; nothing but vague talk, procrastination, hesitation "on the part of Brühl. This wretched little Brühl has twelve "tailors always sewing for him, and three hundred and sixty-"five suits of clothes: so many suits, all pictured in a Book; "a valet enters every morning, proposes a suit, which, after "deliberation, with perhaps amendments, is acceded to, and "worn at dinner. Vainest of human clothes-horses; foolishest

* Valori, i. 211-219.

"coxcomb Valori has seen: it is visibly his notion that it was "he, Brühl, by his Saxon auxiliaries, by his masterly strokes "of policy, that check-mated Friedrich, and drove him from "Bohemia last Year; and, for the rest, that Friedrich is "ruined, and will either shirk out of Silesia, or be cut to rib-"bons there by the Austrian force this Summer. To which "Valori hints dissent; but it is ill received. Valori sees the "King; finds him, as expected, the facsimile of Brühl in this "matter; Jesuit Guarini the like: how otherwise? They "have his Majesty in their leash, and lead him as they "please.

"At four every morning, this Guarini, Jesuit Confessor to "the King and Queen, comes to Brühl; Brühl settles with him "what his Majesty shall think, in reference to current busi-"ness, this day; Guarini then goes, confesses both Majesties; "confesses, absolves, turns in the due way to secular matters. "At nine, Brühl himself arrives, for Privy Council: 'What is "'your Majesty pleased to think on these points of current "'business?' Majesty serenely issues his thoughts, in the "form of orders; which are found correct to pattern. This "is the process with his Majesty. A poor Majesty, taking "deeply into tobacco; this is the way they have him benetted, "as in a dark cocoon of cobwebs, rendering the whole world "invisible to him. Which cunning arrangement is more and "more perfected every year; so that on all roads he travels, "be it to mass, to hunt, to dinner, anywhither in his Palace "or out of it, there are faithful creatures keeping eye, who "admit no unsafe man to the least glimpse of him by night or "by day. In this manner he goes on; and before the end of "him, twenty years hence, has carried it far. Nothing but "disgust to be had out of business; — mutinous Polish Diets "too, some forty of them, in his time, not one of which did "any business at all, but ended in *Liberum Veto*, and Billings-"gate conflagration, perhaps with swords drawn;* — busi-"ness more and more disagreeable to him. What can Valori "expect, on this heroic occasion, from such a King?

"The Queen herself, Maria Theresa's Cousin, an am-"bitious hard-favoured Majesty, — who had sense once to "dislike Brühl, but has been quite reconciled to him by her "Jesuit Messenger of Heaven (which latter is an oily, rather

* See Buchholz, II. 154; &c.

"stupid creature, who really wishes well to her, and loves a "peaceable life at any price), — even she will not take the "bait. Valori was in Dresden nine days (middle part of "February, it is likely); never produced his big bait, his "60,000 men and other brilliancies, at all. He saw old Feld-"marschall Königseck passing from Vienna towards the "Netherlands Camp; where he is to dry-nurse (so they irre-"verently call it, in time coming) his Royal Highness of "Cumberland, that magnificent English Babe of War, and do "feats with him this Summer." Königseck, though Valori did not know it, has endless diplomacies to do withal; inspections of troops, advisings, in Hanover, in Holland, in Dresden here;* — and secures the Saxon Electoral-Vote for his Grand-Duke in passing. "The welcome given to Königs-"eck disgusted Valori; on the ninth day he left; said adieu, "seeing them blind to their interest; and took post for "Berlin," — where he finds Friedrich much out of humour at the Saxon reception of his magnanimities.**

This Saxon intricacy, indecipherable, formidable, contemptible, was the plague of Friedrich's life, one considerable plague, all through this Campaign. Perhaps nothing in the Diplomatic sphere of things caused him such perplexity, vexation, indignation. An insoluble riddle to him; extremely contemptible, yet, — with a huge Russia tacked to it, and looming minatory in the distance, — from time to time, formidable enough. Let readers keep it in mind, and try to imagine it. It cost Friedrich such guessing, computing, arranging, rearranging, as would weary the toughest reader to hear of in detail. How Friedrich did at last

* Anonymous, *Duke of Cumberland*, p. 186.

** Valori, I. 211-219; *Œuvres de Frédéric*, III. 64-66. For details on Brühl, see *Graf von Brühl, Leben und Charakter* (1760, No Place): Anonymous, by one Justi, a noted Pamphleteer of the time: exists in English too, or partly exists; but is unreadable, except on compulsion; and totally unintelligible till after very much inquiry elsewhere.

solve it (in December coming), all readers will see with eyes! —

Middle-Rhine Army in a staggering State; the Bavarian Intricacy settles itself, the wrong Way.

Early in March it becomes surmisable that Maillebois's Middle-Rhine Army will not go a good road. Maillebois has been busy in those countries, working extensive discontent; bullying mankind "to join the Frankfurt Union," to join France at any rate, which nobody would consent to; and exacting merciless contributions, which everybody had to consent to and pay. — And now, on D'Ahremberg's mere advance, with that poor Fraction of Pragmatic Army, roused from its winter sleep, Maillebois, without waiting for D'Ahremberg's attack, rapidly calls in his truculent detachments, and rolls confusedly back into the Frankfurt regions.* Upon which D'Ahremberg, — if by no means going upon Maillebois's throat, — sets, at least, to coercing Wilhelm of Hessen, our only friend in those parts; who is already a good deal disgusted with the Maillebois procedures, and at a loss what to do on the Kaiser's death, which has killed the Frankfurt Union too. Wise Wilhelm consents, under D'Ahremberg's menaces, to become Neutral; and recal his 6,000 out of Baiern, — wishes he had them home beside him even now!

With an Election in the wind, it is doubly necessary for the French, who have not even a Candidate as yet, to stand supreme and minatory in the Frankfurt Country; and to King Friedrich it is painfully

* Adelung, IV. 276-353 (December 1744 — March 1745).

questionable, whether Maillebois can do it. "Do it we will; doubt not that, your Majesty!" answer Valori, and the French; — and study to make improvements, reinforcements, in their Rhine Army. And they do, at least, change the General of their Middle-Rhine Army, — that is to say, recal Prince Conti out of Italy, where he has distinguished himself, and send Maillebois thither in his stead, — who likewise distinguishes himself *there*, if that could be a comfort to us! Whether the distinguished Conti will maintain that Frankfurt Country in spite of the Austrians and their Election movements, is still a question with Friedrich, though Valori continued assuring him (always till July came) that it was beyond question. "Siege of Tournay, vigorous Campaign in the Netherlands (for behoof of Britannic George)!" this is the grand French program for the Year. This good intention was achieved, on the French part; but this, like Aaron's-rod among the serpents, proved to have *eaten* the others as it wriggled along! —

Those Maillebois-D'Ahremberg affairs throw a damp on the Bavarian Question withal; — in fact, settle the Bavarian Question; her Hungarian Majesty, tired of the delays, having ordered Bathyani to shoulder arms again, and bring a decision. Bathyani, with Bärenklau to right of him, and Browne (our old Silesian friend) to left, goes sweeping across those Seckendorf-Ségur posts, and without difficulty tumbles everything to ruin, at a grand rate. The traitor Seckendorf had made such a choice of posts, — left unaltered by Drum Thörring; — what could French valour do? Nothing; neither French valour, nor Bavarian want of valour, could do anything but whirl to the right-about, at sight of the Austrian Sweeping-Apparatus; and go off explosively, as in former instances, at a rate almost unique in military annals. Finished within three weeks or so! — We glance only at two points of it. March 21st, Bathyani stood to arms (to *besoms* we might call it), Browne on the left, Bärenklau on the right: it was March 21st when Bathyani started from Passau, up the Donau Countries; — and within the week coming, see:

"*Vilshofen, 28th March* 1745. Here, at the mouth of the "Vils River (between Inn and Iser), is the first considerable "Post; garrison some 4,000; Hessians and Prince Friedrich "the main part, — who have their share of valour, I dare say; "but with such news out of Hessen, not to speak of the pro-"spects in this Country, are probably in poorish spirits for "acting. General Browne summons them in Vilshofen, this "day; and, on their negative, storms in upon them, bursts "them to pieces; upon which they beat chamade. But the "Croats, who are foremost, care nothing for chamade; go "plundering, slaughtering; burn the poor Town; butcher" (in round numbers) "3,000 of the poor Hessians; and wound "General Browne himself, while he too vehemently inter-"feres." * This was the finale of those 6,000 Hessians, and indeed their principal function, while in French pay; — and must have been, we can judge how surprising to Prince Friedrich, and to his Papa on hearing of it! Note another point.

Precisely about this time twelvemonth, 'March 16th, 1746,' the same Prince Friedrich, with remainder of those Hessians, now again completed to 6,000, and come back with emphasis to the Britannic side of things, was — marching out of Edinburgh, in much state, with streamers, kettle-drums, Highness's coaches, horses, led-horses, on an un-

* Adelung, IV. 358, and the half-intelligible Foot-note in Ranke, III. 220.

expected errand.* Toward Stirling, Perth; towards Killiecrankie, and raising of what is called 'the Siege of Blair in Athol' (most minute of 'sieges,' but subtending a great angle there and then);—much of unexpected, and nearer home than 'Tournay and the Netherlands Campaign,' having happened to Britannic George in the course of this year 1745! "Really "very fine troops, those Hessians" (observes my orthodox Whig friend): "they carry swords as well as guns and bayo-"nets; their uniform is blue turned up with white: the "Hussar part of them, about 500, have scimitars of a great "length; small horses, mostly black, of Swedish breed; "swift durable little creatures, with long tails." Honours, dinners, to his Serene Highness had been numerous, during the three weeks we had him in Edinburgh; "especially that "Ball, February 21st (o. s.), eve of his Consort the Princess "Mary's Birthday" (*eve* of birthday, 'let us dance the auspi-'cious morning *in*') "was, for affluence of Nobility and Gentry "of both sexes," a sublime thing.**

Pfaffenhofen, April 15*th*. "Unfortunate Ségur, the Ségur "of Linz three years ago,—whose conduct was great, accord-"ing to Valori, but powerless against traitors and fate,—"was again, once more, unfortunate in those parts. Unfor-"tunate Ségur drew up at Pfaffenhofen (centre of the Coun-"try, many miles from Vilshofen) to defend himself, when "fallen upon by Bärenklau, in that manner; but could not, "though with masterly demeanour; and had to retreat three "days, with his face to the enemy, so to speak, fighting and "manœuvering all the way: no shelter for him either but "München, and that a most temporary one. Instead of tak-"ing Straubingen, taking Passau, perhaps of pushing on to "Vienna itself, this is what we have already come to. No "Rhine Army, Middle-Rhine Army, Coigny, Maillebois, "Conti, whoever it was, would send us the least reinforce-"ment, when shrieked to. No outlook whatever but rapid "withdrawal, retreat to the Rhine Army, since it will not stir "to help us.**

* Henderson (Whig Eye-witness), *History of the Rebellion*, 1745 *and* 1746 (London, 1748, reprint from the Edinburgh edition), pp. 104, 106, 107.

** Adelung, IV. 360.

"The young Kur-Baiern is still polite, grateful" (to us French), "overwhelms us with politeness; but flies to Augs-"burg, as his Father used to do. Notable, however, his poor "fat little Mother won't, this time: 'No, I will stay here, I "'for one, and have done with flying and running; we have "'had enough of that!' Seckendorf, quite gone from Court "in this crisis, reappears, about the middle of April, in ques-"tionable capacity; at a place called Füssen, not far off, at "the foot of the Tyrol Hills; — where certain Austrian Dig-"nitaries seem also to be enjoying a picturesque Easter! Yes "indeed: and, on *April 22d*, there is signed a '*Peace of Füssen*' "there; general amicable *As-you-were*, between Austria and "Bavaria ('Renounce your Anti-Pragmatic moonshine for-"'evermore, vote for our Grand-Duke; there is your Bavaria "'back, poor wretches!') — and Seckendorf, it is presum-"able, will get his Turkish arrears liquidated.

"The Bavarian Intricacy, which once excelled human "power, is settled, then. Carteret and Haslang tried it in "vain" (dreadful heterodox intentions of secularising Salzburg, secularising Passau, Regensburg, and loud tremulous denial of such); — "Carteret and Wilhelm of Hessen" (Conferences of Hanau, which ruined Carteret), "in vain; King "Friedrich, and many Kings, in vain: a thing nobody could "settle; — and it has at last settled itself, as the generality "of ill-guided and unlucky things do, by collapse. Delirium "once out, the law of gravity acts; and there the mad matter "lies."

"Bought by Austria, that old villain!" cry the French. Friedrich does not think the Austrians bought Seckendorf, having no money at present; but guesses they may have given him to understand that a certain large arrear of payment due ever since those Turkish Wars, — when Seckendorf, instead of payment, was lodged in the Fortress of Grätz, and almost got his head cut off, — should now be paid down in cash, or authentic Paper-money, if matters become amicable.*

* *Œuvres de Frédéric*, III. 22; *Seckendorf's Leben*, pp. 367-378.

As they have done, in Friedrich's despite; — who seems angrier at the old stager for this particular ill-turn than for all the other many; and long remembers it, as will appear.

CHAPTER VII.

FRIEDRICH IN SILESIA; UNUSUALLY BUSY.

HERE, sure enough, are sad new intricacies in the Diplomatic, hypothetic sphere of things; and clouds piling themselves ahead, in a very minatory manner to King Friedrich. Let King Friedrich, all the more, get his Fighting Arrangements made perfect. Diplomacy is clouds; beating of your enemies is sea and land. Austria and the Gazetteer world consider Friedrich to be as good as finished: but that is privately far from being Friedrich's own opinion; — though these occurrences are heavy and dismal to him, as none of us can now fancy.

Herr Ranke has got access, in the Archives, to a series of private utterances by Friedrich, — Letters from him, of a franker nature than usual, and letting us far deeper into his mind; — which must have been well worth reading in the original, in their fully dated and developed condition. From Herr Ranke's Fragmentary Excerpts, let us, thankful for what we have got, select one or two. The Letters are to Minister Podewils at Berlin; written from Silesia (Neisse and neighbourhood), where, since the middle of March, Friedrich has been, personally pushing-on his Army Preparations, while the above sinister things befel.

King Friedrich to Podewils in Berlin (under various dates, March — April 1745).

Neisse, 29th March. * * "We find ourselves in a great crisis. "If we don't, by mediation of England, get Peace, our ene- "mies from different sides" (Saxony, Austria, who knows if not Russia withal!) "will come plunging in against me. Peace "I cannot force them to. But if they must have War, we will "either beat them, or none of us will see Berlin again." *

April (no day given). * * "In any case, I have my troops "well together. The sicknesses are ceasing; the recruit- "ments are coming in: shortly all will be complete. That "does not hinder us from making Peace, if it will only come; "but, in the contrary case, nobody can accuse me of neglecting "what was necessary."

April 17th (still from Neisse). * * "I toil day and night to "improve our situation. The soldiers will do their duty. "There is none among us who will not rather have his back- "bone broken than give up one foot-breadth of ground. They "must either grant us a good Peace, or we will surpass our- "selves by miracles of daring; and force the enemy to accept "it from us."

April 20th. "Our situation is disagreeable; constrained, a "kind of spasm: but my determination is taken. If we needs "must fight, we will do it like men driven desperate. Never "was there a greater peril than that I am now in. Time, at its "own pleasure, will untie this knot; or Destiny, if there is "one, determine the event. The game I play is so high, one "cannot contemplate the issue with cold blood. Pray for the "return of my good luck." — Two days hence, the poor young Kur-Baiern, deaf to the French seductions and exertions which were intense, had signed his 'Peace of Füssen' (22d April 1745), — a finale to France on the German Field, as may be feared! The other Fragments we will give a little farther on.

Friedrich had left Berlin for Silesia, March 15th; rather sooner than he counted on, — Old Leopold

* Ranke, III. 236 et seq.

pleading to be let home. At Glogau, at Breslau, there had been the due inspecting: Friedrich got to Neisse on the 23d (Bathyani just stirring in that Bavarian Business, Vilshofen and the Hessians close ahead); and on the 27th, had dismissed Old Leopold, with thanks and sympathies, — sent him home, "to recover his health." Leopold's health is probably suffering; but his heart and spirits still more. Poor old man, he has just lost, — the other week, '5th February' last, — his poor old Wife, at Dessau; and is broken down with grief. The soft silk lining of his hard Existence, in all parts of it, is torn away. Apothecary Fos's Daughter, Reich's Princess, Princess of Dessau, called by whatever name, she had been the truest of Wives; 'used to attend him in all his Campaigns, for above fifty years back.' "Gone, now, forever gone!" — Old Leopold had wells of strange sorrow in the rugged heart of him, — sorrow, and still better things, — which he does not wear on his sleeve. Here is an incident I never can forget; — dating twelve or thirteen years ago (as is computable), 'middle of July 1732.'

"Louisa, Leopold's eldest Daughter, Wife of Victor Leo-"pold, reigning Prince of Anhalt-Bernburg, lay dying of a "decline." Still only twenty-three, poor Lady, though married seven years ago; — the end now evidently drawing nigh. "A few days before her death, — perhaps some attendant "sorrowfully asking, 'Can we do nothing, then?' — she was "heard to say, 'If I could see my Father at the head of his "'Regiment, yet once!'" — Halle, where the Regiment lies, is some thirty or more miles off; and King Friedrich Wilhelm, I suppose would have to be written to: — Leopold was ready the soonest possible; and, "at a set hour, marched, in all "pomp with banner flying, music playing, into the *Schlosshof*

"(Palace Court) of Bernburg; and did the due salutations and "manœuverings, — his poor Daughter sitting at her window, "till they ended;" — figure them, the last glitter of those muskets, the last wail of that band-music! — "The Regiment "was then marched to the Waisenhaus (*Orphanhouse*), where "the common men were treated with bread and beer; all "the Officers dining at the Prince's Table. All the Officers, "except Leopold alone, who stole away out of the crowd; sat "himself upon the balustrade of the Saale Bridge, and wept "into the river." * — — Leopold is now on the edge of seventy; ready to think all is finished with him. Perhaps not quite, my tough old friend; recover yourself a little, and we shall see!

Old Leopold is hardly home at Dessau, when new Pandour tempests, tides of ravaging War, again come beating against the Giant Mountains, pouring through all passes; from utmost Jablunka, westward by Jägerndorf to Glatz, huge influx of wild riding hordes, each with some support of Austrian grenadiers, cannoniers; threatening to submerge Silesia. Precursors, Friedrich need not doubt, of a strenuous regular attempt that way. Hungarian Majesty's fixed intention, hope and determination is, To expel him straightway from Silesia. Her Patent circulates, these three months; calling on all men to take note of that fixed fact, especially on all Silesian men to note it well, and shift their allegiance accordingly. Silesian men, in great majority, — our friend the Mayor of Landshut, for example? — are believed to have no inclination towards change: and whoever has, had clearly better not show any till he see! ** —

* *Leben* (12mo; not *Ranft's* but Anonymous like his), p. 234 n.

** In Ranke (III. 234), there is vestige of some intended "voluntary subscription by the common people of Glatz," for Friedrich's behoof; — contrariwise, in Orlich (II. 380, "6th February 1745," from the Dessau

Friedrich's thousandfold preliminary orderings, movements, rearrangings in his Army matters, must not detain us here; — still less his dealings with the Pandour element, which is troublesome, rather than dangerous. Vigilance, wise swift determination, valour drilled to its work, can deal with phenomena of that nature, though never so furious and innumerable. Not a cheering service for drilled valour, but a very needful one. Continual bickerings and skirmishings fell out, sometimes rising to sharp fight on the small scale: — Austrian grenadiers with cannon are on that Height to left, and also on this to right, meaning to cut off our march; the difficult landscape furnished out, far and wide, with Pandour companies in position: you must dash in, my Burschen; seize me that cannon-battery yonder; master such and such a post, — there is the heart of all that network of armed doggery; slit asunder that, the network wholly will tumble over the Hills again. Which is always done, on the part of the Prussian Burschen; though sometimes not without difficulty. — His Majesty is forming Magazines at Neisse, Brieg, and the principal Fortresses in those parts; driving on all manner of preparations at the rapidest rate of speed, and looking with his own eyes into everything. The regiments are about what we may call complete, arithmetically and otherwise; the cavalry show good perfection in their new mode of manœuvering; — it is to be hoped the Fighting Apparatus generally will give fair account of itself when the

Archives), notice of one individual, suspected of stirring for Austria, whom "you are to put under lock and key;" — but he runs off, and has no successor, that I hear of.

time comes. Our one anchor of hope, as now more and more appears.

On the Pandour element he first tried (under General Hautcharmoi, with Winterfeld as chief active hand) a direct outburst or two, with a view to slash them home at once. But finding that it was of no use, as they always reappeared in new multitudes, he renounced that; took to calling in his remoter outposts; and, except where Magazines or the like remained to be cared for, let the Pandours baffle about, checked only by the fortified Towns, and more and more submerge the Hill Country. Prince Karl, to be expected in the form of lion, mysteriously uncertain on which side coming to invade us, — he, and not the innumerable weasel kind, is our important matter! By the end of April (news of the *Peace of Füssen* coming withal), Friedrich had quitted Neisse; lay cantoned, in Neisse Valley (between Frankenstein and Patschkau, 'able to assemble in forty-eight hours'); studying, with his whole strength, to be ready for the mysterious Prince Karl, on whatever side he might arrive; — and disregarding the Pandours in comparison.

The points of inrush, the tideways of these Pandour Deluges seem to be mainly three. Direct through the Jablunka, upon Ratibor Country, is the first and chief; less direct (partly supplied by *refluences* from Ratibor, when Ratibor is found not to answer), a second disembogues by Jägerndorf; a third, the westernmost, by Landshut. Three main ingresses: at each of which there fall out little Fights; which are still celebrated in the Prussian Books, and indeed well deserve reading by soldiers that would know their trade. In the Ratibor parts, the invasive leader is a General Karoly, with 12,000 under him, who are the wildest horde of all: "Karoly "lodges in a wood: for himself there is a tent; his companions "sleep under trees, or under the open sky, by the edge of "morasses." * It was against this Karoly and his horde that Hautcharmoi's little expedition, or express attacking party to drive them home again, was shot out (8th–21st April). Which did its work very prettily; Winterfeld, chief hand in it, crowning the matter by a "Fight of Würbitz," ** — where Winterfeld, cutting the taproot, in his usual electric way, tumbles Karoly quite *into* the morasses, and clears the country of him for a time. For a time; though for a time only; — Karoly or others returning in a week or two, to a still higher extent of thousands; mischievous as ever in those Ratibor-Namslau countries. Upon which, Friedrich, finding this an endless business, and nothing like the most important, gives it up for the present; calls-in his remoter detachments; has his Magazines carted home to the Fortress Towns, — Karoly trying, once or so, to hinder in that operation, but only again getting his crown broken. *** Or if carting be too difficult, still do not waste your Magazine: — Margraf Karl, for instance, is ordered to Jägerndorf with his Detachment, "to eat "the Magazine;" hungry Pandours looking on, till he finish. On which occasion a renowned little Fight took place (Fight of Neustadt, or of Jägerndorf-Neustadt), as shall be mentioned farther on.

So that, for certain weeks to come, the Tolpatcheries had free course, in those Frontier parts; and were left to rove about, under check only of the Garrison Towns; Friedrich being obliged to look elsewhere after higher perils, which were now coming in view. In which favourable circumstances, Karoly and Consorts did, at last, make one stroke in those Ratibor countries; that of Kosel, which was greatly consolatory.† "By treachery of an Ensign who had deserted to "them" (provoked by rigour of discipline, or some intolerable thing), "they glided stealthily, one night, across the ditches, "into Kosel" (a half-fortified place, Prussian works only half-finished): which, being the Key of the Oder in those parts, they reckoned a glorious conquest; of good omen, and worthy of *Te-Deums* at Vienna. And they did eagerly, without the least molestation, labour to complete the Prussian works at

* Ranke, III. 244. ** Orlich, II. 136 (21st April).

*** "Fight of Mocker," May 4th (Orlich, II. 141).

† 26th May 1745 (Orlich, II. 156-158).

Kosel: "One garrison already ours!" — which was not had from them without battering (and I believe, burning), when General von Nassau came to inquire after it, in Autumn next.

Friedrich had always hoped that the Saxons, who are not yet in declared War with him, though bound by Treaty to assist the Queen of Hungary under certain conditions, would not venture on actual Invasion of his Territories; but in this, as readers anticipate, Friedrich finds himself mistaken. Weissenfels is hastening from the Leitmeritz north-western quarter, where he has wintered, to join Prince Karl, who is gathering himself from Olmütz and his south-eastern home region; their full intention is to invade Silesia together, and they hope now at length to make an end of Friedrich and it. These Pandour hordes, supported by the necessary grenadiers and cannoniers, are sent as vanguard; these cannot themselves beat him; but they may induce him (which they do not) to divide his Force, they may, in part, burn him away as by slow fire, after which he will be the easier to beat. Instead of which, Friedrich, leaving the Pandours to their luck, lies concentrated in Neisse Valley; watching, with all his faculties, Prince Karl's own advent (coming on like Fate, indubitable, yet involved in mysteries hitherto); and is perilously sensible that only in giving that a good reception is there any hope left him.

Prince Karl, 'who arrived in Olmütz, April 30th,' commands in chief again, — saddened, poor man, by the loss of his young Wife, in December last; willing to still his grief in action for the cause *she* loved; — but old Traun is not with him this year: which is a still more material circumstance. Traun is to go this year, under cloak not of Prince Karl, but of Grand-Duke Franz, to clear those Frankfurt countries for the *Kaiserwahl* and him. Prince Conti lies there, with his famous 'Middle-Rhine Army' (D'Ahremberg, from the western parts, not nearly so diligent upon him as one could wish); and must, at all rates, be cleared away. Traun, taking command of Bathyani's Army (now that it has finished the Bavarian job), is preparing to push down upon Conti, while Bathyani (who is to supersede the laggard D'Ahremberg) shall push vigorously up; — and before summer is over, we shall hear of Traun again, and Conti will have heard! —

Friedrich's indignation, on learning that the Saxons were actually on march, and gradually that they intended to invade him, was great; and the whole matter is portentously enigmatic to him, as he lies vigilant in Neisse Valley, waiting on the When and the How. Indignation; — and yet there is need of caution withal. To be ready for events, the Old Dessauer has, as one sure measure, been requested to take charge, once more, of a "Camp of Observation" on the Saxon Frontier (as of old, in 1741); and has given his consent:* "Camp of Magdeburg," "Camp of Dieskau;" for it had various names and figures; checkings of your hand, then layings of it on, heavier, lighter, and again heavier, according to one's various *readings* of the Saxon Mystery; and we shall hear enough about it, intermittently, till December coming: when it ended in a way we shall not forget! — On which take this Note:

* "April 25th," consents (Orlich. II. 130).

"The Camp of Observation was to have begun, May 1st; "did begin somewhat later, 'near Magdeburg,' not too close "on the Frontier, nor in too alarming strength; was reinforced "to about 30,000; in which state" (middle of August) "it "stept forward to Wieskau, then to Dieskau, close on the "Saxon Border; and became, — with a Saxon Camp lying "close opposite, and War formally threatened, or almost "declared, on Saxony by Friedrich, — an alarmingly serious "matter. Friedrich, however, again checked his hand; and "did not consummate till November — December. But did "then consummate; greatly against his will; and in a way "flamingly visible to all men!" *

Friedrich's own incidental utterances (what more we have of Fractions from the Podewils Letters), in such portentous aspect of affairs, may now be worth giving. It is not now to Jordan that he writes, gaily unbosoming himself, as in the First War, — poor Jordan lies languishing, these many months; consumptive, too evidently dying: — Not to Jordan, this time; nor is the theme "*gloire*" now, but a far different!

Friedrich to Podewils (as before, April — May 1745).

April 20th or so, Orders are come to Berlin (orders, to Podewils's horror at such a thought), Whitherward, should Berlin be assaulted, the Official Boards, the Preciosities and household gods are to betake themselves: — to Magdeburg, all these, which is an impregnable place; to Stettin, the Two 'Queens, and Royal Family, if they like it better. Podewils in horror, 'hair standing on end,' writes thereupon to Eichel, That he hopes the management, 'in a certain contingency,' will be given to Minister Boden: he Podewils, with his hair in that posture, being quite unequal to it. Friedrich answers:

"*April 26th.* * * 'I can understand how you are getting "'uneasy, you Berliners. I have the most to lose of you all;

* Orlich, II. 180, 209, 210; *Helden-Geschichte*, II. 1224-26; I. 1117.

"'but I am quiet, and prepared for events. If the Saxons take "'part,' as they surely will, 'in the Invasion of Silesia, and we "'beat them, I am determined to plunge into Saxony. For "'great maladies, there need great remedies. Either I will "'maintain my all, or else lose my all.' (Hear it, friend; and "understand it, — with hair lying flat!) 'It is true, the dis-"'affection of the Russian Court, on such trifling grounds, "'was not to be expected; and great misfortune can befal us. "'Well; a year or two sooner, a year or two later, — it is not "'worth one's while to bother about the very worst. If things "'take the better turn, our condition will be surer and firmer "'than it was before. If we have nothing to reproach our-"'selves with, neither need we fret and plague ourselves "'about bad events, which can happen to any man.' — 'I am "'causing despatch a secret Order for Boden' (on *you* know "what), 'which you will not deliver him till I give sign.'" — On hearing of the Peace of Füssen, perhaps a day or so later, Friedrich again writes:

"*April*" (no distinct date; Neisse still? *Quits* Neisse, April 28th). ** "Peace of Füssen, Bavaria turned against me? 'I "'can say nothing to it, — except, There has come what had "'to come. To me remains only to possess myself in patience. "'If all alliances, resources, and negotiations fail, and all "'conjunctures go against me, I prefer to perish with honour, "'rather than lead an inglorious life deprived of all dignity. "'My ambition whispers me that I have done more than "'another to the building up of my House, and have played a "'distinguished part among the crowned heads of Europe. "'To maintain myself there, has become as it were a per-"'sonal duty; which I will fulfil at the expense of my happi-"'ness and my life. I have no choice left: I will maintain my "'power, or it may go to ruin, and the Prussian name be "'buried under it. If the enemy attempt anything upon us, "'we will either beat him, or we will all be hewed to pieces, "'for the sake of our Country, and the renown of Branden-"'burg. No other counsel can I listen to.'"

Same Letter, or another? (Herr Ranke having his caprices!) ** "You are a good man, my Podewils, and do what can be "expected of you" (Podewils has been apologising for his terrors; and referring hopefully 'to Providence'): "Perform "faithfully the given work on your side, as I on mine; for "the rest, let what you call 'Providence' decide as it likes:" — (*une Providence aveugle?* Ranke, who alone knows, gives "*blinde Vorsehung.*" What an utterance, on the part of this little Titan! Consider it as exceptional with him, unusual, accidental to the hard moment, and perhaps not so impious as it looks!) — "Neither our prudence nor our courage shall be "liable to blame; but only circumstances that would not "favour us. * *

"I prepare myself for every event. Fortune may be kind "or be unkind, it shall neither dishearten me nor uplift me. If "I am to perish, let it be with honour, and sword in hand. "What the issue is to be — Well, what pleases Heaven, or "the Other Party (*J'ai jeté le bonnet par dessus les moulins*)! "Adieu, my dear Podewils; become as good a philosopher as "you are a politician; and learn from a man who does not go "to Elsner's Preaching" (fashionable at the time), "that one "must oppose to ill fortune a brow of iron; and, during this "life, renounce all happiness, all acquisitions, possessions "and lying shows, none of which will follow us beyond the "grave." *

"By what points the Austrian-Saxon Armament will come through upon us? Together will it be, or separately? Saxons from the Lausitz, Austrians from Böhmen, enclosing us between two fires?" — were enigmatic questions with Friedrich; and the Saxons especially are an enigma. But that come they will, that these Pandours are their preliminary veiling-apparatus as usual, is evident to him; and that he must not spend himself upon Pandours; but coalesce, and lie ready for the main wrestle. So that from April 28th, as above noticed, Friedrich has gone into cantonments, some way up the Neisse Valley, westward of Neisse Town; and is calling-in his outposts, his detachments; emptying his Frontier Magazines; — abandoning his Upper-Silesian Frontier more and more,

* Ranke, III. pp. 236-241.

and in the end altogether, to the Pandour hordes; a small matter they, compared to the grand Invasion which is coming on. Here, with shiftings up the Neisse Valley, he lies till the end of May; watching Argus-like, and scanning with every faculty the Austrian-Saxon motions and intentions, until at length they become clear to him, and we shall see how he deals with them.

His own lodging, or headquarter, most of this time (4th May — 27th May) is in the pleasant Abbey of Camenz (mythic scene of that *Baumgarten-Skirmish* business, in the First Silesian War). He has excellent Tobias Stusche for company in leisure hours; and the outlook of bright Spring all round him, flowering into gorgeous Summer, as he hurries about on his many occasions, *not* of an idyllic nature.* But his Army is getting into excellent completeness of number, health, equipment, and altogether such a spirit as he could wish. May 22d, here is another snatch from some Note to Podewils, from this balmy Locality, potential with such explosions of another kind. "*Camenz, May 22d.* * * "'The Enemies are making move-"'ments; but nothing like enough as yet for our guess-"'ing their designs. Till we see, therefore, the thunder "'lies quiet in us (*la foudre repose en mes mains*). Ah, "'could we but have a Day like that May Eleventh!"**

What "that May Eleventh" is or was? Readers are curious to know; especially English readers, who guess *Fontenoy*. And Historic Art, if she were strict, would decline to inform them at any length; for really the thing is no better than a "Victory on the Scamander,

* Orlich, II. 189; Ranke, III. 242-249. ** Ranke, III. 248 n.

and a Siege of Pekin" (as a certain observer did afterwards define it), in reference to the matter now on hand! Well, Pharsalia, Arbela, the Scamander, Armageddon, and so many Battles and Victories being luminous, by study, to cultivated Englishmen, and one's own Fontenoy such a mystery and riddle, — Art, after consideration, reluctantly consents to be indulgent; will produce from her Paper Imbroglios a slight Piece on the subject; and print instead of burning.

CHAPTER VIII.

THE MARTIAL BOY AND HIS ENGLISH *VERSUS* THE LAWS OF NATURE.

"Glorious Campaign in the Netherlands, Siege of Tournay, final ruin of the Dutch Barrier!" this is the French program for Season 1745, — no Belleisle to contradict it; Belleisle secure at Windsor, who might have leant more towards German enterprises. And to this his Britannic Majesty (small gain to him from that adroitness in the Harz, last winter!) has to make front. And is strenuously doing so, by all methods; especially by heroic expenditure of money, and ditto exposure of his Martial Boy. Poor old Wade, last year, — perhaps Wade did suffer, as he alleged, from "want of sufficient authority in that mixed Army"? Well, here is a Prince of the Blood, Royal Highness of Cumberland, to command in chief. With a Königseck to dry-nurse him, may not Royal Highness, luck favouring, do very well? Luck did not favour; Britannic Majesty, neither in the Netherlands over seas, nor at home (strange new domestic wool, of a tarry *Highland* nature, being thrown him to card, on the sudden!), made a good Campaign, but a bad. And again a bad (1746), and again (1747), ever again, till he pleased to cease altogether. Of which distressing objects we propose that the following one glimpse be our last.

Battle of Fontenoy (11th May 1745).

* * "In the end of April, Marechal de Saxe, now become very famous for his sieges in the Netherlands, opened "trenches before Tournay; King Louis, with his Dauphin, "not to speak of mistresses, playactors and cookery apparatus "(in wagons innumerable) hastens to be there. A fighting "Army, say of 70,000, besides the garrisons; and great things, "it is expected, will be done; Tournay, in spite of strong "works and Dutch garrison of 9,000, to be taken in the first "place.

"Of the Siege, which was difficult and ardent, we will remember nothing, except the mischance that befel a certain "'Marquis de Talleyrand' and his men, in the trenches, one "night. Night of 8th-9th May, by carelessness of somebody, "a spark got into the Marquis's powder, two powder-barrels "that there were; and, with horrible crash, sent eighty men, "Marquis Talleyrand and Engineer Du Mazis among them, "aloft into the other world; raining down their limbs into the "covered-way, where the Dutch were very inhuman to them, "and provoked us to retaliate.* Du Mazis I do not know; "but Marquis de Talleyrand turns out, on study of the French "Peerages, to be Uncle of a lame little Boy, who became "Right Reverend Talleyrand under singular conditions, and "has made the name very current in after times! —

"Hearing of this Siege, the Duke of Cumberland hastened "over from England, with intent to raise the same. Mustered "his 'Allied Army' (once called 'Pragmatic'), — self at the "head of it; old Count Königseck, who was *not* burnt at "Chotusitz, commanding the small Austrian quota" (Austrians mainly are gone laggarding with D'Ahremberg up the Rhine); "and a Prince of Waldeck the Dutch, — on the plain of "Anderlecht near Brussels, May 4th,** and found all things "tolerably complete. Upon which, straightway, his Royal "Highness, 60,000 strong let us say, set forth; by slowish "marches, and a route somewhat leftward of the great Tour-"nay Road" (no place on it, except perhaps *Steenkerke*, ever

* Espagnac, II. 27.

** Anonymous *Life of Cumberland*. p. 190; Espagnac, II. 26.

"heard of by an English reader); "and on Sunday 9th May,*
"precisely on the morrow after poor Talleyrand had gone "aloft, reached certain final Villages: Vezon, Maubray, "where he encamps, Briffoeil to rear; Camp looking towards "Tournay and the setting sun, — with Fontenoy short way "ahead, and Antoine to left of it, and Barry with its Woods "to right: — small peaceable Villages, which become famous "in the Newspapers shortly after.** Royal Highness, resting "here at Vezon, is but some six or seven miles from Tournay; "in low undulating Country, woody here and there, not with-"out threads of running water, and with frequent Villages "and their adjuncts: the part of it now interesting to us lies "all between the Brussels-Tournay Road and the Scheld "River, — all in immediate front of his Royal Highness, — "to south-eastward from beleaguered Tournay, where said "Road and River intersect. How shall he make some im-"pression on the Siege of Tournay? That is now the ques-"tion; and his Royal Highness struggles to manœuvre accord-"ingly.

"Maréchal de Saxe, whose habit is much that of vigilance, "forethought, sagacious precaution, singular in so dissolute "a man, has neglected nothing on this occasion. He knows "every foot of the ground, having sieged here, in his boy-"hood, once before. Leaving the siege-trenches at Tournay, "under charge of a ten or fifteen thousand, he has taken "camp here; still with superior force (56,000 as they count, "Royal Highness being only 50,000 ranked), barring Royal "Highness's way. Tournay, or at least the Maréchal's "trenches there, are on the right bank of the Scheld; which "flows from south-east, securing all on that hand. The "broad Brussels Highway comes in to him from the east; — "north of that, he has nothing to fear, the ground being cut "with bogs; no getting through upon him, that way, to "Tournay and what he calls the 'Under Scheld.' The 'Upper "'Scheld' too, eastward of the Enemy, can, for reasons which "he sees, avail them nothing. There is only that triangle to "the south-east, between Road and River, where the Enemy "is now manœuvering in front of him, from which damage "can well come; and he has done his best to be secure there.

* Espagnac, ii. 27.
** Patch of Map at p. 130.

"Four villages or hamlets, close to the Scheld and onwards to "the Great Road, — Antoine, Fontenoy, Barry, Ramecroix, "with their lanes and boscages, — make a kind of circular "base to his triangle; base of some six or eight miles; with hollows in it, brooks, and northward a considerable Wood" *(Bois de Barry*, enveloping Barry and Ramecroix, which do not prove of much interest to us, though the *Bois* does of a good deal). "In and before each of those villages are posts "and defences; in Antoine and Fontenoy elaborate redoubts, "batteries, redans connecting: in the Wood *(Bois de Barry)*, "an abattis, or wall of felled trees, as well as cannon; and at "the point of the Wood, well within double-range of Fonte-"noy, is a Redoubt, called of Eu *(Redoute d'Eu*, from the re-"giment occupying it), which will much concern his Royal "Highness and us. Saxe has a hundred pieces of cannon" (say the English, which is correct), "consummately disposed "along this space; no ingress possible anywhere, except "through the cannon's throat, torrents of fire and cross-fire "playing on you. He is armed to the teeth, as they say; and "has his 56,000 arranged according to the best rules of tac-"tics, behind this murderous line of works. If his Royal "Highness think of breaking in, he may count on a very warm "reception indeed.

"Saxe is only afraid his Royal Highness will not. Out-"side of these lines, with a 50,000 dashing fiercely round us, "under any kind of leading; pouncing on our convoys; "harassing and sieging *us*, — our siege of Tournay were a "sad outlook. And this is old Austrian Königseck's opinion, "too; though, they say, Waldeck and the Dutch (impetuous "in theory at least) opined otherwise, and strengthened "Royal Highness's view. Two young men against one old: "'Be it so, then!' His Royal Highness, resolute for getting in, "manœuvres and investigates, all Monday 10th; his cannon "is not to arrive completely till night; otherwise he would be "for breaking in at once: a fearless young man, fearless as "ever his poor Father was; certainly a man *sans peur*, this "one too; whether of much *avis*, we shall see anon.

"Tuesday morning early, 11th May 1745, cannon being "up, and dispositions made, his Royal Highness sallies out; "sees his men taking their ground: Dutch and Austrians to "the left, chiefly opposite Antoine; English, with some

"Hanoverians, in the centre and to the right; infantry in "front, facing Fontenoy, cavalry to rear flanking the Wood "of Barry, — Königseck, Ligonier, and others able, assisting "to plant them advantageously; cannon going, on both sides, "the while; radiant enthusiasm, *sans peur et sans avis*, look-"ing from his Royal Highness's face. He has been on horse-"back since two in the morning; cannon started thundering "between five and six, — has killed chivalrous Grammont "over yonder (the Grammont of Dettingen), almost at the "first volley. And now, about the time when ploughers "breakfast (eight A. M., no ploughing hereabouts today!), "begins the attack, simultaneously or in swift succession, on "the various batteries which it will be necessary to attack "and storm.

"The attacks took place; but none of them succeeded. "Dutch and Austrians, on the extreme left, were to have "stormed Antoine by the edge of the River; that was their "main task; right skirt of them to help *us* meanwhile with "Fontenoy. And they advanced, accordingly; but found "the shot from Antoine too fierce: especially when a sub-"sidiary battery opened from across the River, and took them "in flank, the Dutch and Austrians felt astonished; and "hastily drew aside, under some sheltering mound or earth-"work they had found for themselves, or prudently thrown "up the night before. There, under their earthwork, stood "the Dutch and Austrians; patiently expecting a fitter time, "which indeed never occurred; for always, the instant they "drew out, the batteries from Antoine, and from across the "River, instantly opened upon them, and they had to draw in "again. So that they stood there, in a manner, all day; and "so to speak did nothing but patiently expect when it should "be time to run. For which they were loudly censured, and "deservedly. Antoine is and remains a total failure on the "part of the Dutch and Austrians.

"Royal Highness in person, with his English, was to attack "Fontenoy; — and is doing so, by battery and storm, at "various points; with emphasis, though without result. As "preliminary, at an early stage he had sent forward on the "right, by the Wood of Barry, a Brigadier Ingoldsby 'with "'Semple's Highlanders' and other force, to silence 'that "'redoubt yonder at the point of the Wood,' — redoubt, fort, "or whatever it be (famous *Redoute d'Eu*, as it turned out!), "— which guards Fontenoy to north, and will take us in "flank, nay in rear, as we storm the cannon of the Village. "Ingoldsby, speed imperative on him, pushed into the Wood; "found French light-troops ('God knows how many of them!") "prowling about there; found the Redoubt a terribly strong "thing, with ditch, drawbridge, what not; spent thirty or "forty of his Highlanders, in some frantic attempt on it by "rule of thumb; — and found 'He would need artillery' and "other things. In short, Ingoldsby, hasten what he might, "could not perfect the preparations to his mind, had to wait "for this and for that; and did not storm the Redoubt d'Eu at "all; but hung fire, in an unaccountable manner. For which "he had to answer (to Court-Martial, still more to the News- "papers) afterwards; and prove that it was misfortune "merely, or misfortune and stupidity combined. Too evident, "the *Redoute d'Eu* was not taken, then or thenceforth; which "might have proved the saving of the whole affair, could In- "goldsby have managed it. Royal Highness attacked Fonte- "noy, and re-attacked, furiously, thrice over; and had to "desist, and find Fontenoy impossible on those terms.

"Here is a piece of work. Repulsed at all those points; "and on the left and on the right, no spirit visible but what "deserves repulse! His Royal Highness blazes into resplen- "dent *Platt-Deutsch* rage, what we may call spiritual white- "heat, a man *sans peur* at any rate, and pretty much *sans avis*; "decides that he must and will be through those lines, if it "please God; that he will not be repulsed at his part of the "attack, not he for one; but will plunge through, by what "gap there is" (900 yards Voltaire measures it*) "between "Fontenoy and that Redoubt with its laggard Ingoldsby; "and see what the French interior is like! He rallies rapidly, "re-arranges; forms himself in thin column or columns" (three of them, I think, — which gradually got crushed into one, as they advanced, under cannon-shot on both hands), — "wheeling his left round, to be rear, his right to be head of "said column or columns. In column, the cannon-shot from

* *Œuvres*, xxviii. 150 (*Siecle de Louis Quinze*, c. xv. "*Bataille de Fontenoi*," — elaborately exact on all such points).

"Fontenoy on the left, and Redoubt d'Eu on our right, will "tell less on us; and between these two death-dealing locali- "ties, by the hollowest, least shelterless way discoverable, "we mean to penetrate: 'Forward, my men, steady and swift, "'till we are through the shot-range, and find men to grapple "'with, instead of case-shot and projectile iron!' Marechal "de Saxe owned afterwards, 'He should have put an ad- "'ditional redoubt in that place, but he did not think any "'Army would try such a thing' (cannon batteries playing on "each hand at 400 yards distance); — nor has any Army "since or before!

"These columns advance, however; through bushy hollows, "water-courses, through what defiles or hollowest grounds "there are; endure the cannon-shot, while they must; trailing "their own heavy-guns by hand, and occasionally blasting "out of them where the ground favours; — and do, with in- "dignant patience, wind themselves through, pretty much "beyond direct shot-range of either d'Eu or Fontenoy. And "have actually got into the interior mystery of the French "Line of Battle, — which is not a little astonished to see them "there! It is over a kind of blunt ridge, or rising ground, "that they are coming: on the crown of this rising ground, "the French regiment fronting it (*Gardes Françaises* as it "chanced to be) notices, with surprise, field-cannon pointed "the wrong way; actual British artillery unaccountably "showing itself there. Regiment of *Gardes* rushes up to seize "said fieldpieces: but, on the summit, perceives with amaze- "ment that it cannot; that a heavy volley of musketry blazes "into it (killing sixty men); that it will have to rush back "again, and report progress: Huge British force, of unknown "extent, is readjusting itself into column there, and will be "upon us on the instant. Here is news!

"News true enough. The head of the English column "comes to sight, over the rising ground, close by: their offi- "cers doff their hats, politely saluting ours, who return the "civility: was ever such politeness seen before? It is a fact; "and among the memorablest of this Battle. Nay a certain "English Officer of mark, — Lord Charles Hay the name of "him, valued surely in the annals of the Hay and Tweeddale "House, — steps forward from the ranks, as if wishing some- "thing. Towards whom" (says the accurate Espagnac)

"Marquis d'Auteroche, grenadier-lieutenant, with air of polite "interrogation, not knowing what he meant, made a step or "two: 'Monsieur,' said Lord Charles *(Lord Charles-hay)*, "'bid your people fire *(faites tirer vos gens)*!' '*Non, Monsieur,* "'*nous ne tirons jamais les premiers* (We never fire first).'* "After *you*, Sire! Is not this a bit of modern chivalry? A "supreme politeness in that sniffing pococurante kind; pro- "bably the highest point (or lowest) it ever went to. Which I "have often thought of."

It is almost pity to disturb an elegant Historical Passage of this kind, circulating round the world, in some glory, for a century past: but there has a small irrefragable Document come to me, which modifies it a good deal, and reduces matters to the business form. Lord Charles Hay, "Lieutenant-Colonel," practical Head, "of the First Regiment of Foot-guards," wrote, about three weeks after (or dictated in sad spelling, not himself able to write for wounds), a Letter to his Brother, of which here is an Excerpt at first hand, with only the spelling altered: * * "It was our Regiment that "attacked the French Guards: and when we came within "twenty or thirty paces of them, I advanced before our Regi- "ment; drank to them" (to the French, from the pocket-pistol one carries on such occasions), "and told them that "we were the English Guards, and hoped that they would "stand till we came quite up to them, and not swim the "Scheld as they did the Mayn at Dettingen" (shameful *third-bridge*, not of wood, though carpeted with blue cloth there)! "Upon which I immediately turned about to our "own Regiment; speeched them, and made them huzzah," —I hope with a will. "An Officer" (d'Auteroche) "came out "of the ranks, and tried to make his men huzzah; however,

* Espagnac, II. 60 (of the *Original*, Toulouse, 1789); II. 46 of the German Translation (Leipzig, 1774), our usual reference. Voltaire, endlessly informed upon details this time, is equally express: *"Milord Charles Hay "capitaine aux gardes anglaises, cria: 'Messieurs des gardes françaises, "tirez!'* To which Count d'Auteroche with a loud voice answered" &c. (*Œuvres*, vol. XXVIII. p. 155). See also *Souvenirs du Marquis de Valfons* (edited by a Grand-Nephew, Paris, 1860), p. 151; — a poor, considerably noisy and unclean little Book; which proves unexpectedly worth looking at, in regard to some of those poor Battles and personages and occurrences: the Bohemian Belleisle-Broglio part, to my regret, if to no other person's, has been omitted, as extinct, or undecipherable by the Grand-Nephew.

"there were not above three or four in their Brigade that did."† * *

Very poor counter-huzzah. And not the least whisper of that sublime "After you, Sirs!" but rather, in confused form, of quite the reverse; Hay having been himself fired into ("fire had begun on my left;" Hay totally ignorant on which side first), — fired into, rather feebly, and wounded by those d'Auteroche people, while he was still advancing with shouldered arms; — upon which, and not till which, he did give it them: in liberal dose; and quite blew them off the ground, for that day. From all which, one has to infer, That the mutual salutation by hat was probably a fact; that, for certain, there was some slight preliminary talk and gesticulation, but in the Homeric style, by no means in the Espagnac-French, — not chivalrous epigram at all, mere rough banter, and what is called "chaffing;" — and in short, that the French Mess-rooms (with their eloquent talent that way) had rounded off the thing into the current epigrammatic redaction; the authentic business-form of it being ruggedly what is now given. Let our Manuscript proceed.

"D'Auteroche declining the first fire," — or accepting it, if ever offered, nobody can say, — "the three Guards Regi-"ments, Lord Charles's on the right, give it him hot and "heavy, 'tremendous rolling fire;' so that D'Auteroche, "responding more or less, cannot stand it; but has at once "to rustle into discontinuity, he and his, and roll rapidly "out of the way. And the British Column advances, steadily, "terribly, hurling back all opposition from it; deeper and "deeper into the interior mysteries of the French Host; "blasting its way with gunpowder; — in a magnificent "manner. A compact Column, slowly advancing, — ap-"parently of some 16,000 foot. Pauses, readjusts itself a "little, when not meddled with; when meddled with, has "cannon, has rolling fire, — delivers from it, in fact, on both "hands such a torrent of deadly continuous fire as was rarely "seen before or since. '*Feu infernal*,' the French call it. "The French make vehement resistance. Battalions, "squadrons, regiment after regiment, charge madly on this

† "Ath, May ye 30th, o.s." (to John, Fourth Marquis of Tweeddale, last 'Secretary of State for Scotland,' and a man of figure in his day): Letter is at Yester House, East Lothian; Excerpt *penes me*.

"terrible Column; but rush only on destruction thereby. "Regiment This storms in from the right, regiment That "from the left; have their colonels shot, 'lose the half of "'their people;' and hastily draw back again, in a wrecked "condition. The cavalry-horses cannot stand such smoke "and blazing; nor indeed, I think, can the cavaliers. *Regi-"ment du Roi* rushing on, full gallop, to charge this Column, "got one volley from it" (says Espagnac) "which brought to "the ground 460 men. Natural enough that horses take the "bit between their teeth; likewise that men take it, and "career very madly in such circumstances!

"The terrible Column with slow inflexibility advances; "cannon (now in reversed position) from that Redoubt d'Eu "('Shame on you, Ingoldsby!') and irregular musketry from

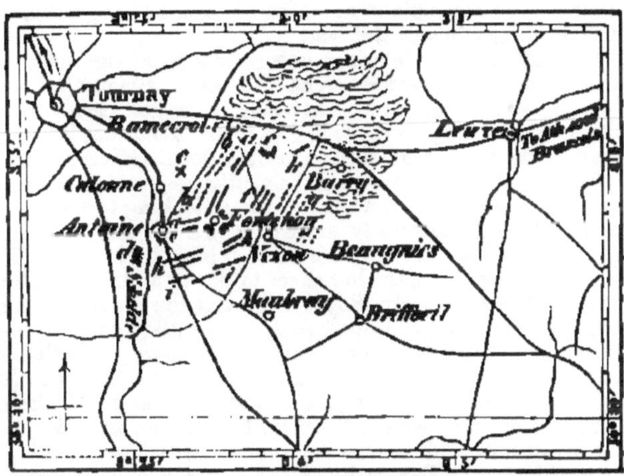

aa. French Infantry.
bb. French Horse.
c. Redoubt d'Eu.
d. Subsidiary French Battery, which takes the Dutch in flank.
e. Gallows-Hill, where King Louis and the Dauphin were.
f. English Foot.
g. English Horse.
hh. Dutch and Austrian Foot.
ii. Dutch and Austrian Horse.
k. Ingoldsby, starting (in vain) to attack Redoubt d'Eu.

"Fontenoy side, playing upon it; defeated regiments making "barriers of their dead men and firing there; Column always "closing its gapped ranks, and girdled with insupportable "fire. It ought to have taken Fontenoy and Redoubt d'Eu, "say military men; it ought to have done several things! It "has now cut the French fairly in two; — and Saxe, who is "earnestly surveying it a hundred paces a-head, sends word, "conjuring the King to retire instantly, — across the Scheld, "by Calonne Bridge and the strong rear-guard there, — who, "however, will not. King and Dauphin, on horseback both, "have stood 'at the Justice (*Gallows*, in fact) of our Lady of "'the Woods,' not stirring much, occasionally shifting to a "windmill higher, — ye Heaven, with what intrepidity, all "day! — 'a good many country-folk in trees close behind "'them.' Country-folk, I suppose, have by this time seen "enough, and are copiously making off: but the King will not, "though things do look dubious.

"In fact, the Battle hangs now upon a hair; the Battle is "as good as lost, thinks Maréchal the Saxe. His battle-lines "torn in two in that manner, hovering in ragged clouds over "the field, what hope is there in the Battle? Fontenoy is firing "blank, this some time; its cannon-balls done. Officers, in An-"toine, are about withdrawing the artillery, — then again (on "new order) replacing it a while. All are looking towards the "Scheld Bridge; earnestly entreating his Majesty to with-"draw. Had the Dutch, at this point of time, broken heartily "in, as Waldeck was urging them to do, upon the redoubts "of Antoine; or had His Royal Highness the Duke, for his "own behoof, possessed due cavalry or artillery to act upon "these ragged clouds, which hang broken there, very fit for "being swept, were there an artillery-and-horse besom to do "it, — in either of these cases, the Battle was the Duke's. "And a right fiery victory it would have been; to make his "name famous; and confirm the English in their mad method "of figthing, like Baresarks or Janizaries rather than stra-"tegic human creatures.*

"But neither of these contingencies had befallen. The

* See, in Büschings *Magazin*, xvi. 169 ("Your illustrious 'Column,' at Fontenoy? It was fortuitous, I say; done like janisaries;" and so forth), a Criticism worth reading by soldiers.

"Dutch-Austrian wing did evince some wish to get possession "of Antoine; and drew out a little; but the guns also awoke "upon them; whereupon the Dutch-Austrians drew in again, "thinking the time not come. As for the Duke, he had taken "with him of cannon a good few: but of horse none at all (im-"possible for horse, unless Fontenoy and the Redoubt d'Eu "were ours!) — and his horse have been hanging about, in the "Wood of Barry all this while, uncertain what to do; their "old Commander being killed withal, and their new a dubi-"tative person, and no orders left. The Duke had left no "orders; having indeed broken in here, in what we called a "spiritual white-heat, without asking himself much what he "would do when in: 'Beat the French, knock them to "'powder, if I can!' — Meanwhile the French clouds are re-"assembling a little: Royal Highness too is readjusting him-"self, now got '300 yards ahead of Fontenoy,' — pauses "there about half an hour, not seeing his way farther.

"During which pause, Duc de Richelieu, famous black-"guard man, gallops up to the Maréchal, gallops rapidly "from Maréchal to King; suggesting, 'Were cannon brought "*ahead* of this close deep Column, might not they shear it "into beautiful destruction; and then a general charge be "made?' So counselled Richelieu: it is said, the Jacobite "Irishman, Count Lally of the Irish Brigade, was prime "author of this notion, — a man of tragic notoriety in time "coming.* Whoever was author of it, Maréchal de Saxe "adopts it eagerly, King Louis eagerly: swift it becomes a "fact. Universal rally, universal simultaneous charge on "both flanks of the terrible Column: this it might resist, as it "has done these two hours past; but cannon ahead, shearing "gaps through it from end to end, this is what no column can "resist; — and only perhaps one of Friedrich's columns (if "even that) with Friedrich's eye upon it, could make its half-"right-about (*quart de conversion*), turn its side to it, and ma-"nœuvre out of it, in such circumstances. The wrathful Eng-"lish Column, slit into ribbons, can do nothing at manœuver-

* "Thomas Arthur Lally Comte de Tollendal," patronymically "O'*Mulally* of *Tullindally*" (a place somewhere in Connaught, undiscoverable where, not material where): see our dropsical friend (in one of his wheezless states), *King James's Irish Army-List* (Dublin, 1855), pp. 594-600.

"ing; blazes and rages, — more and more clearly in vain; "collapses by degrees, rolls into ribbon coils, and winds it- "self out of the field. Not much chased, — its cavalry now "seeing a job, and issuing from the Wood of Barry to cover "the retreat. Not much chased; — yet with a loss, they say "in all, of 7,000 killed and wounded, and about 2,000 pri- "soners; French loss being under 5,000.

"The Dutch and Austrians had found that the fit time was "now come, or taken time by the forelock, — their part of "the loss, they said, was a thousand and odd hundreds. The "Battle ended about two o'clock of the day; had begun about "eight. Tuesday, 11th May 1745: one of the hottest half- "day's works I have known. A thing much to be meditated "by the English mind. — King Louis stept down from the "Gallows-Hill of Our Lady; and *kissed* Maréchal de Saxe. "Saxe was nearly dead of dropsy; could not sit on horseback, "except for minutes; was carried about in a wicker bed; has "had a lead bullet in his mouth, all day, to mitigate the in- "tolerable thirst. Tournay was soon taken; the Dutch gar- "rison, though strong, and in a strong place, making no due "debate.

"Royal Highness retired upon Ath and Brussels; hovered "about, nothing daunted, he or his: 'Dastard fellows, they "'would not come out into the open ground, and try us fairly!' "snort indignantly the Gazetteers and enlightened Public.* "Nothing daunted; — but, as it were, did not do anything "farther, this Campaign; except lose Gand, by negligence "*versus* vigilance, and eat his victuals, — till called home by "the Rebellion Business, in an unexpected manner! Fonte- "noy was the nearest approach he ever made to getting "victory in a battle; but a miss too, as they all were. He was "nothing like so rash, on subsequent occasions; but had no "better luck; and was beaten in all his battles, — except the "immortal Victory of Culloden alone. Which latter indeed, "was it not itself (in the Gazetteer mind) a kind of apotheosis, "or lifting of a man to the immortal gods, — by endless tar- "barrels and beer, for the time being?

"Old Maréchal de Noailles was in this Battle; busy about "the redans, and proud to see his Saxe do well. Chivalrous

* Old Newspapers.

"Grammont, too, as we saw, was there, — killed at the first "discharge. Prince de Soubise too (not killed); a certain Lord "George Sackville (hurt slightly, — perhaps had *better* have "been killed!) — and others known to us, or that will be "known. Army-Surgeon La Mettrie, of busy brain, expert "with his tourniquets and scalpels, but of wildly blusterous "heterodox tongue and ways, is thrice busy in Hospital this "night, — 'English and French all one to you, nay if any-"thing the English better!' those are the Royal orders: — "La Mettrie will turn up, in new capacity, still blusterous, at "Berlin, by and by.

"The French made immense explosions of rejoicing over "this Victory of Fontenoy; Voltaire (now a man well at "Court) celebrating it in prose and verse, to an amazing de-"gree (21,000 copies sold in one day); the whole Nation blaz-"ing out over it into illuminations, arcs of triumph, and uni-"versal three times three: — in short, I think, nearly the "heartiest National Huzzah, loud, deep, long-drawn, that "the Nation ever gave in like case. Now rather curious to "consider, at this distance of time. Miraculous Anecdotes, "true and not true, are many. Not to mention again that "surprising offer of the first fire to us, what shall we say of "'the two camp-suttlers whom I noticed,' English females of "the lowest degree; 'one of whom was busy slitting the gold-"'lace from a dead Officer, when a cannon-ball came whist-"'ling, and shore her head away. Upon which, without "'sound uttered, her neighbour snatched the scissors, and de-"'liberately proceeded.'* A deliberate gloomy People; — "unconquerable except by French prowess, glory to that "same!"

Britannic Majesty is not successful this season; Highland Rebellions rising on him, and much going awry. He is founding his National Debt, poor Majesty; nothing else to speak of. His poor Army, fighting never so well in foreign quarrels, — and generally

* *A French Officer's Account* (translated in *Gentleman's Magazine*, 1745; where, pp. 246, 250, 291, 315, &c., are many confused details and speculations on this subject).

itself standing the brunt, with the copartners looking on till it is time to run (as at Roucoux again next season, and at Lauffeld next), — can win nothing but hard knocks and losses. And is defined by mankind, — in phraseology which we have heard again since then! — as having "the heart of a Lion and the head of an Ass."* Portentous to contemplate! —

Cape Breton was besieged this Summer, in a creditable manner; and taken. The one real stroke done upon France this Year, or indeed (except at sea) throughout the War. "Ruin to their Fisheries, and a clear loss of 1,400,000 *l.* a-year." Compared with which all these fine "Victories in Flanders" are a bottle of moonshine. This was actually a kind of stroke; — and this, one finds, was accomplished under presidency of a small squadron of King's ships, by "New England Volunteers," on funds raised by subscription, in the way of joint-stock. A shining Colonial feat; said to be very perfectly done, both scrip part of it, and fighting part;** — and might have yielded, what incalculable dividends in the Fishery way! But had to be given up again, in exchange for the Netherlands, when Peace came. Alas, your Majesty! Would it be quite impossible, then, to go direct upon your own sole errand, the *Jenkins's-Ear* one; instead of stumbling about among the Foreign chimney-pots, far and wide, under nightmares, in this terrible manner? — Let us to Silesia again.

* Old Pamphlets, *sæpius.*

** Adelung, v. 32-35 ("27th June 1745, after a siege of forty-nine days"): see "Gibson, *Journal of the Siege;*" "Mr. Prince (of the South Church, Boston), *Thanksgiving Sermon* (price fourpence);" &c. &c.: in the Old Newspapers, 1745, 1748, multifarious Notices about it, and then about the "repayment" of those excellent "joint-stock" people.

CHAPTER IX.

THE AUSTRIAN-SAXON ARMY INVADES SILESIA, ACROSS THE MOUNTAINS.

VALORI, who is to be of Friedrich's Campaign this Year, came posting off directly in rear of the glorious news of Fontenoy; found Friedrich at Camenz, rather in spirits than otherwise; and lodged pleasantly with Abbot Tobias and him, till the Campaign should begin. Two things surprise Valori: first, the great strength, impregnable as it were, to which Neisse has been brought since he saw it last, — superlative condition of that Fortress, and of the Army itself, as it gathers daily more and more about Frankenstein here: — and then secondly, and contrariwise, the strangely neglected posture of mountainous or Upper Silesia, given up to Pandours. Quite submerged, in a manner: Margraf Karl lies quiet among them at Jägerndorf, "eating his magazine;" General Hautcharmoi (Winterfeld's late chief in that Würben affair), with his small Detachment, still hovers about in those Ratibor parts, "with the Strong Towns to fall back upon," or has in effect fallen back accordingly; and nothing done to coerce the Pandours at all. While Prince Karl and Weissenfels are daily coming on, in force 100,000, their intention certain; force, say, about 100,000 regular! Very singular to Valori.

"Sire, will not you dispute the Passes, then?"

asks Valori, amazed: "Not defend your Mountain rampart, then?" "*Mon cher*, the Mountain rampart is three or four hundred miles long; there are twelve or twenty practicable roads through it. One is kept in darkness, too; endless Pandour doggery shutting out your daylight: — ill defending such a rampart," answers Friedrich. "But how, then," persists Valori; "but —?" "One day the King answered me," says Valori, '"*Mon* "*ami*, if you want to get the mouse, don't shut the "trap; leave the trap open (*on laisse la souricière ou-* "*verte*)!"' Which was a beam of light to the inquiring thought of Valori, a military man of some intelligence.*

That, in fact, is Friedrich's purpose privately formed. He means that the Austrians shall consider him cowed into nothing, as he understands they already do; that they shall enter Silesia in the notion of chasing him; and shall, if need be, have the pleasure of chasing him, — till perhaps a right moment arrive. For he is full of silent finesse, this young King; soon sees into his man, and can lead him strange dances on occasion. In no man is there a plentifuller vein of cunning, nor of a finer kind. Lynx-eyed perspicacity, inexhaustible contrivance, prompt ingenuity, — a man very dangerous to play with at games of skill. And it is cunning regulated always by a noble sense of honour, too; instinctively abhorrent of attorneyism and the swindler element: a cunning, sharp as the vulpine, yet always strictly human, which is rather beautiful to see. This is one of Friedrich's marked endowments. Intellect sun-clear, wholly practical (need not be specially deep), and entirely loyal to the fact before it; this, —

* *See Valori*, i. 223, 224, 226.

if you add rapidity and energy, prompt weight of stroke, such as was seldom met with, — will render a man very dangerous to his adversary in the game of war. — Here is the last of our Pandour Adventures, for the present:

"From May 12th, Friedrich had been gathering closer and "closer about Frankenstein; by the end of the month (28th, "as it proved) he intends that all Detachments shall be home, "and the Army take Camp there. The most are home; Mar-"graf Karl, at Jägerndorf, has not yet done eating his maga-"zine; but he too must come home. Summon the Margraf "home: — it is not doubted he will cut himself through, he and "his 12,000; but such is the swarm of Pandours hovering be-"tween him and us, no estafette, or cleverest letterbearer, can "hope to get across to him. Ziethen with 500 Hussars, he "must take the Letter; there is no other way. Ziethen mounts; "fares swiftly forth, towards Neustadt, with his Letter; lodges "in woods; dodges the thick-crowding Tolpatcheries (passes "himself off for a Tolpatchery, say some, and captures "Hungarian Staff-Officers who come to give him orders*); is "at length found out, and furiously set upon, 'Ziethen, Hah!' "— but gets to Jägerndorf, Margraf Karl coming out to the "rescue, and delivers his Letter. 'Home, then', all of us "'tomorrow!' And so, Saturday, 22d May, before we get to "Neustadt on the way home, there is an authentic passage of "arms, done very brilliantly by Margraf Karl against Pandours "and others.

"To right of us, to left, barring our road, the enemy, "20,000 of them, stand ranked on heights, in chosen positions; "cannon-batteries, grenadiers, dragoons of Gotha, and infinite "Pandours: military jungle bristling far and wide. And you "must push it heartily, and likewise cut the tap-root of it "(seize its big guns), or it will not roll away. Margraf Karl "shoots forth his steady infantry ('Silent till you see the "'whites of their eyes!'), — his cavalry with new manœuvres;

* Frau von Blumenthal, *Life of De Ziethen*, pp. 171-181 (extremely romantic; now given up as mythical, for most part): see Orlich (II. 150); but also Ranke (III. 245), Preuss, &c.

"whose behaviour is worthy of Ziethen himself: — in brief, "the jungle is struck as by a whirlwind, the tap-root of it cut, "and rolls simultaneously out of range, leaving only the "Regiment of Gotha, Regiment of Ogilvy, and some Regulars, "who also get torn to shreds, and utterly ruined. Seeing which, "the Pandour jungle plunges wholly into the woods, uttering "horrible cries (*en poussant des cris terribles*), says Friedrich.* "Our new cavalry manœuvres deserve praise. Margraf Karl "had the honour to gain his Cousin's approbation this day; "and to prove himself, says the Cousin, 'worthy of the grand-"'father he came from,' — my own great-grandfather; Great "Elector, Friedrich-Wilhelm; whose style of motion at Fehr-"bellin, or on the ice of the Frische Haf (soldiers all in sledges, "tearing along to be at the Swedes), was probably somewhat "of this kind." * *

"Some days ago, Winterfeld had been pushed out to "Landshut, with Detachment of 2,000, to judge a little for "himself which way the Austrians were coming, and to scare "off certain Uhlans (the *Saxon* species of Tolpatchery), who "were threatening to be mischievous thereabouts. The Uhlans, "at sound of Winterfeld, jingled away at once: but, in a day "or two, there came upon him, on the sudden, Pandour out-"burst in quite other force; — and in the very hours while "Ziethen was struggling into Jägerndorf, and still more em-"phatically next day, while Margraf Karl was handling his "Pandours, — Colonel Winterfeld, a hundred miles to west-"ward lapped among the Mountains, chanced to be dealing "again with the same article. Very busy with it, from 4 o'clock "this morning; likely to give a good account of the job. "Steadily defending Landshut and himself, against the grena-"dier battalions, cannon, and furious overplus of Pandours "(8,000 or 9,000, it is said, six to one or so in the article of "cavalry), which General Nadasti, a scientific leader of men "or Pandours, skilfully and furiously hurls upon Landshut "and him, in an unexpected manner. Colonel Winterfeld had "need of all his art and energy, in the intricate ground; "against the furious overplus well manœuvred: but in him too "there are manœuvres; if he fall back here, it is to rush-on

* *Œuvres de Frédéric*, III. 108. More specially *Bericht von der am 22 Mai 1745 bei Neustadt in Ober-Schlesien vorgefallenen Action* (Seyfarth, *Beylage*, I. 158-166).

"double strong there; hour after hour he inexpugnably "defends himself, — till General Stille, Friedrich's old Tutor, "our worthy writing friend, whom we occasionally quote, "comes up with help; and Nadasti is at once brushed home "again, with sore smart of failure, and 'the loss of 600 killed,' "among other items.* Colonel Winterfeld was made Major-"General next day, for this action. Colonel Winterfeld is "cutting out a high course for himself, by his conduct in these "employments; solidity, brilliant effectuality, shining through "all he does; his valour and value, his rapid just insight, fiery "energy, and nobleness of mind, more and more disclosing "themselves,—to one who is a judge of men, and greatly needs "for his own use the first-rate quality in that article."

Friedrich has left the mousetrap open; — and latterly has been baiting it with a pleasant spicing of toasted cheese. One of his Spies, reporting from Prince Karl's quarters, Friedrich has at this time discovered to be a Double-Spy, reporting thither as well. Double-Spy, there is an ugly fact; — perhaps not quite convenient to abolish it by hemp and gibbet; perhaps it could be turned to use, as most facts can? "Very good, my expert Herr von Schönfeld" (that was the knave's name): "and now of all things, whenever the Prince does get across, — instant word to us of that! Nothing so important to us. If he should get *between* us and Breslau, for example, what would the consequence be!" To this purport Friedrich instructs his Double-Spy; sends him off, unhanged, to Prince Karl's Camp, to blab this fresh bit of knowledge. "We likewise," says Friedrich, "ordered some repairs on the roads leading "to Breslau;" — last turn of the hand to our bit of toasted fragrancy. And Prince Karl is actually striding

* *Bericht von der am 21 Mai 1745 bei Landshut vorgefallenen Action*, in *Feldzüge*, i. 302-305 (or in Seyfarth, *Beylage*, i. 155-158); *Œuvres de Frédéric*, iii. 105; Stille, pp. 120-124 (who misdates, "23d May" for 22d).

forward, at an eager pace: — and Nadasti *versus* Winterfeld, the other day, could Winterfeld have guessed it, was the actual vanguard of the march; and will be up again straightway! Whereupon Winterfeld too is called home; and all eyes are bent on the Landshut side.

Prince Karl, under these fine omens, had been urgent on the Saxons to be swift; Saxons under Weissenfels did at last "get their cannon up," and we hear of them for certain, in junction with the Austrians, at Schatzlar, on the Bohemian side of the Giant-Mountains; climbing with diligence those wizard solitudes and highland wastes. In a word, they roll across into Silesia, to Landshut (29th May); nothing doubting but Friedrich has cowered into what retreats he has, as good as desperate of Silesia, and will probably be first heard of in Breslau, when they get thither with their sieging guns. No cautious sagacious old Feldmarschall Traun is in that Host, at present; nothing but a Prince Karl, and a poor Duke of Weissenfels; who are too certain of several things; — very capable of certainty, and also of doubt, the wrong way of the facts. Their force is, by strict count, 75,000; and they march from Landshut, detained a little by provender concerns, on the last day of May.*

May 28th, Friedrich had encamped at Frankenstein; May 30th, he sets forth north-westward, to be nearer the new scene; encamps at Reichenbach, that night; pushes forward again, next day, for Schweidnitz, for Striegau (in all, a shift north-west of some forty miles); — and from June 1st, lies stretched out between Schweidnitz and Striegau, nine miles long; well hidden

* Orlich, ii. 146; Ranke, iii. 247; Stenzel, iv. 245.

in the hollows of the little Rivers thereabouts (Schweidnitz Water, Striegau Water), with their little knolls and hills; watching Prince Karl's probable place of egress from the Mountain Country opposite. His main Camp is from Schweidnitz to Jauernik, some five miles long; but he has his vanguard up as far as Striegau, Dumoulin and Winterfeld as vanguard, in good strength, a little way behind or westward of that Town and Stream; Nassau and his Division are screened in the Wood called Nonnenbusch (*Nun's Bush*), and there are outposts sprinkled all about, and vedettes watching from the hill-tops, from the Stanowitz Foxhill; the Zedlitz "Cowhill," "Winehill:" an Army not courting observation, but intent very much to observe. Nadasti has appeared again; at Freyburg, few miles off, on this side of the Mountains; goes out scouting, reconnoitering; but is "fired at from the growing corn," and otherwise hoodwinked by false symptoms, and makes little of that business. Friedrich's Army we will compute at 70,000.* Not quite equal in number to Prince Karl's; and in other particulars, willing and longing that Prince Karl would arrive, and try its quality.

Friedrich's headquarter is at Jauernik: he goes daily riding hither, thither; to the top of the Fuchsberg (*Foxhill* at Stanowitz) with eager spyglass; daily many times looks with his spyglass to the ragged peaks about Bolkenhayn, Kauder, Rohnstock; expecting the throw of the dice from that part. On Thursday, 3d June: Do you notice that cloud of dust rising among the peaks over yonder? Dust-cloud mounting higher and higher.

* General Lieutenant Freiherr Leo von Lützow, *Die Schlacht von Hohenfriedberg* (Potsdam, 1845), pp. 18, 21.

There comes the big crisis, then! There are the combined Weissenfels and Karl with their Austrian Saxons, issuing proudly from their stone labyrinth; guns, equipments, baggages, all perfectly brought through; rich Silesian plain country now fairly at their feet, Breslau itself but a few marches off: — at sight of all which, the Austrian big host bursts forth into universal field-music, and shakes out its banners to the wind. Thursday, 3d June 1745; a dramatic Entry of something quite considerable on the Stage of History.

Friedrich, with Nassau and generals round, stands upon the Fuchsberg, — his remarks not given, his looks or emotions not described to us, his thought well known, — and looks at it through his *tubus* (or spy-glass): There they are, then, and the big moment is come! Friedrich had seen the dust and the manœuvering of them, deeper in the Hills, from this same Fuchsberg yesterday, and inferred what was coming; calculated by what roads or hill-tracks they could issue; and how he, in each case, was to deal with them; his march-routes are all settled, plank-bridges repaired, all privately is ready for these proud Austrian musical gentlemen, here in the hollow. Friedrich has been upon this Fuchsberg with his *tubus* daily, many times since Monday last: it is our general observatorium, says Stille, and commands a fine view into the interior of these Hills. A Fuchsberg which has become notable in the Prussian maps: "the Stanowitz Fuchsberg," east side of Striegau Water, — let no tourist mistake himself; for there are two or even three other Fuchsbergs, a mile or so northward on the western side of that Stream, which need to be distinguished by epithets, as the Striegau Fuchsberg, the Gräben Fuchsberg, and perhaps still others: comparable to the *four* Neisse rivers, three besides the one we know, which occur in this piece of Country! Our German cousins, I have often sorrowed to find, have practically a most poor talent for *giving names;* and indeed much, for ages back, is lying in a sad state of confusion among them. Many confused things, rotting far and wide, in contradiction to the plainest laws of Nature; things as well as names! All the welcomer this Prussian Army, this young Friedrich leading it; they, beyond all earthly entities of their epoch, are not in a state of confusion, but of most strict conformity to the laws of Arithmetic and facts of Nature: perhaps a very blessed phenomenon for Germany in the long-run.

Prince Karl with Weissenfels, General Berlichingen, and many plumed dignitaries, are dining on the Hill-top near Hohenfriedberg: after having given order about everything, they witness there, over their wine, the issue of their Columns from the Mountains; which goes on all afternoon, with field-music, spread banners; and the oldest General admits he never saw a finer review-manœuvre, or one better done, if so well. Thus sit they on the Hill-top (*Galgenberg*, not far from the gallows of the place, says Friedrich), in the beautiful June afternoon. Silesia lying beautifully azure at their feet; the Zobtenberg, enchanted Mountain, blue and high on one's eastern horizon; Prussians noticeable only in weak hussar parties four or five miles off, which vanish in the hollow grounds again. All intending for Breslau, they, it is like; — and here, red wine and the excellent manœuvre going on. "The Austrian-and-"Saxon Army streamed out all afternoon," says a

Country Schoolmaster of those parts, whose Daybook has been preserved,* "each regiment or division taking "the place appointed it; all afternoon, till late in the "night, submerging the Country as in a deluge," five miles long of them; taking post at the foot of the Hills there, from Hohenfriedberg round upon Striegau, looking towards the morrow's sunrise. To us poor country-folk not a beautiful sight; their light troops flying ahead, and doing theft and other mischief at a sad rate.

On the other hand, the Austrian and Saxon gentlemen, from their Gallows-Hill at Hohenfriedberg, notice, four or five miles in the distance, opposite them, or a little to the left of opposite, a Body of Prussian horse and foot, visibly wending northward; like a long glittering serpent, the glitter of their muskets flashing back yonder on the afternoon sun and us, as they mount from hollow to height. Ten or twelve thousand of them; making for Striegau, to appearance. Intending to bivouac or billet there, and keep some kind of watch over us; belike with an eye to being rearguard, on the retreat towards Breslau to-morrow? Or will they retreat without attempting mischief? Serenity of Weissenfels engages to seize the heights and proper posts, over yonder, this night yet; and will take Striegau itself, the first thing, to-morrow morning.

Yes, your Serenities, those are Prussians in movement: Vanguard Corps of Dumoulin, Winterfeld; — Rittmeister Seydlitz rides yonder: — and it is not their notion to retreat without mischief. For there stands, not so far off, on the Stanowitz Fuchsberg, a brisk little Gentleman, if you could notice him; with

* In Lützow, pp. 128-132.

his eyes fixed on you, and plans in the head of him now getting nearly mature. For certain, he is pushing out that column of men; and all manner of other columns are getting order to push out, and take their ground; and to-morrow morning,—you will not find him in retreat! Such are the phenomena in that Striegau-Hohenfriedberg region, while the sun is bending westward, on Thursday, 3d June 1745.

"From Hohenfriedberg, which leans against the higher "Mountains, there may be, across to Striegau north-east, which "stands well apart from them, among lower Hills of its own, a "distance of about five English miles. The intervening "country is of flat, though upland nature: the first broad "stage, or *stair-step*, so to speak, leading down into the general "interior levels of Silesia in those parts. A tract which is now "tolerably dried by draining, but was then marshy as well as "bushy:—flat to the eye, yet must be imperceptibly convexed "a little, for the line of watershed is hereabouts: walk from "Hohenfriedberg to Striegau, the water on your left hand "flows, though mainly in ditches or imperceptible oozings, to "the north and west,— there to fall into an eastern fork of the "Roaring Neisse" (one of our three new Neisses, which is a very quiet stream here; runs close by the Mountain base, fed by many torrents, and must get its name, *Wüthende* or Roaring, from the suddenness of its floods): "into this, bound northward "and westward, run or ooze all waters on your left hand as you "go to Striegau. Right hand, again, or to eastward, you will "find all sauntering, or running in visible brooks into Striegau "Water" (little River notable to us), "which comes circling "from the Mountains, past Hohenfriedberg, farther south; "and has got to some force as a stream before it reaches "Striegau, and turns abruptly eastward; — eastward, to join "Schweidnitz Water, and form with it the *second* stair-step "downwards to the Plain Country. Has its Fuchsbergs, Kuh-"bergs, and little knolls and heights interspersed, on both "sides of it, in the conceivable way.

"So that, looking eastward from the heights of Hohen-"friedberg, our broad stage or stair-step has nothing of the "nature of a valley, but rather is a kind of insensibly swelling "plain between two valleys, or hollows, of small depth; and "slopes both ways. Both ways; but *more* towards the Striegau-"Water valley or hollow; and thence, in a lazily undulating "manner, to other hollows and waters farther down. Fried-"rich's Camp lies in the next, the Schweidnitz-Water hollow; "and is five, or even nine miles long, from Schweidnitz north-"ward; — much hidden from the Austrian-Saxon gentlemen "at present. No hills farther, more flat country, to eastward "of that. But to the north, again, about Striegau, the hollow "deepens, narrows; and certain Hills," much notable at present, "rise to west of Striegau, definite peaked Hills, with "granite quarries in them and basalt blocks atop:—Striegau, "it appears, is, in old Czech dialect, *Trzica*, which means "*Triple Hill*, the 'Town of the Three Hills.'* An ancient "quaint little Town, of perhaps 2,000 souls: brown-gray, the "stones of it venerably weathered; has its wide big market-"place, piazza, plain-stones, silent enough except on market-"days: nestles itself compactly in the shelter of its Three "Hills, which screen it from the north-west; and has a pictur-"esque appearance, its Hills and it, projected against the big "Mountain range beyond, as you approach it from the Plain "Country.

"Hohenfriedberg, at the other corner of our battle-stage, "on the road to Landshut, is a Village of no great compass; "but sticks pleasantly together, does not straggle in the usual "way; climbs steep against its Gallows-Hill (now called "'*Siegesberg*, Victory Hill,' with some tower or steeple-monu-"ment on it, built by subscription); — and would look better, "if trimmed a little and habitually well swept. The higher "Mountain summits, Landshut way, or still more if you look "south-eastward, Glatz-ward, rise blue and huge, remote on "your right; to left, the Roaring-Neisse range close at hand, "is also picturesque, though less Alpine in type."† * * And of all Hills, the notablest, just now to us, are those "Three" at Striegau.

Those Three Hills of Striegau his Serenity of Weissenfels is to lay hold of, this night, with his ex-

* Lützow, p. 23. † Tourist's Note (1858).

treme left, were it once got deployed and bivouacked. Those Hills, if he can: but Prussian Dumoulin is already on march thither; and privately has his eye upon them, on Friedrich's part! — For the rest, this upland platform, insensibly sloping two ways, and as yet undrained, is of scraggy boggy nature in many places; much of it damp ground, or sheer morass; better parts of it covered, at this season, with rank June grass, or greener luxuriance of oats and barley. A humble peaceable scene; peaceable till this afternoon; dotted, too, with six or seven poor Hamlets, with scraggy woods, where they have their fuel; most sleepy littery ploughman Hamlets, sometimes with a *Schloss* or Mansion for the owner of the soil (who has absconded in the present crisis of things), — their evening smoke rising rather fainter than usual; much cookery is not advisable with Uhlans and Tolpatches flying about. Northward between Striegau and the higher Mountains there is an extensive *Teichwirthschaft*, or "Pond-Husbandry" (gleaming visible from Hohenfriedberg Gallows-Hill just now); a combination of stagnant pools and carp-ponds, the ground much occupied hereabouts with what they name Carp-Husbandry. Which is all drained away in our time, yet traceable by the studious: — quaggy congeries of sluices and fish-ponds, no road through them except on intricate dams; have scrubby thickets about the border; — this also is very strong ground, if Weissenfels thought of defence there.

Which Weissenfels does not, but only of attack. He occupies the ground nevertheless, rearward of this Carp-Husbandry, as becomes a strategic man; gradually bivouacking all round there, to end on the Three Hills, were his last regiments got up. The Carp-Husbandry is mainly about Eisdorf Hamlet: — in Pilgramshayn, where Weissenfels once thought of lodging, lives our Writing-Schoolmaster. The Mountains lie to westward; flinging longer shadows, as the invasive troops continually deploy, in that beautiful manner; and coil themselves strategically on the ground, a bent rope, cordon, or line (*three* lines in depth), reaching from the front skirts of Hohenfriedberg to the Hills at Striegau again, — terrible to behold.

In front of Hohenfriedberg, we say, is the extremity or right wing of the Austrian-Saxon bivouac, or will be when the process is complete; five miles to north-east, sweeping round upon Striegau region, will be their left, where mainly are the Saxons, — to nestle upon those Three Hills of Striegau: whitherward, however, Dumoulin, on Friedrich's behalf, is already on march. Austrian-Saxon bivouac, as is the way in regulated hosts, can at once become Austrian-Saxon order-of-battle: and then, probably, on the Chord of that Arc of five miles, the big Fight will roll tomorrow; Striegau one end of it, Hohenfriedberg the other. Flattish, somewhat elliptic upland, stair-step from the Mountains, as we called it; tract considerably cut with ditches, carp-husbandries, and their tufts of wood; line from Striegau to Hohenfriedberg being axis or main diameter of it, and in general the line of watershed: there, probably, will the tug of war be. Friedrich, on his Fuchsberg, knows this; the Austrian-Saxon gentlemen, over their wine on the Gallows-Hill, do not yet know it, but will know.

It was about four in the afternoon, when Valori,

with a companion, waiting a good while in the King's Tent at Jauernik, at last saw his Majesty return from the Fuchsberg observatory. Valori and friend have great news: "Tournay fallen; siege done, your Majesty!" Valori's friend is one De Latour; who had brought word of Fontenoy ("important victory on the Scamander," as Friedrich indignantly defined it to himself); and was bid wait here till this Siege-of-Tournay consummation ("as helpful to me as the Siege of Pekin!") should supervene. They hasten to salute his Majesty with the glorious tidings. Hmph! thinks Friedrich; and we are at death-grips here, little to be helped by your taking Pekin! However, he lets wit of nothing. "I make my compliments; mean to fight to-morrow."* Valori, as old soldier and friend, volunteers to be there and assist: — Good.

Friedrich, I presume, at this late hour of four, may be snatching a morsel of dinner; his orderlies are silently speeding, plans taken, orders given: To start all, at eight in the evening, for the Bridge of Striegau; there to cross, and spread to the right and to the left. Silent, not a word spoken, not a pipe lighted: silently across the Striegau Water there. A march of three miles for the nearest, who are here at Jauernik; of nine miles for the farthest about Schweidnitz; at Schweidnitz leave all your baggage, safe under the guns there. To the Bridge of Striegau, diligently, silently march along; Bridge of Striegau, there cross Striegau Water, and deploy to right and to left, in the way each of you knows. These are Friedrich's orders.

* Valori, i. 228.

Late in the dusk, Dumoulin and Winterfeld, whom we saw silently on march some hours ago, have silently glided past Striegau, and got into the Three-Hill region, which is some furlong or so farther north: — to his surprise, Dumoulin finds Saxon parties posting themselves thereabouts. He attacks said Saxon parties; and, after some slight tussle, drives them mostly from their Three Hills; mostly, not altogether; one Saxon Hill is precipitous on our hither side of it, and we must leave that till the dawn break. Of the other Heights Dumoulin takes good possession, with cannon too, to be ready against dawn; — and ranks himself out to leftward withal, along the plain ground; for he is to be right wing, had the other troops come up. These are now all under way; astir from Jauernik and Schweidnitz, silently streaming along; and Dumoulin bivouacks here, — very silent he: not so silent the Saxons; who are still marching in, over yonder, to westward of Dumoulin, their rearguard groping out its posts as it best can in the dark. Elsewhere, miles and miles along the foot of the Mountains, Austrian-Saxon watchfires flame through the ambrosial night; and it is an impressive sight for Dumoulin, — still more for the poor Schoolmaster at Pilgramshayn and others, less concerned than Dumoulin. "It was beautiful," says Stille, who was there, "to see how the plain about "Rohnstock, and all over that way, was ablaze with "thousands of watchfires (*tausend und aber tausend*); by "the light of these, we could clearly perceive the "enemy's troops continually defile from the Hills the "whole night through." *

* Cited in Seyfarth, i. 650.

Serenity of Weissenfels, after all, does not lodge at Pilgramshayn; far in the night, he goes to sleep at Rohnstock, a Schloss and Hamlet on that fork of Roaring Neisse, by the foot of the Mountains; three or four miles off, yet handy enough for picking up Striegau the first thing tomorrow. His Highness Prince Karl lies in Hausdorf, tolerable quarters, pretty much in the centre of his long bivouac; day's business well done, and bottle (as one's wont rather is) well enjoyed. Nadasti has been out scouting; but was pricked into by hussar parties, fired into from the growing corn; and could make out little, but the image of his own ideas. Nadasti's ultimate report is, That the Prussians are perfectly quiet in their camp; from Jauernik to Schweidnitz, watchfires all alight, sentries going their rounds. And so they are, in fact; sentries and watch-fires, — but now nothing else there, a mere shell of a camp; the men of it streaming steadily along, without speech, without tobacco; and many of them are across Striegau Bridge by this time! —

It was past eleven, so close and continuous went this march, before Valori and his Latour, with their carriages and furnitures, could find an interval, and get well into it. Never will Valori forget the discipline of these Prussians, and how they marched. Difficult ways; the hard road is for their artillery; the men march on each side, sometimes to mid-leg in water, — never mind. Wholly in order, wholly silent; Valori followed them three leagues close, and there was not one straggler. Every private man, much more every officer, knows well what grim errand they are on; and they make no remarks. Steady as Time; and, except that their shoes are not of felt, silent as he. The Austrian watch-fires glow silent manifold to leftward yonder; silent overhead are the stars: the path of all duty, too, is silent (not about Striegau alone) for every well-drilled man. Tomorrow; — well, tomorrow?

A grimmish feeling against the Saxons is understood to be prevalent among these men. Brühl, Weissenfels himself, have been reported talking high, — "Reduce our King to the size of an Elector again," and other foolish things; — indeed, grudges have been accumulating for some time. "*Kein Pardon* (No quarter)!" we hear has been a word among the Saxons, as they came along; the Prussians growl to one another, "Very well, then, None!" Nay Friedrich's general order is, "No prisoners, you cavalry, in the heat of fight; cavalry, strike at the faces of them: you infantry, keep your fire till within fifty steps; bayonet withal is to be relied on." These were Friedrich's last general orders, given in the hollow of the night, near the foot of that Fuchsberg where he had been so busy all day; a widish plain space hereabouts, Striegau Bridge now near: he had lain some time in his cloak, waiting till the chief generals, with the heads of their columns, could rendezvous here. He then sprang on horseback; spoke briefly the essential things (one of them the above); — "Had meant to be more minute, in regard to positions and the like; but all is so in darkness, embroiled by the flare of the Austrian watch-fires, we can make nothing farther of localities at present: Striegau for right wing, left wing opposite to Hohenfriedberg — so, and Striegau Water well to rear of us. Be diligent, exact, all faculties awake: your own sense, and the Order of Battle which you know, must do the rest. Forward; steady: can I doubt but you will acquit yourselves like Prussian men?" And so they march, across the Bridge at Striegau, south outskirt of the Town, — plank Bridge, I am afraid; — and pour themselves, to right and to left, continually the livelong night.

To describe the Battle which ensued, Battle named of Striegau or Hohenfriedberg, excels the power of human talent, — if human talent had leisure for such employment. It is the huge shock and clash of 70,000 against 70,000, placed in the way we said. An enormous furious *simultas* (or "both-at-once," as the Latin phrase it), spreading over ten square miles. Rather say, a wide congeries of electric simultaneities; all *electric*, playing madly into one another; most loud, most mad: the aspect of which is smoky, thunderous, abstruse; the true *sequences* of which, who shall unravel? There are five accounts of it, all modestly written, each true-looking from its own place: and a thrice-diligent Prussian Officer, stationed on the spot in late years, has striven well to harmonise them all.* Well worth the study of military men; — who might

* Five Accounts: 1°. The Prussian Official Account, in *Helden-Geschichte*, I. 1098-1102. 2°. The Saxon, ib. 1102-1108. 3°. The Austrian, ib. 1109-1115. 4°. Stille's (II. 125-133, of English Translation). 5°. Friedrich's own, *Œuvres*, III. 108-118. Lütsow, above cited, is the harmoniser. Besides which, two of value, in *Feldzüge*, I. 310-323, 328-336; not to mention Cogniazzo, *Confessions of an Austrian Veteran* (Breslau, 1788-1791: strictly Anonymous at that time, and candid or almost more to Prussian merit; — still worth reading, here and throughout), II. 123-135; &c. &c.

make tours towards this and the other great battlefield, and read such things, were they wise. For us, a feature or two, in the huge general explosion, to assist the reader's fancy in conceiving it a little, is all that can be pretended to.

CHAPTER X.

BATTLE OF HOHENFRIEDBERG.

WITH the first streak of dawn, the dispute renewed itself between those Prussians and Saxons who are on the Heights of Striegau. The two Armies are in contact here; they lie wide apart as yet at the other end. Cannonading rises here, on both sides, in the dim gray of the morning, for the possession of these Heights. The Saxons are out-cannonaded and dislodged, other Saxons start to arms in support: the cry "To arms!" spreads everywhere, rouses Weissenfels to horseback; and by sunrise a furious storm of battle has begun, in this part. Hot and fierce, on both sides; charges of horse, shock after shock, bayonet-charges of foot; the great guns going like Jove's thunder, and the continuous tearing storm of small guns, very loud indeed: such a noise, as our poor Schoolmaster, who lives on this spot, thinks he will hear only once again, when the Last Trumpet sounds! It did indeed, he informs us, resemble the dissolution of Nature: "For all fell dark too;" a general element of sulphurous powder-smoke, streaked with dull blazes; and death and destruction very nigh. What will become of poor pacific mortals hereabouts? Rittmeister Seydlitz, Winterfeld his patron, ride, with knit brows, in these horse-charges; fiery Rothenburg too; Truchsess von Waldburg, at the head of his Division, — poor Truchsess known in

London society, a cannon-ball smites the life out of him, and he ended here.

At the first clash of horse and foot, the Saxons fancied they rather had it; at the second, their horse became distressed; at the third, they rolled into disorderly heaps. The foot also, stubborn as they were, could not stand that swift firing, followed by the bayonet and the sabre; and were forced to give ground. The morning sun shone into their eyes, too, they say; and there had risen a breath of easterly wind, which hurled the smoke upon them, so that they could not see. Decidedly staggering backwards; getting to be taken in flank and ruined, though poor Weissenfels does his best. About five in the morning, Friedrich came galloping hitherward; Valori with him: "*Mon ami*, this is looking well! This will do, won't it?" The Saxons are fast sinking in the scale; and did nothing thenceforth but sink ever faster; though they made a stiff defence, fierce exasperation on both sides; and disputed every inch. Their position, in these scraggy Woods and Villages, in these Morasses and Carp-Husbandries, is very strong.

It had proved to be farther north, too, than was expected; so that the Prussians had to wheel round a little (right wing as a centre, fighting army as radius) before they could come parallel, and get to work: a delicate manœuvre, which they executed to Valori's admiration, here in the storm of battle; tramp, tramp, velocity increasing from your centre outwards, till at the end of the radius, the troops are at treble quick, fairly running forward, and the line straight all the while. Admirable to Valori, in the hot whirlwind of battle here. For the great guns go, in horrid salvoes, unabated, and the crackling thunder of the small guns; "terrible tusselling about those Carp-ponds, that quaggy "Carp-husbandry," says the Schoolmaster, "and the "Heavens blotted out in sulphurous fire-streaked smoke. "What had become of us pacific? Some had run in "time, and they were the wisest; others had squatted, "who could find a nook suitable. Most of us had "gathered into the Nursery-garden at the foot of our "Village; we sat quaking there, — our prayers grown "tremulously vocal; — in tears and wail, at least the "women part. Enemies made reconcilement with each "other," says he, "and dear friends took farewell." * One general Alleleu; the Last Day, to all appearance, having come. Friedrich, seeing things in this good posture, gallops to the left again, where much urgently requires attention from him.

On the Austrian side, Prince Karl, through his morning sleep at Hausdorf, had heard the cannonading: "Saxons taking Striegau!" thinks he; a pleasant lullaby enough; and continues to sleep and dream. Agitated messengers rush in, at last; draw his curtains: "Prussians all in rank, this side Striegau Water; Saxons beaten, or nearly so, at Striegau: we must stand to arms, your Highness!" — "To arms, of course," answers Karl; and hurries now, what he can, to get everything in motion. The bivouac itself had been in order of battle; but naturally there is much to adjust, to put in trim; and the Austrians are not distinguished for celerity of movement. All the worse for them just now.

On Friedrich's side, so far as I can gather, there

* His Narrative, in Lüttow, *ubi suprà.*

have happened two cross accidents. First, by that wheeling movement, done to Valori's admiration in the Striegau quarter, the Prussian line has hitched itself up towards Striegau, has got curved inward, and covers less ground than was counted on; so that there is like to be some gap in the central part of it; — as in fact there was, in spite of Friedrich's efforts, and hitchings of battalions and squadrons: an indisputable gap, though it turned to rich profit for Friedrich; Prince Karl paying no attention to it. Upon such indisputable gap a wakeful enemy might have done Friedrich some perilous freak; but Karl was in his bed, as we say; — in a terrible flurry, too, when out of bed. Nothing was done upon the gap; and Friedrich had his unexpected profit by it before long.

The second accident is almost worse. Striegau Bridge (of planks, as I feared), creaking under such a heavy stream of feet and wheels all night, did at last break, in some degree, and needed to be mended; so that the rearward regiments, who are to form Friedrich's left wing, are in painful retard; — and are becoming frightfully necessary, the Austrians as yet far outflanking us, capable of taking us in flank with that right wing of theirs! The moment was agitating to a General-in-chief: Valori will own this young King's bearing was perfect; not the least flurry, though under such a strain. He has aides-de-camp, dashing out everywhither with orders, with expedients; Prince Henri, his younger Brother, galloping the fastest; nay, at last, he begs Valori himself to gallop, with orders to a certain General Gessler, in whose Brigade are Dragoons. Which Valori does, — happily without effect on Gessler; who knows no Valori for an aide-de-camp, and keeps the ground appointed him; rearward of that gap we talked of.

Happily the Austrian right wing is in no haste to charge. Happily Ziethen, blocked by that incumbrance of the Bridge mending, "finds a ford higher up,' the assiduous Ziethen; splashes across, other regiments following; forms in line well leftward; and instead of waiting for the Austrian charge, charges home upon them, fiercely through the difficult grounds. No danger of the Austrians outflanking us now; they are themselves likely to get hard measure on their flank. By the ford and by the Bridge, all regiments, some of them at treble quick, get to their posts still in time. Accident second has passed without damage. Forward, then; rapid, steady; and reserve your fire till within fifty paces! — Prince Ferdinand of Brunswick (Friedrich's Brother-in-law, a bright-eyed steady young man, of great heart for fight) tramps forth with his Division: — steady! — all manner of Divisions tramp forth; and the hot storm, Ziethen and cavalry dashing upon that left wing of theirs, kindles here also far and wide.

The Austrian cavalry on this wing and elsewhere, it is clear, were ill off. "We could not charge the "Prussian right wing, say they, partly because of the "morasses that lay between us; *and* partly" (which is remarkable) "because they rushed across and charged "us."* Prince Karl is sorry to report such things of his cavalry; but their behaviour was bad and not good. The first shock threw them wavering; the second, — nothing would persuade them to dash forth and meet it. High officers commanded, obtested, drew out pistols, Prince Karl himself shot a fugitive or two, —

* Austrian report, *Helden-Geschichte*, i. 1113.

it was to no purpose; they wavered worse at every new shock; and at length a shock came (sixth it was, as the reporter counts) which shook them all into the wind. Decidedly shy of the Prussians with their new manœuvres, and terrible way of coming on, as if sure of beating. In the Saxon quarter, certain Austrian regiments of horse would not charge at all; merely kept firing from their carbines, and when the time came ran.

As for the Saxons, they have been beaten these two hours; that is to say, hopeless these two hours, and getting beaten worse and worse. The Saxons cannot stand, but neither generally will they run; they dispute every ditch, morass, and tuft of wood, especially every village. Wrecks of the muddy desperate business last, hour after hour. "I gave my men a little rest under "the garden walls," says one Saxon gentleman, "or "they would have died, in the heat and thirst and "extreme fatigue: I would have given 100 gulden" (10*l*. sterling) "for a glass of water."* The Prussians push them on, bayonet in back; inexorable, not to be resisted; slit off whole battalions of them (prisoners now, and quarter given); take all their guns, or all that are not sunk in the quagmires; — in fine, drive them, part into the Mountains direct, part by circuit thither, down upon the rear of the Austrian fight: through Hausdorf, Seifersdorf and other Mountain gorges, where we hear no more of them, and shall say no more of them. A sore stroke for poor old Weissenfels; the last public one he has to take, in this world, for the poor man died before long. Nobody's blame,

* *Helden-Geschichte*, ubi supra.

he says; every Saxon man did well; only some Austrian horse-regiments, that we had among us, were too shy. Adieu to poor old Weissenfels. Luck of war, what else, — thereby is he in this pass.

And now new Prussian force, its Saxons being well abolished, is pressing down upon Prince Karl's naked left flank. Yes; — Prince Karl too will have to go. His cavalry is, for most part, shaken into ragged clouds; infantry, steady enough men, cannot stand everything. "I have observed," says Friedrich, "if you step sharply "up to an Austrian battalion" (within fifty paces or so), "and pour in your fire well, in about a quarter of an "hour, you see the ranks beginning to shake, and jum-"ble towards indistinctness;" * a very hopeful symptom to you!

It was at this moment that Lieutenant-General Gessler, under whom is the Dragoon regiment Baireuth, who had kept his place in spite of Valori's message, determined on a thing, — advised to it by General Schmettau (younger Schmettau) who was near. Gessler, as we saw, stood in the rear line, behind that gap (most likely one of several gaps, or wide spaces, left too wide as we explained): Gessler, noticing the jumbly condition of those Austrian battalions, heaped now one upon another in this part, — motions to the Prussian Infantry to make what further room is needful; then dashes through, in two columns (self and the Dragoon-Colonel heading the one, French Chasot, who is Lieutenant-Colonel, heading the other), sabre in hand, with extraordinary impetus and fire, into the belly of these jumbly Austrians; and slashes them to rags, "twenty

* *Military Instructions.*

battalions of them," in an altogether unexampled manner. Takes "several thousand prisoners," and such a haul of standards, kettledrums, and insignia of honour, as was never got before at one charge. Sixty-seven standards by the tale, for the regiment (by most All-Gracious Permission) wears, ever after, "67" upon its cartridge-box, and is allowed to beat the grenadier march;* — how many kettledrums memory does not say.

Prince Karl beats retreat, about 8 in the morning; is through Hohenfriedberg about 10 (cannon covering there, and Nadasti as rearguard): back into the Mountains; a thoroughly well-beaten man. Towards Bolkenhayn, the Saxons and he; their heavy artillery and baggage had been left safe there. Not much pursued, and gradually rearranging himself; with thoughts, — no want of thoughts! Came pouring down, triumphantly invasive, yesterday; returns, on these terms, in about fifteen hours. Not marching with displayed banners and field-music, this time; this is a far other march. The mouse-trap had been left open, and we rashly went in! — Prince Karl's loss, including that of the Saxons (which is almost equal, though their number in the field was but *half*), is 9,000 dead and wounded, 7,000 prisoners, 66 cannon, 73 flags and standards; the Prussian is about 5,000 dead and wounded.** Friedrich, at sight of Valori, embraces his *gros Valori;* says, with a pious emotion in voice and look, "My friend, God has helped me wonderfully this day!" Actually there was a kind of devout feeling visible in

* Orlich, II. 179 (173 n., 179 n., slightly wrong); *Militair-Lexikon*, II. 9, IV. 465, 466. See Preuss, I. 212; *Œuvres de Frédéric;* &c. &c.

** In Orlich (II. 182) all the details.

him, thinks Valori: "A singular mixture, this Prince, "of good qualities and of bad; I never know which "preponderates."* As is the way with fat Valoris, when they come into such company.

Friedrich is blamed by some military men, and perhaps himself thought it questionable, that he did not pursue Prince Karl more sharply. He says his troops could not; they were worn out with the night's marching and the day's fighting. He himself may well be worn out. I suppose, for the last four-and-twenty hours he, of all the contemporary sons of Adam, has probably been the busiest. Let us rest this day; rest till tomorrow morning, and be thankful. "So decisive "a defeat," writes he to his Mother (hastily, misdating "6th" June for 4th), "has not been since Blenheim"** (which is tolerably true); and "I have made the Princes "sign their names," to give the good Mother assurance of her children in these perils of war. Seldom has such a deliverance come to a man.

* Valori, *sæpius*.
** Letter in *Œuvres de Frédéric*, xxvi. 71.

CHAPTER XI.

CAMP OF CHLUM: FRIEDRICH CANNOT ACHIEVE PEACE.

FRIEDRICH marched, on the morrow, likewise to Bolkenhayn; which the enemy have just left; our hussars hanging on their rear, and bickering with Nadasti. Then again on the morrow, Sunday, — "twelve hours of continuous rain," writes Valori; but there is no down-pour, or distress, or disturbance that will shake these men from their ranks, writes Valori. And so it goes on, march after march, the Austrians ahead, Dumoulin and our hussars infesting their rear, which skilfully defended itself: through Landshut down into Bohemia; where are new successive marches, the Prussian quarterstaff stuck into the back of defeated Austria, "Home with you; farther home!" — and shogging it on, — without pause, for about a fortnight to come. And then only with temporary pause; that is to say, with intricate manœuvrings of a month long, which shove it to Königsgrätz, its ultimatum, beyond which there is no getting it. The stages and successive campings, to be found punctually in the old Books and new, can interest only military readers. Here is a small theological thing at Landshut, from first hand:

June 8th, 1745. "The Army followed Dumoulin's Corps, "and marched upon Landshut. On arriving in that neigh-"bourhood, the King was surrounded by a troop of 2,000

"Peasants," — of Protestant persuasion, very evidently! (which is much the prevailing thereabouts) — "who begged "permission of him 'to massacre the Catholics of those parts, "'and clear the country of them altogether.' This animosity "arose from the persecutions which the Protestants had "suffered during the Austrian domination, when their "churches used to be taken from them and given to the popish "priests," — churches and almost their children, such was the anxiety to make them orthodox. The patience of these peasants had run over; and now, in the hour of hope, they proposed the above sweeping measure. "The King was very "far from granting them so barbarous a permission. He told "them, 'They ought rather to conform to the Scripture "'precept, to bless those that cursed them, and pray for those "'that despitefully used them; such was the way to gain the "'Kingdom of Heaven.' The peasants," rolling dubious eyes for a moment, "answered, His Majesty was right; and desisted "from their cruel pretension." † * * — "On Hohenfriedberg "Day," says another Witness, "as far as the sound of the "cannon was heard, all round, the Protestants fell on their "knees, praying for victory to the Prussians;"* and at Breslau that evening, when the "Thirteen trumpeting Postillions" came tearing in with the news, what an enthusiasm without limit!

Prince Karl has skill in choosing camps and positions: his Austrians are much cowed; that is the grievous loss in his late fight. So, from June 8th, when they quit Silesia, — by two roads to go more readily, — all through that month and the next, Friedrich spread to the due width, duly pricking into the rear of them, drives the beaten hosts onward and onward. They do not think of fighting; their one thought is to get into positions where they can have living conveyed to them, and cannot be attacked; for the former of which objects, the farther homewards

† *Œuvres de Frédéric*, III. 318. * In Ranke, III. 259.

they go, it is the better. The main pursuit, as I gather, goes leftward from Landshut, by Friedland — the Silesian Friedland, once Wallenstein's. Through rough wild country, the southern slope of the Giant Mountains, goes that slow pursuit, or the main stream of it, where Friedrich in person is; intricate savage regions, out by precipitous rocks and soaking quagmires, shaggy with woods: watershed between the Upper Elbe and Middle Oder; Glatz on our left, — with the rain of its mountains gathering to a Neisse River, eastward, which we know; and on their west or hither side, to a Metau, Adler, Aupa, and other many-branched feeders of the Elbe. Most complex military ground, the manœuverings on it endless, — which must be left to the reader's fancy here.

About the end of June, Karl and his Austrians find a place suitable to their objects: Königsgrätz, a compact little Town, in the nook between the Elbe and Adler; covered to west and to south by these two streams; strong enough to east withal; and sure and convenient to the southern roads and victual. Against which Friedrich's manœuvres avail nothing; so that he at last (20th July) crosses Elbe River; takes, he likewise, an inexpugnable Camp on the opposite shore, at a Village called Chlum; and lies there, making a mutual dead-lock of it, for six weeks or more. Of the prior Camps, with their abundance of strategic shufflings, wheelings, pushings, all issuing in this of Chlum, we say nothing: none of them, — except the immediately preceding one, called of Nahorzan, called also of Drewitz (for it was in parts a shifting entity, and flung the *limbs* of it about, strategically clutching at Königsgrätz), — had any permanency: let us take

Chlum (the longest, and essentially the last in those parts) as the general summary of them, and alone rememberable by us.*

Friedrich's purposes, at Chlum, or previously, are not towards conquests in Bohemia, nor of fighting farther, if he can help it. But, in the mean while, he is eating out these Bohemian vicinages; no invasion of Silesia possible from that quarter soon again. That is one benefit: and he hopes always his enemies, under screw of military pressure with the one hand, and offer of the olive-branch with the other, will be induced to grant him Peace. Britannic Majesty, after Fontenoy and Hohenfriedberg, not to mention the first rumours of a Jacobite Rebellion, with France to rear of it, is getting eager to have Friedrich settled with, and withdrawn from the game again; — the rather, as Friedrich, knowing his man, has ceased latterly to urge him on the subject. Peace with George the Purseholder, does not that mean Peace with all the others? Friedrich knows the high Queen's indignation; but he little guesses, at this time, the humour of Brühl and the Polish Majesty. He has never yet sent the Old Dessauer in upon them; always only keeps him on the slip, at Magdeburg; still hoping actualities may not be needed. He hopes too, in spite of her indignation, the Hungarian Majesty, with an Election on hand, with the Netherlands at such a pass, not to

* "Camp of Gross-ParALitz" (across the Metau, to dislodge Prince Karl from his shelter behind that stream), "June 14th:" "Camp of Nahorzan, June 18th" (and abstruse manœuvrings, of a month, for Königsgrätz): "20th July," cross Elbe for Chlum; and lie, yourself also inexpugnable, there. See *Œuvres de Frédéric* (III. 120 et seq.); especially see Orlich (II. pp. 193, 194, 203, &c. &c.), — with an amplitude of inorganic details, sufficient to astonish the robustest memory!

speak of Italy and the Middle Rhine, will come to moderate views again. On which latter points, his reckoning was far from correct! Within three months, Britannic Majesty and he did get to explicit Agreement (*Convention of Hanover*, 26th August): but in regard to the Polish Majesty and the Hungarian there proved to be no such result attainable, and quite other methods necessary first!

"Of military transactions in this Camp of Chlum, or in all "these Bohemian-Silesian Camps, for near four months, there "is nothing, or as good as nothing: Chlum has no events; "Chlum vigilantly guards itself; and expects, as the really "decisive to it, events that will happen far away. We are to "conceive this military business as a deadlock; attended with "hussar skirmishes; attacks, defences, of outposts, of provi- "sion-wagons from Moravia or Silesia: — Friedrich has his "food from Silesia chiefly, by several routes, 'convoys come "'once in the five days.' His horse-provender he forages; "with Tolpatches watching him, and continual scufflings of "fight: 'for hay and glory,' writes one Prussian Officer, 'I "'assure you we fight well!' Endless enterprising, manœuver- "ing, counter-manœuvering there at first was; and still is, if "either party stir: but here, in their mutually fixed camps, "tacit mutual observances establish themselves; and amid the "rigorous armed vigilances, there are traits of human neigh- "bourship. As usual in such cases. The guard-parties do "not fire on one another, within certain limits: a signal that "there are dead to bury, or the like, is strictly respected. On "one such occasion it was (June 30th, Camp-of-Nahorzan "time) that Prince Ferdinand of Brunswick, — Prince Ferdi- "nand, with a young Brother Albert volunteering and learn- "ing his business here, who are both Prussian, — had a snatch "of interview with a third much-loved Brother, Ludwig, who "is in the Austrian service. A Prussian Officer, venturing "beyond the limits, had been shot; Ferdinand's message, "'Grant us burial of him!" found, by chance, Brother Lud- "wig in command of that Austrian outpost; who answers: "'Surely; — and beg that I may embrace my Brothers!' And "they rode out, those three, to the space intermediate; "talked there for half an hour, till the burial was done.* "Fancy such an interview between the poor young fellows, "the soul of honour each, and tied in that manner!

"Trenck of the Life-guard was not quite the soul of "honour. It was in the Nahorzan time too that Trenck, who "had, in spite of express order to the contrary, been writing "to his Cousin the indigo Pandour, was put under arrest when "found out. 'Wrote merely about horses: purchase of "'horses, so help me God!' protests the blusterous Life-"guardsman, loud as lungs will, — whether with truth in "them, nobody can say. 'Arrest for breaking orders!' "answers Friedrich, doubting or disbelieving the horses; and "loud Trenck is packed over the Hills to Glatz; to Governor "Fouqué, or Substitute; — where, by *not* submitting and "repenting, by resisting and rebelling, and ever again doing "it, he makes out for himself, with Fouqué and his other "Governors, what kind of life we know! '*Gardez étroitement ce* "'*drôle-là, il a voulu devenir Pandour auprès de son oncle* (Keep "'a tight hold of this fine fellow; he wanted to become "'Pandour beside his Uncle)!' writes Friedrich: — 'Uncle' "instead of 'Cousin,' all one to Friedrich. This he writes "with his own hand, on the margin: 28th June 1745; the "inexorable Records fix that date.† Which I should not "mention, except for another inexorable date (30th Septem-"ber), that is coming; and the perceptible slight comfort "there will be in fixing down a loud-blustering, extensively "fabulous blockhead, still fit for the Nurseries, to one unde-"niable premeditated lie, and tar-marking him therewith, for "benefit of more serious readers." As shall be done, were the 30th of September come!

Here is still something, — if it be not rather nothing, by a great hand! Date uncertain; Camp-of-Chlum time, pretty far on: * * "There are continual foragings, on both sides; "with parties mutually dashing out to hinder the same. The "Prussians have a detached post at Smirzitz; which is much "harassed by Hungarians lurking about, shooting our sentry "and the like. An inventive head contrives this expedient. "Stuff a Prussian uniform with straw; fix it up, by aid of

* Mauvillon, *Geschichte Ferdinands von Braunschweig-Lüneburg*, I. 118.

† Rödenbeck, III. 381. Copy of the Warrant, once *penes me*.

"ropes and cheek-strings, to stand with musket shouldered, "and even to glide about to right and left, on judicious pull-"ing. So it is done: straw man is made; set upon his ropes, "when the Tolpatches approach; and pensively saunters to "and fro, — his living comrades crouching in the bushes near "by. Tolpatches fire on the walking straw sentry; straw "sentry falls flat; Tolpatches rush in, esurient, triumphant; "are exploded in a sharp blast of musketry from the bushes "all round, every wounded man made prisoner; — and come "no more back to that post." Friedrich himself records this little fact: "slight pleasantry to relieve the reader's mind," says he, in narrating it.* — Enough of those small matters, while so many large are waiting.

June 26th, a month before Chlum, General Nassau had been detached, with some 8 or 10,000, across Glatz Country, into Upper Silesia, to sweep that clear again. Hautcharmoi, quitting the Frontier Towns, has joined, raising him to 15,000; and Nassau is giving excellent account of the multitudinous Pandour doggeries there; and will retake Kosel, and have Upper Silesia swept before very long.** On the other hand, the Election matter (*Kaiserwahl*, a most important point) is obviously in threatening, or even in desperate state! That famed Middle-Rhine Army has gone to the — what shall we say?

July 5th-19th, Middle-Rhine Country. "The first Election-"news that reaches Friedrich is from the Middle-Rhine "Country, and of very bad complexion. Readers remember "Traun, and his Bathyanis, and his intentions upon Conti "there. In the end of May, old Traun, things being all com-"pleted in Bavaria, had got on march with his Bavarian

* *Œuvres*, III. 123.

** Kosel, "September 5th:" Excellent, lucid and even entertaining Account of Nassau's Expedition, in the form of *Diary* (a model, of its kind), in *Feldzüge*, IV. 357-371-582.

"Army, say 40,000, to look into Prince Conti down in those "parts; a fact very interesting to the Prince. Traun held "leftward, westward, as if for the Neckar Valley,—'Perhaps "intending to be through upon Elsass, in those southern "undefended portions of the Rhine?' Conti, and his Ségur, "and Middle-Rhine Army stood diligently on their guard; "got their forces, defences, apparatuses, hurried southward, "from Frankfurt quarter where they lay on watch, into those "Neckar regions. Which seen to be done, Traun whirled "rapidly to rightward, to northward; crossed the Mayn at "Wertheim, wholly leaving the Neckar and its Conti; having "weighty business quite in the other direction, — on the "north side of the Mayn, namely; on the Kinzig River, where "Bathyani (who has taken D'Ahremberg's command below "Frankfurt, and means to bestir himself in another than the "D'Ahremberg fashion) is to meet him on a set day. Traun "having thus, by strategic suction, pulled the Middle-Rhine "Army out of his and Bathyani's way, hopes they two will "manage a junction on the Kinzig; after junction they will be "a little stronger than Conti, though decidedly weaker taken "one by one. Traun, in the long June days, had such a "march, through the Spessart Forest (Mayn River to his left, "with our old friends Dettingen, Aschaffenburg, far down in "the plain), as was hardly ever known before: pathless "wildernesses, rocky steeps and chasms; the sweltering June "sun sending down the upper snows upon him in the form of "muddy slush; so that 'the infantry had to wade haunch-"'deep in many of the hollow parts, and nearly all the cavalry "'lost its horse-shoes.' A strenuous march; and a well-"schemed. For at the Kinzig River (Conti still far off in the "Neckar country), Bathyani punctually appeared, on the "opposite shore; and Traun and he took camp together; "July 5th, at Langen-Selbord (few miles north of Hanau, "which we know); — and rest there; calculating that Conti is "now a manageable quantity; — and comfortably wait till "the Grand-Duke arrives.* For this is, theoretically, *his* "Army; Grand-Duke Franz being the Commander's Cloak, "this season; as Karl was, last, — a right lucky Cloak he, "while Traun lurked under him, not so lucky since! July "13th, Franz arrived; and Traun, under Franz, instantly

* Adelung, IV. 421; V. 36.

"went into Conti (now again in those Frankfurt parts); "clutched at Conti, Briareus-like, in a multiform alarming "manner: so that Conti lost head; took to mere retreating, "rushing about, burning bridges; — and, in fine, July 19th, "had flung himself bodily across the Rhine (clouds of Tol-"patches sticking to him), and left old Traun and his Grand-"Duke supreme lord in those parts. Who did *not* invade "Elsass, as was now expected; but lay at Heidelberg, intend-"ing to play pacifically a surer card. All French are out of "Teutschland again; and the game given up. In what a "premature and shameful manner! thinks Friedrich.

"Nominally it was the Grand-Duke that flung Conti over "the Rhine; and delivered Teutschland from its plagues. "After which fine feat, salvatory to the Cause of Liberty, and "destructive to French influence, what is to prevent his elec-"tion to the Kaisership? Friedrich complains aloud: "Conti "has given it up; you drafted '15,000 from him (for imaginary "'uses in the Netherlands) — you have given it up, then! "'Was that our bargain?' 'We have given it up,' answers "D'Argenson the War-minister, writing to Valori; 'but' — "And supplies, instead of performance according to the laws "of fact, eloquent logic; very superfluous to Friedrich and "the said laws! — Valori, and the French Minister at Dres-"den, had again been trying to stir up the Polish Majesty to "stand for Kaiser; but of course that enterprise, eager as the "Polish Majesty might be for such a dignity, had now to "collapse, and become totally hopeless. A new offer of Fried-"rich's to coöperate had been refused by Brühl, with a "brevity, a decisiveness — 'Thinks me finished (*aux abois*),' "says Friedrich; 'and not worth giving terms to, on sur-"'rendering!' The foolish little creature; insolent in the "wrong quarter!" *

The German Burden, then, — which surely was mutual, at lowest, and lately was French altogether, — the French have thrown it off; the French have dropped their end of the *bearing-poles* (so to speak), and left Friedrich by himself, to stand or stagger,

* *Œuvres de Frédéric*, III. 128.

under the beweltered broken harness-gear and intolerable weight! That is one's payment for cutting the rope from their neck last year! — Long since, while the present Campaign was being prepared for under such financial pressures, Friedrich had bethought him, "The French might at least give me money, if they can nothing else?" — and he had one day penned a Letter with that object; but had thrown it into his desk again, "No; not till the very last extremity, that!" Friedrich did at last despatch the unpleasant missive: "Service done you in Elsass, let us say little of it; but the repayment has been zero hitherto: your Bavarian expenses (poor Kaiser gone, and Peace of Füssen come!) are now ended: — A round sum, say of 600,000 *l.*, is becoming indispensable here, if we are to keep on our feet at all!" Herr Ranke, who has seen the Most Christian King's response (though in a capricious way), finds "three or four successive redactions" of the difficult passage; all painfully meaning, "Impossible, alas!" — painfully adding, "We will try, however!" And, after due cunctations, Friedrich waiting silent the while, — Louis, Most Christian King, who had failed in so many things towards Friedrich, does empower Valori To offer him a subsidy of 500,000 livres a-month, till we see farther. Twenty thousand pounds a-month; he hopes this will suffice, being himself run terribly low. Friedrich's feeling is to be guessed: "Such a dole might answer to a Landgraf of Hessen-"Darmstadt; but to me is not in the least suitable;" — and flatly refuses it; *fièrement*, says Valori.*

Mon gros Valori, who could not himself help all

* Ranke, iii. 235, 299 n. (not the least of *date* allowed us in either case,); Valori, i. 240.

this, poor soul, "falls now into complete disgrace;" waits daily upon Friedrich at the giving out of the parole, "but frequently his Majesty does not speak to me at all." Hardly looks at me, or only looks as if I had suddenly become Zero Incarnate. It is now in these days, I suppose, that Friedrich writes about the "Scamander Battle" (of Fontenoy), and "Capture of Pekin," by way of helping one to fight the Austrians according to Treaty. And has a touch of bitter sarcasm in uttering his complaints against such treatment, — the heart of him, I suppose, bitter enough. Most Christian King has felt this of the Scamander, Friedrich perceives; Louis's next letter testifies pique; — and of course we are farther from help, on that side, than ever. "From the *Stände* of the Kur-Mark" (Brandenburg) "Friedrich was offered a considerable "subsidy instead; and joyfully accepted the same, 'as "'a loan:'" — paid it punctually back, too; and never, all his days, forgot it of those *Stände*.*

Camp of Dieskau: Britannic Majesty makes Peace, for himself, with Friedrich; but cannot for Austria or Saxony.

About the middle of August, there are certain Saxon phenomena which awaken dread expectation in the world. Friedrich, watching, Argus-like, near and far, in his Chlum observatory, has noticed that Prince Karl is getting reinforced in Königsgrätz; 10,000 lately, 7,000 more coming; — and contrariwise that the Saxons seem to be straggling off from him; ebbing away, corps after corps, — towards Saxony, can it be?

* Stenzel, IV. 256; Ranke, &c.

There are whispers of "Bavarian auxiliaries" being hired for them, too. And little Brühl's late insolence; Brühl's evident belief that "we are finished (*aux abois*)?" Putting all this together, Friedrich judges, — with an indignation very natural, — that there is again some insidious Saxon mischief, most likely an attack on Brandenburg, in the wind. Friedrich orders the Old Dessauer: "March into them, delay no longer!" and publishes a clangorously indignant Manifesto (evidently his own writing, and coming from the heart):* "How they have, *not* bound by their Austrian Treaty, wantonly invaded our Silesia; have, since and before, in spite of our forbearance, done so many things: — and, in fact, have finally exhausted our patience; and are forcing us to seek redress and safety by the natural methods," which they will see how they like! —

Old Leopold advances straightway, as bidden, direct for the Saxon frontier. To whom Friedrich shoots off detachments, — Prince Dietrich, with so many thousands, to reinforce Papa; then General Gessler with so many, — till Papa is 30,000 odd; and could eat Saxony at a mouthful; nothing whatever being yet ready there on Brühl's part, though he has such immense things in the wind! — Nevertheless Friedrich again paused; did not yet strike. The Saxon question has Russian bugbears, no end of complications. His Britannic Majesty, now at Hanover, and his prudent Harrington with him, are in the act of labouring, with all earnestness, for a general Agreement with Friedrich. Without further bitterness, embroilment and bloodshed: how much preferable for

* In Adelung, v. 64-71 (no date; "middle of August," say the Books).

Friedrich! Old Dessauer, therefore, pauses: "Camp of Dieskau," which we have often heard of, close on the Saxon Border; stands there, looking over, as with sword drawn, 30,000 good swords, — but no stroke, not for almost three months more. In three months, wretched Brühl had not repented; but, on the contrary, had completed his preparations, and gone to work; — and the stroke did fall, as will be seen. That is Brühl's posture in the matter.*

To Britannic George, for a good while past, it has been manifest that the Pragmatic Sanction, in its original form, is an extinct object; that reconquest of Silesia, and such-like, is melancholy moonshine; and that, in fact, towards fighting the French with effect, it is highly necessary to make peace with Friedrich of Prussia again. This once more is George's and his Harrington's fixed view. Friedrich's own wishes are known, or used to be, ever since the late Kaiser's death, — though latterly he has fallen silent, and even avoids the topic when offered (knowing his man)! Harrington has to apply formally to Friedrich's Minister at Hanover. "Very well, if they are in earnest this time," so Friedrich instructs his Minister: "My terms are known to you; no change admissible in the terms; — do not speak with me on it farther: and, observe, within four weeks, the thing finished, or else broken off!"** And in this sense they are labouring incessantly, with Austria, with Saxony, — without the least success; — and Excellency Robinson has again a panting uncomfortable time. Here is a scene Robinson transacts at Vienna, which gives us a curious face-

* Ranke, III. 281, 314.

** Ranke, III. 277-281.

to-face glimpse of her Hungarian Majesty, while Friedrich is in his Camp at Chlum.

Schönbrunn, 2d August 1745, *Robinson has Audience of her Hungarian Majesty.*

Robinson, in a copious sonorous speech (rather apt to be copious, and to fall into the Parliamentary *canto-fermo*), sets forth how extremely ill we Allies are faring on the French hand; nothing done upon Silesia either; a hopeless matter that, — is it not, your Majesty? And your Majesty's forces all lying there, in mere dead-lock; and we in such need of them! 'Peace with Prussia is indispensable." — To which her Majesty listened, in statuesque silence mostly; "never "saw her so reserved before, my Lord.' * *

Robinson. * * "'Madam, the Dutch will be obliged to "accept 'Neutrality'" (and plump down again, after such hoisting)!

Queen. "Well, and if they did, they? 'It would be "'easier to accommodate with France itself, and so finish the "'whole matter, than with Prussia.' My Army could not get "to the Netherlands this season. No General of mine would "undertake conducting it at this day of the year. Peace with "Prussia, what good could it do at present?"

Robinson. "'England has already found, for subsidies, "'this year, 1,178,753*l*. Cannot go on at that rate. Peace "'with Prussia is one of the returns the English Nation ex-"'pects for all it has done.'"

Queen. "I must have Silesia again; without Silesia the "Kaiserhood were an empty title. 'Or would you have us "'administer it under the guardiancy of Prussia!' * *

Robinson. "In Bohemia itself things don't look well; no-"thing done on Friedrich: your Saxons seem to be quarrel-"ling with you, and going home."

Queen. "Prince Karl is himself capable of fighting the "Prussians again. Till that, do not speak to me of Peace! "Grant me only till October!"

Robinson. "Prussia will help the Grand-Duke to Kaiser-ship."

Queen. "The Grand-Duke is not so ambitious of an empty

"honour as to engage in it under the tutelage of Prussia. "Consider farther: the Imperial dignity, is it compatible with "the fatal deprivation of Silesia? 'One other battle, I say! "'Good God, give me only till the month of October!'"

Robinson. "A battle, Madam, if won, won't reconquer "Silesia; if lost, your Majesty is ruined at home."

Queen. "'*Dussé-je conclure avec lui le lendemain, je lui livre*-"'*rais bataille ce soir*' (Had I to agree with him tomorrow, I "would try him in a battle this evening)!" *

Her Majesty is not to be hindered; deaf to Robinson, to her Britannic George who pays the money. "Cruel man, is that what you call keeping the Pragmatic Sanction; dismembering me of Province after Province, now in Germany, then in Italy, on pretext of necessity? Has not England money, then? Does not England love the Cause of Liberty? Give me till October!" Her Majesty did take till October, and later, as we shall see; poor George not able to hinder, by power of the purse or otherwise: who can hinder high females, or low, when they get into their humours? Much of this Austrian obstinacy, think impartial persons, was of female nature. We shall see what profit her Majesty made by taking till October.

As for George, the time being run, and her Majesty and Saxony unpersuadable, he determined to accept Friedrich's terms himself, in hope of gradually bringing the others to do it. August 26th, at Hanover, there is signed a *Convention of Hanover* between Friedrich and him: "Peace on the old Breslau-Berlin terms, — precisely the same terms, but Britannic Majesty to

* Robinson's Despatch, 4th August 1745. Ranke, III. 267; Raumer, pp. 161, 162.

have them guaranteed by All the Powers, on the General Peace coming, — so that there be no snake-procedure henceforth." Silesia Friedrich's without fail, dear Hanover unmolested even by a thought of Friedrich's; — and her Hungarian Majesty to be invited, nay urged by every feasible method, to accede.* Which done, Britannic Majesty, — for there has hung itself out, in the Scotch Highlands, the other day ("Glenfinlas, August 12th"), a certain Standard '*Tandem Triumphans*,' and unpleasant things are imminent! — hurries home at his best pace, and has his hands full there, for some time. On Austria, on Saxony, he could not prevail: "By no manner of means!" answered they; and went their own road, — jingling his Britannic subsidies in their pocket; regardless of the once Supreme Jove, who is sunk now to a very different figure on the German boards.

Friedrich's outlook is very bad: such a War to go on, and not even finance to do it with. His intimates, his Rothenburg one time, have "found him sunk in gloomy thought." But he wears a bright face usually. No wavering or doubting in him, his mind made up; which is a great help that way. Friedrich indicates, and has indicated everywhere, for many months, that Peace, precisely on the old footing, is all he wants: "The Kaiser being dead, whom I took up arms to defend, what further object is there?" says he. "Renounce Silesia, more honestly than last time; engage to have it guaranteed by everybody at the General Peace (or perhaps Hohenfriedberg will help to guarantee

* Adelung, v. 75; in "in Rousset, xix. 441;" in &c &c.

it), — and I march home!" My money is running down, privately thinks he; guarantee Silesia, and I shall be glad to go. If not, I must raise money somehow; melt the big silver balustrades at Berlin, borrow from the *Stände*, or do something; and, in fact, must stand here, unless Silesia is guaranteed, and struggle till I die.

That latter withal is still privately Friedrich's thought. Under his light air, he carries unspoken that grimly clear determination, at all times, now and henceforth; and it is an immense help to the guidance of him. An indispensable, indeed. No king or man, attempting anything considerable in this world, need expect to achieve it except, tacitly, on those same terms, "I will achieve it or die!" For the world, in spite of rumours to the contrary, is always much of a bedlam to the sanity (so far as he may have any) of every individual man. A strict place, moreover; its very bedlamisms flowing by law, as do alike the sudden mud-deluges, and the steady Atlantic tides, and all things whatsoever: a world inexorable, truly, as gravitation itself; — and it will behove you to front it in a similar humour, as the tacit basis for whatever wise plans you lay. In Friedrich, from the first entrance of him on the stage of things, we have had to recognise this prime quality, in a fine tacit form, to a complete degree; and till his last exit, we shall never find it wanting. Tacit enough, unconscious almost, not given to articulate itself at all; — and if there be less of piety than we could wish in the silence of it, there is at least no play-actor mendacity, or cant of devoutness, to poison the high worth of it. No braver little figure stands on the Earth at that epoch. Ready, at the due season, with his mind silently made up; — able to answer diplomatic Robinsons, Bartensteins, and the very Destinies when they apply. If you will withdraw your snakish notions, will guarantee Silesia, will give him back his old Treaty of Berlin in an irrefragable shape, he will march home; if not, he will never march home, but be carried thither dead rather. That is his intention, if the gods permit.

Grand-Duke Franz is elected Kaiser (13th September 1745); *Friedrich, the Season and Forage being done, makes for Silesia.*

There occurred at Frankfurt, — the clear majority, seven of the nine Electors, Bavaria itself (nay Bohemia, this time, "distaff" or not), and all the others but Friedrich and Kur-Pfalz, being so disposed or so disposable, Traun being master of the ground, — no difficulty about electing Grand-Duke Franz Stephan of Tuscany, Joint-King of Bohemia, to be Kaiser of the Holy Romish Reich. Friedrich's envoy protested; — as did Kur-Pfalz's, with still more vehemence, and then withdrew to Hanau: the other Seven voted, September 13th, 1745: and it was done. A new Kaiser, Franz Stephan, or Franz I., — with our blessing on him, if that can avail much. But I fear it cannot. Upon such mendacious Empty-Case of Kaiserhood, without even money to feed itself, not to speak of governing, of defending and coercing; upon such entities the blessings of man avail little; the gods, having warned them to go, do not bless them for staying! — However, tar-barrels burn, the fountains play (wine in some of them, I hope); Franz is to be crowned in a fortnight hence, with extraordinary magnificence. At this last part of it Maria Theresa will, in her own high person, attend; and proceeds accordingly towards Frankfurt, in the end of September (say the old Books), so soon as the Election is over.

Hungarian Majesty's bearing was not popular there, according to Friedrich, — who always admires her after a sort, and always speaks of her like a king and gentleman: — but the High Lady, it is intimated, felt somewhat too well that she was high. Not sorry to have it known, under the due veils, that her Kaiser-Husband is but of a mimetic nature; that it is she who has the real power; and that indeed she is in a victorious posture at present. Very high in her carriage towards the Princes of the Reich, and their privileges: — poor Kur-Pfalz's notary, or herald, coming to protest (I think, it was the second time) about something, she quite disregarded his tabards, pasteboards, or whatever they were, and clapt him in prison. The thing was commented upon; but Kur-Pfalz got no redress. Need we repeat, — lazy readers having so often met him, and forgotten him again, — this is a new younger Kur-Pfalz: August Theodor, this one; not Friedrich Wilhelm's old Friend, but his Successor, of the Sulzbach line; of whom, after thirty years or so, we may again hear. He can complain about his violated tabard; will get his notary out of jail again, but no redress.

Highish even towards her friends, this "Empress-Queen" (*Kaiserin-Königin*, such her new title), and has a kind of 'Thank-you-for-Nothing' air towards them. Prussian Majesty, she said, had unquestionable talents; but, oh, what a character! Too much levity, she said, by far; heterodox too, in the extreme; a *böser Mann;* — and what a neighbour has he been! As to Silesia, she was heard to say, she would as soon part with her petticoat as part with it.* — So that there is not the least prospect of peace here? "None," answer Friedrich's emissaries, whom he had empowered to hint the thing. Which is heavy news to Friedrich.

Early in August, not long after that Audience of Robinson's, her Majesty, after repeated written-messages to Prince Karl, urging him to go into fight again or attempt something, had sent two high messengers: Prince Lobkowitz, Duke d'Ahremberg, high dignitaries from Court, have come to Königsgrätz with the latest urgencies, the newest ideas; and would fain help Prince Karl to attempt something. Daily they used to come out upon a little height, in view of Friedrich's tent, and gaze in upon him, and round all Nature, 'with big tubes,' he says, 'as if they had been astronomers;' but never attempted anything. We remember D'Ahremberg, and what part he has played, from the Dettingen times and onward. "A debauched old fellow," says Friedrich; "gone all to hebetude by his labours in that line; agrees always with the last speaker." Prince Karl seems to have little stomach himself; and does not see his way into (or across) another Battle. Lobkowitz, again, is always saying: "Try something! We are now stronger than they, by their detachings, by our reinforcings" (indeed, about twice their number, regular and irregular), though most of the Saxons are gone home. After much gazing through their tubes, the Austrians (August 23d) do make a small shift of place, insignificant otherwise; the Prussians, next day,

* *Œuvres de Frédéric,* III. 126, 128.

do the like, in consequence; quit Chlum, burning their huts; post themselves a little farther up the Elbe, — their left at a place called Jaromirz, embouchure of the Aupa into Elbe,* — and are again unattackable.

The worst fact is the multitude of Pandours, more and more infesting our provision roads; and that horse-forage itself is, at last, running low. Detachments lie all duly round to right and left, to secure our communications with Silesia, especially to left, out of Glatz, where runs one of the chief roads we have. But the service is becoming daily more difficult. For example:

"*Neustadt, 8th September.* In that left-hand quarter, com-"ing out of Glatz at a little Bohemian Town called Neustadt, "the Prussian Commander, Tauenzien by name, was re-"peatedly assaulted; and from September 8th, had to stand "actual siege, gallantly repulsing a full 10,000 with their big "artillery, though his walls were all breached, for about a "week, till Friedrich sent him relief. Prince Lobkowitz, our "old anti-Belleisle friend, who is always of forward fiery "humour, had set them on this enterprise; which has turned "out fruitless. The King is much satisfied with Tauenzien;** "of whom we shall hear again. Who indeed becomes notable "to us, were it only for getting one Lessing as secretary, by "and by: Gotthold Ephraim Lessing, whose fame has since "gone into all countries; the man having been appointed a "'Secretary' to the very Destinies, in some sort; that is to "say, a Writer of Books which have turned out to have truth "in them! Tauenzien, a grimmish aquiline kind of man, of "no superfluous words, has distinguished himself for the pre-"sent by defending Neustadt, which the Austrians fully "counted to get hold of."

Let us give another little scene; preparatory to quitting this Country, as it is evident the King and

* *Œuvres de Frédéric*, III. 129. ** Ib. III. 132.

we will soon have to do; Country being quite eaten out, Pandours getting ever rifer, and the Season done:

Jaromirz, "early in September" 1745. "Jaromirz is a little "Bohemian Town on the Aupa, or between the Aupa and Me-"tau branches of the upper Elbe; four or five miles north of "Semonitz, where Friedrich's quarter now is. Valori, so "seldom spoken to, is lodged in a suburb there: 'Had not "'you better go into the town itself?' his Majesty did once "say; but Valori, dreading nothing, lodged on, — 'Landlord "'a Burgher whom I thought respectable.' Respectable, yes "he; but his son had been dealing with Franquini the Pan-"dour, and had sold Valori, — night appointed, measures all "taken; a miracle if Valori escape. Franquini, chief of "30,000 Pandours, has come in person to superintend this im-"portant capture; and lies hidden, with a strong party, in "the woods to rearward. Prussians about 200, scattered in "posts, occupy the hedges in front, for guard of the ovens; "to rear, Jaromirz being wholly ours, there is no suspicion.

"In the dead of the night, Franquini emerges from the "woods; sends forward a party of sixty, under the young "Judas; who, by methods suitable, gets them stealthily con-"ducted into Papa's Barn, which looks across a courtyard "into Valori's very windows. From the Barn it is easy, on "paws of velvet, to get into the House, if you have a Judas "to open it. Which you have: — bolts all drawn for you, and "even beams ready for barricading if you be meddled with. "'Up stairs is his Excellency asleep; Excellency's room is — "'to right, do you remember; or to left' — 'Pshaw, we shall "'find it!' The Pandours mount; find a bedroom, break it "open, — some fifteen or sixteen of them, and one who knows "a little French; — come crowding forward: to the horror "and terror of the poor inhabitant. '*Que voulez-vous donc?*' "'His Excellency Valori!' 'Well, no violence; I am your "'prisoner: let me dress!' answers the supposed Excellency, "— and contrives to secrete portfolios, and tear, or make "away with papers. And is marched off, under a select "guard, who leave the rest to do the pillage. And was not "Valori at all; was Valori's Secretary, one D'Argot, who "had called himself Valori on this dangerous occasion! Va-"lori sat quaking behind his partition; not till the Pandours "began plundering the stables, did the Prussian sentry catch "sound of them, and plunge in."

Friedrich had his amusement out of this adventure; liked D'Arget, the clever Secretary; got D'Arget to himself before long, as will be seen; — and, in quieter times, dashed-off a considerable Explosion of Rhyme, called *Le Palladion* (Valori as Prussia's "Palladium," with Devils attempting to steal him, and the like), which was once thought an exquisite Burlesque, — Kings coveting a sight of it, in vain, — but is now wearisome enough to every reader.* — Let us attend his Majesty's exit from Bohemia.

* Valori, i. 242; *Œuvres de Frédéric*, III. 130: for the Fact. Exquisite Burlesque, *Palladion* itself, is in *Œuvres*, XI. 179-272 (see *ib.* 139): a bad copy of that very bad Original, *Jeanne d'Arc*, — the only thing now good in it, Friedrich's polite yet positive refusal to gratify King Louis and his Pompadour with a sight of it (see *ib. Preface*, x.-xiv., Friedrich's Letter to Louis; date of request and of refusal, March 1750).

CHAPTER XII.

BATTLE OF SOHR.

THE famed beautiful Elbe River rises in romantic chasms, terrible to the picturesque beholder, at the roots of the Riesengebirge; overlooked by the Hohe-Kamms, and highest summits of that chain. "Out of eleven wells," says gentle Dulness, "*Eilf* or *Elf Quellen*, whence its name, Elbe for *Elf*." Sure enough, it starts out of various wells;* rushes out, like a great peacock's or pasha's tail, from the roots of the Giant Mountains thereabouts; and hurries southward, — or even rather eastward, at first; for (except the Iser to westward, which does not fall in for a great while) its chief branches come from the eastern side: Aupa, Metau, Adler, the drainings of Glatz, and of that rugged Country where Friedrich has been camping and manœuvering all summer. On the whole, its course is southward for the first seventy or eighty miles, washing Jaromirz, Königshof, Königsgrätz, down to Pardubitz: at Pardubitz it turns abruptly westward, and holds on so, bending even northward, by hill and plain, through the rest of its five or six hundred miles.

Its first considerable branch, on that eastern or left bank, is the Aupa, which rises in the Pass of Schatz-

* Description, in Zöllner, *Briefe über Schlesien*, II. 806; in &c. &c.

lar (great struggling there, for convoys, just now); goes next by Trautenau, which has lately been burnt; and joins the Elbe at Jaromirz, where Valori was stolen, or nearly so, from under the Prussian left wing. The Aupa runs nearly straight south; the Elbe, till meeting it, has run rather south-east; but after joining they go south together, augmented by the Metau, by the Adler, down to Pardubitz, where the final turn to west occurs. Jaromirz, which lies in the very angle of Elbe and Aupa, is the left wing of Friedrich's Camp; main body of the Camp lies on the other side of the Elbe, but of course has bridges (as at Smirzitz, where that straw sentry did his pranks lately); bridges are indispensable, part of our provision coming always by that *Bohemian* Neustadt, from the northeast quarter out of Silesia; though the main course of our meal (and much fighting for it) is direct from the north by the Pass of Schatzlar, — "Chaslard," as poor Valori calls it.

Thus Friedrich lay, when Valori escaped being stolen; when Tauenzien was assailed by the 10,000 Pandours with siege artillery, and stood inexpugnable in the breach till Friedrich relieved him. Those Pandours "had cut away his water, for the last two days;" so that, except for speedy relief, all valour had been in vain. Water being gone, not recoverable without difficulties, Neustadt was abandoned (September 16th, as I guess); — one of our main Silesian roads for meal has ceased. We have now only Schatzlar to depend on; where Franquini, — lying westward among the glens of the Upper Elbe, and possessed of abundant talent in the Tolpatch way (witness Valori's narrow miss lately), — gives us trouble enough. Friedrich determines to move towards Schatzlar. Homewards, in fact; eating the Country well as he goes.

Saturday, 18th September, Friedrich crosses the Elbe at Jaromirz. Entirely unopposed; the Austrians were all busy firing *feu-de-joie* for the Election of their Grand-Duke: Election done five days ago at Frankfurt, and the news just come. So they crackle about, and deliver rolling fire, at a great rate; proud to be "*Imperial* Army" henceforth, as if that could do much for them. There was also vast dining, for three days, among the high heads, and a great deal of wine spent. That probably would have been the chance to undertake something upon them, better than crossing the Elbe, says Friedrich looking back. But he did not think of it in time; took second-best in place of best.

He is now, therefore, over into that Triangular piece of Country between Elbe and Aupa; in that triangle, his subsequent notable operations all lie. He here purposes to move northward, by degrees, — through Trautenau, Schatzlar, and home; well eating this bit of Country too, the last uneaten bit, as he goes. This well eaten, there will be no harbour anywhere for Invasion, through the Winter coming. One of my old Notes says of it, in the topographic point of view:

"It is a triangular patch of Country, which has lain asleep "since the Creation of the World; traversed only by Boii "(*Boi-heim-ers*, Bohemians), Czechs, and other such popu-"lations, in Human History; but which Friedrich has been "fated to make rather notable to the Moderns henceforth. "Let me recommend it to the picturesque tourist, especially "to the military one. Lovers of rocky precipices, quagmires, "brawling torrents, and the unadulterated ruggedness of "Nature, will find scope there; and it was the scene of a "distinguished passage of arms, with notable display of "human dexterity and swift presence of mind. For the rest, "one of the wildest, and perhaps (except to the picturesque "tourist) most unpleasant regions in the world. Wild stony "upland; topmost Upland, we may say, of Europe in "general, or portion of such Upland; for the rain-storms "hereabouts run several roads, — into the German Ocean "and Atlantic by the Elbe, into the Baltic by the Oder, into "the Black Sea by the Donau; — and it is the waste Out-"field whither you rise, by long weeks-journeys, from many "sides.

"Much of it, towards the angle of Elbe and Aupa, is "occupied by a huge waste Wood, called 'Kingdom Forest' "(*Königreich Sylva* or *Wald*, peculium of Old Czech Majesties, "I fancy); may be sixty square miles in area, the longer side "of which lies along the Elbe. A Country of rocky defiles; "lowish hills chaotically shoved together, not wanting their "brooks and quagmires, strait labyrinthic passages; shaggy "with wild wood. Some poor Hamlets here and there, pro-"bably the sleepiest in Nature, are scattered about; there "may be patches ploughable for rye" (modern Tourist says snappishly, There are many such; whole region now drained; reminded you of Yorkshire Highlands, with the Western Sun gilding it, that fine afternoon!) — "ploughable for "rye, buckwheat; boggy grass to be gathered in summer; "charcoaling to do; pigs at least are presumable, among "these straggling outposts of humanity in their obscure Ham-"lets: poor ploughing, moiling creatures, they little thought "of becoming notable so soon! None of the Books (all intent "on mere soldiering) take the least notice of them; not at "the pains to spell their Hamlets right: no more notice than "if they also had been stocks and moss-grown stones. Never-"theless, there they did evidently live, for thousands of "years past, in a dim manner; — and are much terrified to "have become the seat of war, all on a sudden. Their poor "Hamlets, Sohr, Staudentz, Prausnitz, Burgersdorf, and "others still send up a faint smoke; and have in them, "languidly, the live-coal of mysterious human existence, in "those woods, — to judge by the last maps that have come "out. A thing worth considering by the passing tourist, "military or other."

It is in this Kingdom Forest (which he calls *Royaume de Silva*, instead of *Sylva de Royaume*) that Friedrich now marches; keeping the body of the Forest well on his left, and skirting the southern and eastern sides of it. Rough marching for his Majesty; painfully infested by Nadastian Tolpatches; who run out on him from ambushes, and need to be scourged; one ambush in particular, at a place called Liebenthal (second day's march, and near the end of it), — where our Prussian Hussars, winding like fiery dragons on the dangerous precipices, gave them better than they brought, and completely quenched their appetite for that day. After Liebenthal, the march soon ends; three miles farther on, at the dim wold-hamlet of Staudentz: here a camp is pitched; here, till the Country is well eaten out, or till something else occur, we propose to tarry for a time.

Horse-forage abounds here; but there is no getting of it without disturbance from those dogs; you must fight for every truss of grass: if a meal-train is coming, as there does every five days, you have to detach 6,000 foot and 3,000 horse to help it safe in. A fretting fatiguing time for regular troops. Our bakery is at Trautenau, — where Valori is now lodging. The Tolpatchery, unable to take Trautenau, set fire to it, though it is their own town, their own Queen's town: thatchy Trautenau, wooden too in the upper stories of it, takes greedily to the fire; goes all aloft in flame, and then lies black. A scandalous transaction, thinks Friedrich. The Prussian corn lay nearly all in cellars; little got, even of the Prussians, by such an atrocity: and your own poor fellow-subjects, where are they? Valori was burnt out here; again exploded from his quarters, poor man; — seems to have thought it a mere fire in his own lodging, and that he was an unfortunate diplomatist. Happily he got notice (*privatissime*, for no officer dare whisper in such cases) that there is an armed party setting out for Silesia, to guard meal that is coming: Valori yokes himself to this armed party, and gets safe over the Hills with it, — then swift, by extra post, to Breslau and to civilised (partially civilised) accommodation, for a little rest after these hustlings and tossings.

Friedrich had lain at Staudentz, in this manner, bickering continually for his forage, and eating the Country, for about ten days: and now, as the latter process is well on, and the season drawing to a close, he determines on a shift northward. Thursday, 30th September next, let there be one other grand forage, the final one in this eaten tract, then northward to fresh grounds. That, it appears, was the design. But, on Wednesday, there came in an Austrian deserter; who informs us that Prince Karl is not now in Königsgrätz, but in motion up the Elbe; already some fifty miles up; past Jaromirz; his rear at Königshof, his van at Arnau, — on a level with burnt Trautenau, and farther north than we ourselves are. This is important news. "Intending to block us out from Schatzlar? Hmh!" Single scouts, or small parties, cannot live in this Kingdom Wood, swarming with Pandours: Friedrich sends out a Colonel Katzler, with 500 light horse, to investigate a little. Katzler pushes forward, on such lane or forest road-track as there is, towards Königshof; beats back small hussar parties; — comes, in about an hour's space, not upon hussars merely, but upon dense masses of heavy horse winding through the forest lanes; and, with that imperfect intelligence, is obliged to return. The deserter spake truth, apparently; and that is all we can know. Forage scheme is given up; the order is, "Baggage packed, and *march* tomorrow morning at ten." Long before ten, there had great things befallen on the morrow! — Try to understand this Note a little:

"The Camp of Staudentz, — which two persons (the "King, and General Stille, a more careful reporter, who "also was an eyewitness) have done their best to describe, — "will, after all efforts, and an Ordnance Map to help, remain "considerably unintelligible to the reader; as is too usual in "such cases. A block of high-lying ground; Friedrich's "Camp on it, perhaps two miles long, looks to the south; "small Village of Staudentz in front; hollow beyond that, "and second small Village, Deutsch Prausnitz, hanging on "the opposite slope, with shaggy heights beyond, and the "Kingdom Forest there beginning; on the left, defiles, "brooks, and strait country, leading towards the small town "of Eypel: that is our left and front aspect, a hollow well "isolating us on those sides. Hollow continues all along the "front; hollow definite on our side of it, and forming a "tolerable defence: — though again, I perceive, to right-"ward at no great distance, there rise High Grounds which "considerably overhang us." A thing to be marked! "These "we could not occupy, for want of men; but only maintain "vedettes upon them. Over these Heights, a mile or two "westward of this hollow of ours, runs the big winding hollow "called Georgengrund (*George's bottom*), which winds up and "down in that Kingdom Forest, and offers a road from "Königshof to Trautenau, among other courses it takes.

"From the crown of those Heights on our right flank here, "looking to the west, you might discern (perhaps three "miles off, from one of the sheltering nooks in the hither "side of that Georgengrund), rising faintly visible over "knolls and dingles, the smoke of a little Forest Village. "That Village is Sohr; notable ever since, beyond others, "in the Kingdom Wood. Sohr, like the other Villages, has "its lane-roads; its road to Trautenau, to Königshof, no "doubt; but much nearer you, on our eastern slope of the "Heights, and far hitherward of Sohr, which is on the "western, goes the great road" (what is now the great road) "from Königshof to Trautenau, well visible from Friedrich's "Camp, though still at some distance from it. Could these "Heights between us and Sohr, which lie beyond the great "road, be occupied, we were well secured; isolated on the "right too, as on the other sides, from Kingdom Forest and "its ambushes. 'Should have been done,' admits Friedrich; "'but then, as it is, there are not troops enough:' with "18,000 men you cannot do everything!"

Here, however, is the important point. In Sohr, this night, 29th September, in a most private manner, the Austrians, 30,000 of them and more, have come gliding through the woods, without even their pipe lit, and with thick veil of hussars ahead! Outposts of theirs lie squatted in the bushes behind Deutsch Prausnitz, hardly 500 yards from Friedrich's Camp. And eastward, leftward of him, in the defiles about Eypel, lie Nadasti and Ruffian Trenck, with ten or twelve thousand, who are to take him in rear. His "Camp of Staudentz" will be at a fine pass tomorrow morning. The Austrian Gentlemen had found, last week, a certain bare Height in the Forest (Height still known), from which they could use their astronomer tubes, day after day;* and now they are about attempting something!

Thursday morning, very early, 30th September 1745, Friedrich was in his tent, busy with generals and march-routes, — when a rapid orderly comes in, from that Vedette, or strong Piquet, on the Heights to

* Orlich, ii. 225.

our right: "Austrians visibly moving, in quantity, near by!" and before he has done answering, the officer himself arrives: "Regular Cavalry in great force; long dust-cloud in Kingdom Forest, in the gray dawn; and, so far as we can judge, it is their Army coming on." Here is news for a poor man, in the raw of a September morning, by way of breakfast to him! "To arms!" is, of course, Friedrich's instant order; and he himself gallops to the Piquet on the Heights, glass in hand. "Austrian Army sure enough, thirty to thirty-five thousand of them, we only eighteen.* Coming to take us on the right flank here; to attack our Camp by surprise: will crush us northward through the defiles, and trample us down in detail? Hmh! To run for it, will never do. We must fight for it, and even attack *them*, as our way is, though on such terms. Quick, a plan!" The head of Friedrich is a bank you cannot easily break by coming on it for plans: such a creature for impromptu plans, and unexpected dashes swift as the panther's, I have hardly known, — especially when you squeeze him into a corner, and fancy he is over with it! Friedrich gallops down, with his plan clear enough; and already the Austrians, horse and foot, are deploying upon those Heights he has quitted; Fifty Squadrons of Horse for left wing to them, and a battery of Twenty-eight big Guns is establishing itself where Friedrich's Piquet lately stood.

Friedrich's right flank has to become his front, and face those formidable Austrian Heights and Batteries; and this with more than Prussian velocity, and under

* *Œuvres de Frédéric,* III. 139.

the play of those twenty-eight big guns, throwing case-shot (*grénades royales*) and so forth, all the while. To Valori, when he heard of the thing, it is inconceivable how mortal troops could accomplish such a movement; Friedrich himself praises it, as a thing honourably well done. Took about half an hour; case-shot raining all the while; soldier honourably never-minding: no flurry, though a speed like that of spinning tops. And here we at length are, Staudentz now to rear of us, behind our centre a good space; Burgersdorf in front of us to right, our left reaching to Prausnitz: Austrian lines, three deep of them, on the opposite Height; we one line only, which matches them in length.

They, that left wing of horse, should have thundered down on us, attacking us, not waiting our attack, thinks Friedrich; but they have not done it. They stand on their height there, will perhaps fire carbines, as their wont is. "You, Buddenbrock, go into them with your Cuirassiers!" Buddenbrock and the Cuirassiers, though it is uphill, go into them at a furious rate; meet no countercharge, mere sputter of carbines; — tumble them to mad wreck, back upon their second line, back upon their third: absurdly crowded there on their narrow height, no room to manœuvre; so that they plunge, fifty squadrons of them, wholly into the Georgengrund rearward, into the Kingdom Wood, and never come on again at all. Buddenbrock has done his job right well.

Seeing which, our Infantry of the right wing, which stood next to Buddenbrock, made impetuous charge uphill, emulous to capture that Battery of Twenty-eight; but found it, for some time, a terrible attempt. These Heights are not to be called "hills," still less "mountains" (as in some careless Books); but it is a stiff climb at double-quick, with twenty-eight big guns playing in the face of you. Storms of case-shot shear away this Infantry, are quenching its noble fury in despair; Infantry visibly recoiling, when our sole Three Regiments of Reserve hurry up to support. Round these all rallies; rushes desperately on, and takes the Battery, — of course, sending the Austrian left wing rapidly adrift, on loss of the same.

This, I consider, is the crisis of the Fight; the back of the Austrian enterprise is already broken, by this sad winging of it on the left. But it resists still; comes down again, — the *reserve* of their left wing seen rapidly making for Burgersdorf, intending an attack there; which we oppose with vigour, setting Burgersdorf on fire for temporary screen; and drive the Austrian reserve rapidly to rearward again. But there is rally after rally of them. They rank again on every new height, and dispute there; loth to be driven into Kingdom Wood, after such a flourish of arms. One height, "bushy steep height," the light-limbed valiant Prince, little Ferdinand of Brunswick, had the charge of attacking; and he did it with his usual impetus and irresistibility: — and, strangely enough, the defender of it chanced to be that Brother of his, Prince Ludwig, with whom he had the little Interview lately. Prince Ludwig got a wound, as well as lost his height. The third Brother, poor Prince Albrecht, who is also here, as volunteer apprentice, on the Prussian side, gets killed. There will never be another Interview, for all three, between the Camps! Strange times for those poor Princes, who have to seek soldiering for their existence.

Meanwhile the Cavalry of Buddenbrock, that is to

say of the right wing, having now no work in that quarter, is despatched to reinforce the left wing, which has stood hitherto apart on its own ground; not attacked or attacking, — a left wing *refused*, as the soldiers style it. Reinforced by Buddenbrock, this left wing of horse does now also storm forward; — "near the Village of Prausnitz" (Prausnitz a little way to rear of it), thereabouts, is the scene of its feat. Feat done in such fashion that the Austrians opposite will not stand the charge at all; but gurgle about in a chaotic manner; then gallop fairly into Kingdom Wood, without stroke struck; and disappear, as their fellows had done. Whereupon the Prussian horse breaks in upon the adjoining Infantry of that flank (Austrian right flank, left bare in this manner); champs it also into chaotic whirlpools; cuts away an outskirt of near 2,000 prisoners, and sets the rest running. This seems to have been pretty much the *coup-de-grace* of the Fight; and to have brought the Austrian dispute to finis. From the first, they had rallied on the heights; had struggled and disputed. Two general rallies they made, and various partial, but none had any success. They were driven on, bayonet in back, as the phrase is: with this sad slap on their right, added to that old one on their left, what can they now do but ebb rapidly; pour in cataracts into Kingdom Wood, and disappear there.*

Prince Karl's scheme was good, says Friedrich, but it was ill executed. He never should have let us form; his first grand fault was that he waited to be attacked, instead of attacking. Parts of his scheme were never

* *Œuvres de Frédéric*, III. 135-143; Stille, pp. 144-163; Orlich, II. 237-245; *Feldzüge*, I. 857-863-874.

executed at all. Duke d'Ahremberg, for instance, it is said, had so dim a notion of the ground, that he drew up some miles off, with his *back* to the Prussians. Such is the rumour, — perhaps only a rumour, in mockery of the hebetated old gentleman fallen unlucky? On the other hand, that Nadasti made a failure which proved important, is indubitable. Nadasti, with some thousands of Tolpatchery, was at Liebenthal, four miles to south-east of the action; Ruffian Trenck lay behind Eypel, perhaps as far to east of it: Trenck and Nadasti were to rendezvous, to unite, and attack the Prussian Camp on its rear, — "Camp," so ran the order, for it was understood the Prussians would all be there, we others attacking it in front and both flanks; — which turned out otherwise, not for Nadasti alone!

Nadasti came to his rendezvous in time; Ruffian Trenck did not: Nadasti grew tired of waiting for Trenck, and attacked the Camp by himself: — Camp, but not any men; Camp being now empty, and the men all fighting, ranked at right angles to it, furlongs and miles away. Nadasti made a rare hand of the Camp; plundered everything, took all the King's Camp-furniture, ready money, favourite dog Biche, — likewise poor Eichel his Secretary, who, however, tore the papers first. Tolpatchery exultingly gutted the Camp; and at last set fire to it, — burnt even some eight or ten poor Prussian sick, and also "some women whom "they caught. We found the limbs of these poor men "and women lying about," reports old General Lehwald; who knew about it. A doggery well worthy of the gallows, think Lehwald and I. "Couldn't help it; ferocity of wild men," says Nadasti. "Well; but why not attack, then, with your ferocity?" Confused Court-martial put these questions, at Vienna subsequently; and Ruffian Tronck, some say, got injustice, Nadasti shuffling things upon him; for which one cares almost nothing. Lehwald, lying at Trautenau, had heard the firing at sunrise; and instantly marched to help: he only arrived to give Nadasti a slash or two, and was too late for the Fight. One Schlichtling, on guard with a weak party, saved what was in the right wing of the Camp, — small thanks to him, the Main Fight being so near: Friedrich's opinion is, an Officer, in Schlichtling's place, ought to have done more, and not have been so helpless.

This was the Battle of Sohr; so called because the Austrians had begun there, and the Prussians ended there. The Prussian pursuit drew bridle at that Village; unsafe to prosecute Austrians farther, now in the deeps of Kingdom Forest. The Battle has lasted five hours. It must be now getting towards noon; and time for breakfast, — if indeed any were to be had; but that is next to impossible, Nadasti having been so busy. Not without extreme difficulty, is a manchet of bread, with or without a drop of wine, procured for the King's Majesty this day. Many a tired hero will have nothing but tobacco, with spring-water, to fall back upon. Never mind! says the King, says everybody. After all, it is a cheap price to pay for missing an attack from Pandours in the rear, while such crisis went on ahead.

Lying *Cousin* Tronck, of the Lifeguard, who is now in Glatz, gives vivid eye-witness particulars of these things, time of the morning and so on; says expressly he was there, and what he did there,* — though in Glatz under lock and key, three good months before. "How could I help mistakes," said he afterwards, when people objected to this and that in his blusterous mendacity of a Book: "I had nothing but my poor agitated memory to trust to!" A man's memory, when it gets the length of remembering that he was in the Battle of Sohr while bodily absent, ought it not to — in fact, to strike work; to *still* its agitations altogether, and call halt? Treuck, some months after, got clambered out of Glatz, by sewers, or I forget how; and leaped, or dropped, from some parapet into the River Neisse, — sinking to the loins in tough mud, so that he could not stir farther. "Fouqué let me stand there, half a day, before he would pick me out again." Rigorous Fouqué, human mercy forbidding, could not let him stand there in permanence, — as we, better circumstanced, may with advantage try to do, in time coming!

Friedrich lay at Sohr five days; partly for the honour of the thing, partly to eat out the Country to perfection. Prince Karl, from Königshof, soon fell back to Königsgrätz; and lay motionless there, nothing but his Tolpatcheries astir. Sohr Country all eaten, Friedrich, in the due Divisions, marched northward. Through Trautenau, Schatzlar, his own Division, which was the main one; — and, fencing off the Tolpatches successfully with trouble, brings all his men into Silesia again. A good job of work behind them, surely! Cantons them to right and left of Landshut, about Rohn-

* Frédéric Baron de Trenck, *Mémoires, traduits par lui-même* (Strasburg and Paris, 1789), i. 74-78, 79.

stock and Hohenfriedberg, hamlets known so well; and leaving the Young Dessauer to command, drives for Berlin (30th October), — rapidly, as his wont is. Prince Karl has split up his force at Königsgrätz; means, one cannot doubt, to go into winter-quarters. If he think of invading, across that eaten Country and those bad Mountains, — well, our troops can all be got together in six hours' time.

At Trautenau, a week after Sohr, Friedrich had at last received the English ratification of that Convention of Hanover, signed 26th August, almost a month ago; not ratified till September 22d. About which there had latterly been some anxiety, lest his Britannic Majesty himself might have broken off from it. With Austria, with Saxony, Britannic Majesty has been entirely unsuccessful: — "May not Sohr, perhaps, be a fresh persuasive?" hopes Friedrich; — but as to Britannic Majesty's breaking off, his thoughts are far from that, if we knew! Poor Majesty: not long since, Supreme Jove of Germany; and now — is like to be swallowed in ragamuffin street-riots; not a thunderbolt within clutch of him (thunderbolts all sticking in the mud of the Netherlands, far off), and not a constable's staff of the least efficacy! Consider these dates in combination. Battle of Sohr was on *Thursday, September 30th:*

"*Sunday* preceding, *September 26th*, was such a Lord's "Day in the City of Edinburgh, as had not been seen there, "— not since Jenny Geddes's stool went flying at the Bishop's "head, a hundred years before. Big alarm-bell bursting "out in the middle of divine service; emptying all the "Churches ('Highland rebels just at hand!') — into General "Meeting of the Inhabitants, into Chaos come again, for the "next forty hours. Till, in the gaunt midnight, Tuesday, "2 a. m., Lochiel with about 1,000 Camerons, waiting slight "opportunity, crushed in through the Netherbow Port; and" — And, about noon of that day, a poor friend of ours, loitering expectant in the road that leads by St. Anthony's Well, saw making entry into paternal Holyrood, — the Young Pretender, in person, who is just being proclaimed Prince of Wales, up in the High-Street yonder! "A tall slender young "man, about five feet ten inches high; of a ruddy complexion, "high-nosed, large rolling brown eyes; long-visaged, red-"haired, but at that time wore a pale periwig. He was in a "Highland habit" (coat); "over the shoulder a blue sash "wrought with gold; red velvet breeches; a green velvet "bonnet, with white cockade on it and a gold lace. His "speech seemed very like that of an Irishman; very sly" (how did you know, my poor friend?); — "spoke often to "O'Sullivan" (thought to be a person of some counsel; had been Tutor to Maillebois's Boys, had even tried some irregular fighting under Maillebois) — "to O'Sullivan and"† * * And on Saturday, in short, came *Prestonpans.* Enough of such a Supreme Jove; good for us here as a time-table chiefly, or marker of dates!

Sunday, 3d October, King's Adjutant, Captain Möllendorf, a young Officer deservedly in favour, arrives at Berlin with the joyful tidings of this Sohr business ("Prausnitz" we then called it): to the joy of all Prussians, especially of a Queen Mother, for whom there is a Letter in pencil. After brief congratulation, Möllendorf rushes on; having next to give the Old Dessauer notice of it in his Camp at Dieskau, in the Halle neighbourhood. Möllendorf appears in Halle suddenly next morning, Monday, about ten o'clock, sixteen postillions trumpeting, and at their swiftest trot, in front of him; — shooting like a melodious morning-star, across the rusty old city, in this manner, — to Dieskau Camp, where he gives the Old Dessauer his good news. Excellent Victory indeed; sharp

* Henderson, *Highland Rebellion*, p. 14.

striking, swift self-help on our part. Halle and the Camp have enough to think of, for this day and the next. Whither Möllendorf went next, we will not ask: perhaps to Brunswick and other consanguineous places? — Certain it is,

"On Wednesday the 6th, about two in the afternoon, the "Old Dessauer has his whole Army drawn out there, with "green sprigs in their hats, at Dieskau, close upon the Saxon "Frontier: and, after swashing and manœuvering about in "the highest military style of art, ranks them all in line, "or two suitable lines, 30,000 of them; and then, with "clangorous outburst of trumpet, kettledrum and all manner "of field-music, fires off his united artillery a first time; "almost shaking the very hills by such a thunderous peal, in "the still afternoon. And mark, close fitted into the artillery "peal, commences a rolling fire, like a peal spread out in "threads, sparkling strangely to eye and ear; from right to "left, long spears of fire and sharp strokes of sound, darting "aloft, successive-simultaneous, winding for the space of "miles, then back by the rear line, and home to the starting "point: very grand indeed. Again, and also again, the artillery "peal, and rolling small-arms fitted into it, is repeated; a "second and a third time, kettledrums and trumpets doing "what they can. That was the Old Dessauer's bonfiring (what "is called *feu-de-joie*), for the Victory of Sohr; audible "almost at Leipzig, if the wind were westerly. Overpower-"ing to the human mind; at least, to the old Newspaper "reporter of that day. But what was strangest in the busi-"ness," continues he (*das Curieuseste dabey*), "was that the "Saxon Uhlans, lying about in the villages across the Border, "were out in the fields, watching the sight, hardly 300 yards "off, from beginning to end; and little dreamed that his "High-Princely Serenity," blue of face and dreadful in war, "was quite close to them, on the Height called Bornhöck; "condescending to 'take all this into High-Serene Eye-shine "'there; and, by having a white flag waved, deigning to "'give signal for the discharges of the artillery.'"*

* *Helden-Geschichte*, I. 1124.

By this the reader may know that the Old Dessauer is alive, ready for action if called on; and Brühl ought to comprehend better how riskish his game with edgetools is. Brühl is not now in an unprepared state: — here are Uhlans at one's elbow looking on. Rutowski's Uhlans; who lies encamped, not far off, in good force, posted among morasses; strongly entrenched, and with schemes in his head, and in Brühl's, of an aggressive, thrice-secret, and very surprising nature! I remark only that, in Heidelberg Country, victorious old Traun is putting his people into winter-quarters; himself about to vanish from this History,* — and has detached General Grüne with 10,000 men; who left Heidelberg, October 9th, on a mysterious errand, heeded by nobody; and will turn up in the next Chapter.

* Went to *Siebenbürgen* (Transylvania) as Governor; died there, February 1748, age seventy-one (*Maria Theresiens Leben*, p. 86 n.).

CHAPTER XIII.

SAXONY AND AUSTRIA MAKE A SURPRISING LAST ATTEMPT.

After this strenuous and victorious Campaign, which has astonished all public men, especially all Pragmatic Gazetteers, and with which all Europe is disharmoniously ringing, Friedrich is hopeful there will be Peace, through England; — cannot doubt, at least, but the Austrians have had enough for one year; and looks forward to certain months, if not of rest, yet of another kind of activity. Negotiation, Peace through England, if possible; that is the high prize: and in the other case, or in any case, readiness for next Campaign; — which with the treasury exhausted, and no honourable subsidy from France, is a difficult problem.

That was Friedrich's, and everybody's, program of affairs for the months coming: but in that Friedrich and everybody found themselves greatly mistaken. Brühl and the Austrians had decided otherwise. "Open mousetrap," at Striegau; claws of the sleeping cat, at Sohr: these were sad experiences; ill to bear, with the Sea-Powers grumbling on you, and the world sniffing its pity on you; — but are not conclusive, are only provoking and even maddening, to the sanguine mind. Two sad failures; but let us try another time. "A tricky man; cunning enough, your King of Prussia!" thinks Brühl, with a fellness of humour against Friedrich which is little conceivable to us now: "Cunning enough. But it is possible cunning may be surpassed by deeper cunning!" — and decides, Bartenstein and an indignant Empress-Queen assenting eagerly, That there shall, in the profoundest secrecy till it break out, be a third, and much fiercer trial, this Winter yet. The Brühl-Bartenstein plan (owing mainly to the Russian Bugbear which hung over it, protective, but with whims of its own) underwent changes, successive redactions or editions; which the reader would grudge to hear explained to him.* Of the final or acted edition, some loose notion, sufficient for our purpose, may be collected from the following fractions of Notes:

November 17th (Interior of Germany). * * "Feldmarschall-"Lieutenant von Grüne, a General of mark, detached by "Traun not long since, from the Rhine Country, with a force "of 10,000 men, why is he marching about: first to Baireuth "Country, 'at Hof, November 9th,' as if for Bohemia; then "north, to Gera ('lies at Gera till the 17th'), as if for Saxony "Proper? Prince Karl, you would certainly say, has gone "into winter-quarters; about Königsgrätz, and farther on? "Gone or going, sure enough, is Prince Karl, into the con-"venient Bohemian districts, — uncertain which particular "districts; at least the Young Dessauer, watching him from "the Silesian side, is uncertain which. Better be vigilant, "Prince Leopold! — Grüne, lying at Gera yonder, is not in-"tending for Prince Karl, then? No, not thither. Then "perhaps towards Saxony, to reinforce the Saxons? Or "somewhither to find fat winter-quarters: who knows? In-"deed who cares particularly, for such inconsiderable Grüne "and his 10,000! —

"The Saxons quitted their inexpugnable Camp towards "Halle, some time ago; went into cantonments farther in-

* Account of them in Orlich, ii. 273-278 (from various *Rutowski* Papers; and from the contemporary satirical Pamphlet, "*Mondscheinwürfe*, Mirror-"castings of Moonshine, by *Zebedäus* Cuckoo, beaten Captain of a beaten "Army.")

"land; — the Old Dessauer (middle of October) having done "the like, and gone home: his force lies rather scattered, for "convenience of food and forage. From the Silesian side, "again, Prince Leopold, whose head-quarters are about "Striegau, intimates, That he cannot yet say, with certainty, "what districts Prince Karl will occupy for winter-quarters "in Bohemia. Prince Karl is vaguely roving about; de-"taching Pandours to the Silesian Mountains, as if for check-"ing our victorious Nassau there; — always rather creeping "northward; skirting Western Silesia with his main force; "30,000 or better, with Lobkowitz and Nadasti ahead. Mean-"ing what? Be vigilant, my young friend.

"The private fact is, Prince Karl does not mean to go into "winter-quarters at all. In private fact, Prince Karl is one "of Three mysterious Elements or Currents, sent on a far "errand: Grüne is another: Rutowski's Saxon Camp (now "become Cantonment) is a third. Three Currents instinct "with fire and destruction, but as yet quite opaque; which "have been launched, — whitherward thinks the reader? On "Berlin itself, and the Mark of Brandenburg; there to col-"lide, and ignite in a marvellous manner. There is their "meeting-point: there shall they, on a sudden, smite one "another into flame; and the destruction blaze, fiery enough, "round Friedrich and his own Brandenburg homesteads "there! —

"It is a grand scheme; scheme at least on a grand scale. "For the *legs* of it, Grüne's march and Prince Karl's, are "about 500 miles long! Plan due chiefly, they say, to the "yellow rage of Brühl; aided by the contrivance of Rutowski, "and the counsel of Austrian military men. For there is "much consulting about it, and redacting of it; Polish Majesty "himself very busy. To Brühl's yellow rage it is highly "solacing and hopeful. 'Rutowski, lying close in his Canton-"ments, and then suddenly springing out, will overwhelm the "Old Dessauer, who lies wide; — can do it, surely; and Grüne "is there to help if necessary. Dessauer blown to pieces, "Grüne, with Rutowski combined, push in upon Branden-"burg, — Grüne himself upon Berlin, — from the west and "south, nobody expecting him. Prince Karl, not taking into "winter-quarters in Bohemia, as they idly think; but falling "down the Valley of the Bober, or Bober and Queiss, into the

"Lausitz (to Görlitz, Guben, where we have Magazines for "him), comes upon it from the south-east, — nobody expect-"ing any of them. Three simultaneous Armies hurled on "the head of your Friedrich; combustible deluges flowing "towards him, as from the ends of Germany; so opaque, "silent, yet of fire wholly: 'will not that surprise him!' "thinks Brühl. These are the schemes of the little man."

Brühl, having constituted himself rival to Friedrich, and fallen into pale or yellow rage by the course things took, this Plan is naturally his chief joy, or crown of joys; a bubbling well of solace to him in his parched condition. He should, obviously, have kept it secret; thrice-secret, the little fool; — but a poor parched man is not always master of his private bubbling wells in that kind! Wolfstierna is Swedish Envoy at Dresden; Rudenskjöld, Swedish Envoy at Berlin, has run over to see him in the dim November days. Swedes, since Ulrique's marriage, are friendly to Prussia. Brühl has these two men to dinner; talks with them, over his wine, about Friedrich's insulting usage of him, among other topics. "Insulting; how, your Excellency?" asks Rudenskjöld, privately a friend of Friedrich. Brühl explains, with voice quivering, those cuts in the Friedrich manifesto of August last, and other griefs suffered; the two Swedes soothing him with what oil they have ready. "No matter!" hints Brühl; and proceeds from hint to hint, till the two Swedes are fully aware of the grand scheme: Grüne, Prince Karl; and how Destruction, with legs 500 miles long, is steadily advancing to assuage one with just revenge. "Right, your Excellency!" — only that Rudenskjöld proceeds to Berlin; and there straightway ("8th November") punctually makes Friedrich also aware.* Foolish Brühl: a man that has a secret should not only hide it, but hide that he has it to hide.

Friedrich goes out to meet his Three-legged Monster; cuts one Leg of it in two (Fight of Hennersdorf, 23d November 1745).

Friedrich, having heard the secret, gazes into it with horror and astonishment: "What a time I have! "This is not living; this is being killed a thousand "times a day!"** — with horror and astonishment; but also with what most luminous flash of eyesight is in him; compares it with Prince Karl's enigmatic motions, Grüne's open ones, and the other phenomena; — perceives that it is an indisputable fact, and a thrice formidable; requiring to be instantly dealt with by the party interested! Whereupon, after hearty thanks to Rudenskjöld, there occur these rapidly successive phases of activity, which we study to take up in a curt form.

First (probably 9th or 10th November), there is Council held with Minister Podewils and the Old Dessauer; Council from which comes little benefit, or none. Podewils and Old Leopold stare incredulous; cannot be made to believe such a thing. "Impossible any Saxon minister or man would voluntarily bring the theatre of war into his own Country, in this manner!" thinks the Old Dessauer, and persists to think, — on

* Stenzel, IV. 262; Ranke, III. 317-323; Friedrich's own narrative of it, *Œuvres*, III 148.

** Ranke (III. 321 n.): *to whom said, we are not told.*

what obstinate ground Friedrich never knew. To which Podewils, "who has properties in the Lausitz, "and would so fain think them safe," obstinately though more covertly adheres. "Impossible!" urge both these Councillors; and Friedrich cannot even make them believe it. Believe it; and, alas, believing it is not the whole problem!

Happily Friedrich has the privilege of ordering, with or without their belief. "You, Podewils, announce the matter to foreign Courts. You, Serene Highness of Anhalt, at your swiftest, collect yonder, and encamp again. Your eye well on Grüne and Rutowski; and the instant I give you signal —! I am for Silesia, to look after Prince Karl, the other long leg of this Business." Old Leopold, according to Friedrich's account, is visibly glad of such opportunity to fight again before he die: and yet, for no reason except some senile jealousy, is not content with these arrangements; perversely objects to this and that. At length the King says, — think of this hard word, and of the eyes that accompany it! — "When your High-"ness gets Armies of your own, you will order them "according to your mind; at present, it must be ac-"cording to mine." On, then; and not a moment lost: for of all things we must be swift!

Old Leopold goes accordingly. Friedrich himself goes in a week hence. Orders, correspondences from Podewils and the rest, are flying right and left; — to Young Leopold in Silesia, first of all. Young Leopold draws out his forces towards the Silesian-Lausitz border, where Prince Karl's intentions are now becoming visible. And, — here is the *second* phase notable, —

"On Monday 15th,* at 7 A.M.," Friedrich rushes off, by Crossen, full speed for Liegnitz; "with Rothen-"burg, with the Prince of Prussia, and Ferdinand of "Brunswick accompanying." With what thoughts, — though, in his face, you can read nothing; all Berlin being already in such tremor! Friedrich is in Liegnitz next day; and after needful preliminaries there, does, on the Thursday following, "at Nieder-Adelsdorf" not far off, take actual command of Prince Leopold's Army, which had lain encamped for some days, waiting him. And now with such force in hand, — 35,000, soldiers every man of them, and freshened by a month's rest, — one will endeavour to do some good upon Prince Karl. Probably sooner than Prince Karl supposes. For there is great velocity in this young King; a panther-like suddenness of spring in him: cunning, too, as any Felis of them; and with claws like the Felis Leo on occasion. Here follows the brief Campaign that ensued, which I strive greatly to abridge.

Prince Karl's intentions towards Frankfurt-on-Oder Country, through the Lausitz, are now becoming practically manifest. There is a Magazine for him at Guben, within thirty miles of Frankfurt; arrangements getting ready all the way. A winter march of 150 miles; — but what, say the spies, is to hinder it? Prince Karl dreams not that Friedrich is on the ground, or that anybody is aware. Which notion Friedrich finds that it will be extremely suitable to maintain in Prince Karl. Friedrich is now at Adelsdorf, some thirty miles eastward of the Lausitz Border, perhaps

* "16th," *Feldzüge*, i. 402 (see Rödenbeck, i. 123.).

forty or more from the route Prince Karl will follow through that Province.

"It is a high-lying irregularly hilly Country; hilly, not "mountainous. Various streams rise out of it that have a "long course, — among others, the Spree, which washes "Berlin; — especially three Valleys cross it, three Rivers "with their Valleys: Bober, Queiss, Neisse (the *third* Neisse "we have come upon); all running northward, pretty much "parallel, though all are branches of the Oder. This is "Neisse *Third*, we say; not the Neisse of Neisse City, which "we used to know at the north base of the Giant Mountains, "nor the Roaring Neisse, which we have seen at Hohenfried-"berg; but a third" — (and the *fourth* and last, "Black Neisse," thank Heaven, is an upper branch of this, and we have, and shall have, nothing to do with it!) — "third Neisse, "which we may call the Lausitz Neisse. On which, near "the head of it, there is a fine old spinning, linen-weaving "Town called Zittau, — where, to make it memorable, one "Tourist has read, on the Townhouse, an Inscription worth "repeating: '*Bene facere et male audire regium est*, To do "'good and have evil said of you, is a kingly thing.' Other "Towns, as Görlitz, and seventy miles farther, the above-"said Guben, lie on this same Neisse, — shall we add that "Herrnhuth stands near the head of it? The wondrous "Town of Herrnhuth (*Lord's-Keeping*), founded by Count "Zinzendorf, twenty years before those dates;* where are a "kind of German Methodist-Quakers to this day, who have "become very celebrated in the interim. An opulent enough, "most silent, strictly regular, strange little Town. The "women are in uniform; wives, maids, widows, each their "form of dress. Missionaries, speaking flabby English, who "have been in the West Indies or are going thither, seem to "abound in the place; male population otherwise, I should "think, must be mainly doing trade elsewhere; nothing but "prayers, preachings, charitable boarding-schooling and the "like, appeared to be going on. Herrnhuth is 'a Sabbath "'Petrified; Calvinistic Sabbath done into Stone,' as one of "my companions called it." **

* "In 1722, the first tree felled" (*Lives of Zinzendorf*).

** Tourist's Note (Autumn 1858).

Herrnhuth, of which all Englishmen have heard, stands near the head of this our third Neisse; as does Zittau, a few miles higher up. I can do nothing more to give it mark for them. Bober Valley, then Queiss Valley, which run parallel though they join at last, and become Bober wholly before getting into the Oder, — these two Valleys and Rivers lie in Friedrich's own Territory; and are between him and the Lausitz, Queiss River being the boundary of Silesia and the Lausitz here. It is down the Neisse that Prince Karl means to march. There are Saxons already gathering about Zittau; and down as far as Guben, they are making Magazines and arrangements, — for it is all their own Country in those years, though most of it is Prussia's now. Prince Karl's march will go parallel to the Bober and the Queiss; separated from the Queiss in this part by an undulating Hill-tract of twenty miles or more.

Friedrich has had somewhat to settle for the Southern Frontier of Silesia withal, which new doggeries of Pandours are invading, — to lie ready for Prince Karl on his return thither, whose grand meaning all this while (as Friedrich well knows), is "Silesia in the lump" again, had he once cut us off from Brandenburg and our supplies! General Nassau, far eastward, who is doing exploits in Moravia itself, — him Friedrich has ordered homeward, westward to his own side of the Mountains, to attend these new Pandour gentlemen; Winterfeld he has called home, out of those Southern mountains, as likely to be usefuller here on this Western frontier. Winterfeld arrived in Camp the same day with Friedrich; and is sent forward with a body of 3,000 light troops, to keep watch about the Lausitz Frontier and the River Queiss; "careful not to quit our own side of that stream," — as we mean to hoodwink Prince Karl, if we can!

Friedrich lies strictly within his own borders, for a

day or two; till Prince Karl march, till his own arrangements are complete. Friedrich himself keeps the Bober, Winterfeld the Queiss; "all pass freely out of "the Lausitz; none are allowed to cross into it: thereby "we hear notice of Prince Karl, he none of us." Perfectly quiescent, we, poor creatures, and aware of nothing! Thus, too, Friedrich, — in spite of his warlike Manifesto, which the Saxons are on the eve of answering with a formal Declaration of War, — affects great rigour in considering the Saxons as not yet at war with him: respects their frontier, Winterfeld even punishes hussars "for trespassing on Lausitz ground." Friedrich also affects to have roads repaired, which he by no means intends to travel: — the whole with a view of lulling Prince Karl; of keeping the mousetrap open, as he had done in the Striegau case. It succeeded again, quite as conspicuously, and at less expense.

Prince Karl, — whose Tolpatch doggery Winterfeld will not allow to pass the Queiss, and to whom no traveller or tidings can come from beyond that River, — discerns only, on the farther shore of it, Winterfeld with his 3,000 light troops. Behind these, he discerns either nothing, or nothing immediately momentous; but contentedly supposes that this, the superficies of things, is all the solid-content they have. Prince Karl gets under way, therefore, nothing doubting; with his Saxons as vanguard. Down the Neisse Valley, on the right or Queissward side of it: Saturday, 20th November, is his first march in Lusatian territory. He lies that night spread out in three Villages, Schönberg, Schönbrunn, Kieslingswalde;* some ten miles long; parallel to the Neisse River, and about four miles from it, east or Queissward of it. Karl himself is rear, at Schönberg; fierce Lobkowitz is centre; the Saxons are vanguard, 6,000 in all, posted in Villages, which again are some ten or twelve miles ahead of Prince Karl's forces; the Queiss on their right hand, and the Naumburg Bridge of Queiss, where Winterfeld now is, about fifteen miles to east. Their Uhlans circulate through the intervening space (were much patrolling needed, in such quiet circumstances), and maintain the due communication. There lies Prince Karl, on Saturday night, 20th November 1745; an Army of perhaps 40,000, dangerously straggling out above twenty miles long; and appears to see no difficulty ahead. The Saxons, I think, are to continue where they are; guarding the flank, while the Prince and Lobkowitz push forward, closer by Neisse River. In four marches more, they can be in Brandenburg, with Guben and their Magazines at hand.

Seeing which state of matters, Winterfeld gives Friedrich notice of it; and that he, Winterfeld, thinks the moment is come. "Pontoons to Naumburg, then!" orders Friedrich. Winterfeld, at the proper moment, is to form a Bridge there. One permanent Bridge there already is; and two fords, one above it, one below: with a second Bridge, there will be roadway for four columns, and a swift transit when needful. Sunday 21st, Friedrich quits the Bober, diligently towards Naumburg; marches Sunday, Monday; Tuesday 23d, about eleven A.M., begins to arrive there; Winterfeld and

* *Feldzüge*, i. 407 (Bericht von der Action bey Katholisch-Hennersdorf, &c.).

passages all ready. Forward, then, and let us drive in upon Prince Karl; and either cut him in two, or force him to fight us; he little thinks where or on what terms. Sure enough, in the worst place we can choose for him! Friedrich begins crossing in four columns at one P.M.; crosses continuously for four hours; unopposed, except some skirmishing of Uhlans, while his Cavalry is riding the Fords to right and left; Uhlans were driven back swiftly, so soon as the Cavalry got over. At five in the evening, he has got entirely across, 35,000 horse and foot: Ziethen is chasing the Uhlans, at full speed; who at least will show us the way, — for by this time a mist has begun falling, and the brief daylight is done.

Friedrich himself, without waiting for the rear of his force, and some while before this mist fell (as I judge), is pushing forward, "a miller lad for his guide," across to Hennersdorf, — Katholisch-Hennersdorf, a long straggling Village, eight or ten miles off, and itself two miles long, — where he understands the Saxons are. Miller lad guides us, over height and hollow, with his best skill, at a brisk pace; — through one hollow, where he has known the cattle pasture in summer time; but which proves impassable, and mere quagmire, at this season. No getting through it, you unfortunate miller lad (*garçon de meunier*). Nevertheless, we did find passage through the skirts of it: nay this quagmire proved the luck of us; for the enemy, trusting to it, had no outguard there, never expecting us on that side. So that the vanguard, Ziethen and rapid Hussars, make an excellent thing of it. Ziethen sends us word, That he has got into the body of Hennersdorf, — "found the Saxon Quartermaster quietly paying his men;" — that he, Ziethen, is tolerably master of Hennersdorf, and will amuse the enemy till the other force come up.

Of course Friedrich now pushes on, double speed; detaches other force, horse and foot: which was lucky, says my informant; for the Ziethen Hussars, getting good plunder, had by no means demolished the Saxons; but had left them time to draw up in firm order, a hedge in front, a little west of the Village; — from which post, unassailable by Ziethen, they would have got safe off to the main body, with little but an affront and some loss of goods. The new force, — a rapid Katzler with light horse in the van, cuirassiers and foot rapidly following him, — sweeps past the long Village, "through a thin wood and a defile;" finds the enemy firmly ranked as above said; cavalry their left, infantry on right, flanked by an impenetrable hedge; and at once strikes in. At once, Katzler does, on order given; but is far too weak. Charges, he; but is countercharged, tumbled back; the Saxons, horse and foot, showing excellent fight. At length, more Prussian force coming up, cuirassiers charge them in front, dragoons in flank, hussars in rear; all attacking at once, and with a will; and the poor Saxon Cavalry is entirely cut to shreds.

And now there remains only the Infantry, perhaps about 1,000 men (if one must guess); who form a square; ply vigorously their field-pieces, and their firearms; and cannot be broken by horse-charges. In fact, these Saxons made a fierce resistance; — till, before long, Prussian Infantry came up; and, with counter field-pieces and musketries, blasted gaps in them; upon which the Cavalry got admittance, and reduced the gallant fellows nearly wholly to annihilation either by death or capture. There are 914 Prisoners in this Action, 4 big guns, and I know not how many kettle-drums, standards and the like, — all that were there, I suppose. The number of dead not given.* But, in brief, this Saxon Force is utterly cut to pieces; and only scattered twos and threes of it rush through the dark mist; scattering terror to this hand and that. The Prussians take their post at and round Hennersdorf that night; — bivouacking, though only in sack trowsers, a blanket each man: — "We work hard, my men, and "suffer all things for a day or two, that it may save "much work afterwards," said the King to them; and they cheerfully bivouacked.

This was the Action of Katholisch-Hennersdorf, fought on Tuesday, 23d November 1745; and still celebrated in the Prussian Annals, and reckoned a brilliant passage of war. *Katholisch*-Hennersdorf, some ten miles south-west of Naumburg *on the Queiss* (for there are, to my knowledge, Twenty-five other Villages called Hennersdorf, and Three several Towns of Naumburg, and many Castles and Hamlets so named, in dear Germany of the Nomenclatures): — Katholisch-Hennersdorf is the place, and Tuesday about dusk the time. A sharp brush of fighting; not great in quantity, but laid in at the right moment, in the right place. Like the prick of a needle, duly sharp, into the spinal marrow of a gigantic object; totally ruinous to such object. Never, or rarely, in the Annals of War, was as much good got of so little fighting. You may, with labour and peril, plunge a hundred dirks into your boa-constrictor; hack him with axes, bray him with

* Orlich, ii. 291; *Feldzüge*, i. 400-413.

sledge-hammers; that is not uncommon: but the one true prick in the spinal marrow, and the Artist that can guide you well to that, he and it are the notable and beneficent phenomena.

Prince Karl, cut in two, tumbles home again double-quick.

Next morning, Wednesday, 24th, the Prussians are early astir again; groping, on all manner of roads, to find what Prince Karl is doing, in a world all covered in thick mist. They can find nothing of him, but broken tumbrils, left baggage-wagons, rumour of universal marching hither and marching thither; — evidences of an Army fallen into universal St. Vitus's Dance; distractedly hurrying to and fro, not knowing whitherward for the moment, except that it must be homewards, homewards with velocity.

Prince Karl's farther movements are not worth particularising. Ordering and cross-ordering; march this way; no, back again; such a scene in that mist. Prince Karl is flowing homeward; confusedly deluging and gurgling southward, the best he can. Next afternoon, near Görlitz, and again one other time, he appears drawn up, as if for fighting; but has himself no such thought; flies again, without a shot; leaves Görlitz to capitulate, that afternoon; all places to capitulate or be evacuated. We hear he is for Zittau; Winterfeld with light horse hastens after him, gets sight of him on the Heights at Zittau yonder,* "about two in the morning:" but the Prince has not the least notion to fight. Prince leaves Zittau to capitulate, — quits silently the Heights

* *Œuvres de Frédéric*, III. 157; Orlich, II. 296.

of Zittau at two A. M. (Winterfeld, very lively in the rear of him, cutting off his baggage); — and so tumbles, pellmell, through the Passes of Gabel, home to Bohemia again. Let us save this poor Note from the fire:

"On Saturday night, November 27th, the Prussians, "pursuing Prince Karl, were cantoned in the Herrnhuth "neighbourhood, — my informant's regiment in the Town of "Herrnhuth itself.* Yes, there lay the Prussians over Sun-"day; and might hear some weighty expounder, if they liked. "Considerably theological, many of these poor Prussian "soldiers; carrying a Bible in their knapsack, and devout "Psalms in the heart of them. Two-thirds of every regiment "are *Landeskinder*, native Prussians; each regiment from a "special canton, — generally rather religious men. The "other third are recruits, gathered in the Free Towns of the "Reich, or where they can be got; not distinguished by de-"votion these, we may fancy, only trained to the uttermost by "Spartan drill."

Before the week is done, that "first leg" of the grand Enterprise (the Prince-Karl leg) is such a leg as we see. "Silesia in the lump," — fond dream again, what a dream! Old Dessauer getting signal, where now, too probably, is Saxony itself? — Ranking again at Aussig in Bohemia, Prince Karl, — 5,000 of his men lost, and all impetus and fire gone, — falls gently down the Elbe, to join Rutowski at least; and will reappear within four weeks, out of Saxon Switzerland, still rather in dismal humour.

The Prussian Troops, in four great Divisions, are cantoned in that Lausitz Country, now so quiet; in and about Bautzen, and three other Towns of the

* *Feldzüge*, i. ubi suprà.

neighbourhood; to rest, and be ready for the Old Dessauer, when we hear of him. The "Magazine at Guben in 138 wagons," the Görlitz and other Magazines of Prince Karl in the due number of wagons, supply them with comfortable unexpected provender. Thus they lie cantoned; and have with despatch effectually settled their part of the problem. Question now is, How will it stand with the Old Dessauer, and his part? Or, better still, Would not perhaps the Saxons, in this humiliated state, accept Peace, and finish the matter?

CHAPTER XIV.

BATTLE OF KESSELSDORF.

A "CORRESPONDENCE" of a certain Excellency Villiers, English Minister at Dresden, — Sir Thomas Villiers, Grand-father of the present Earl of Clarendon, — was very famous in those weeks; and is still worth mention, as a trait of Friedrich's procedure in this crisis. Friedrich, not intoxicated with his swift triumph over Prince Karl, but calculating the perils and the chances still ahead, — miserably off for money too, — admits to himself that not revenge or triumph, that Peace is the one thing needful to him. November 29th, Old Leopold is entering Saxony; and in the same hours, Podewils at Berlin, by order of Friedrich, writes to Villiers who is in Dresden, about Peace, about mediating for Peace: "My King ready and desirous, now as at all times, for Peace; the terms of it known; terms not altered, not alterable, no bargaining or higgling needed or allowable. *Convention of Hanover*, let his Polish Majesty accede honestly to that, and all these miseries are ended." *

Villiers starts instantly on this beneficent business; "goes to Court, on it, that very night;" Villiers shows

* "*Correspondance du Roi avec Sir Thomas Villiers;*" commences, on Podewils's part, 28th November; on Friedrich's, 4th December; ends, on Villiers's, 18th December; fourteen Pieces in all, four of them Friedrich's: Given in *Œuvres de Frédéric*, III. 183-216 (see *ib.* 158), and in many other Books.

himself really diligent, reasonable, loyal; doing his very best now and afterwards; but has no success at all. Polish Majesty is obstinate, — I always think, in the way sheep are, when they feel themselves too much put upon; — and is deaf to everybody but Brühl. Brühl answers: "Let his Prussian Majesty retire from our Territory; — what is he doing in the Lausitz just now! Retire from our Territory; *then* we will treat!" Brühl still refuses to be desperate of his bad game; — at any rate, Brühl's rage is yellower than ever. That very evening, while talking to Villiers, he has had preparations going on; — and next morning takes his Master, Polish Majesty August III., with some comfortable minimum of apparatus (cigar-boxes not forgotten), off to Prag, where they can be out of danger till the thing decide itself. Villiers follows to Prag; desists not from his eloquent Letters, and earnest persuasions at Prag; but begins to perceive that the means of persuading Brühl will be a much heavier kind of artillery.

On the whole, negotiations have yet done little. Britannic George, though Purse-holder, what is his success here? As little is the Russian Bugbear persuasive on Friedrich himself. The Czarina of the Russias, a luxurious lady, of far more weight than insight, has just notified to him, with more emphasis than ever, That he shall not attack Saxony; that if he do, she with considerable vigour will attack him! That has always been a formidable puzzle for Friedrich: however, he reflects that the Russians never could draw sword, or be ready with their Army, in less than six months, probably not in twelve; and has answered, translating it into polite official terms: "Fee-faw-fum, your Czarish Majesty! Question is not now of attacking, but of being myself attacked!" — and so is now running his risks with the Czarina.

Still worse was the result he got from Louis XV. Lately, "for form's sake," as he tells us, "and not expecting anything," he had (November 15th) made a new appeal to France: "Ruin menacing your Most Christian Majesty's Ally, in this huge sudden crisis of invasive Austrian-Saxons; and for your Majesty's sake, may I not in some measure say?" To which Louis's Answer is also given. A very sickly, unpleasant Document; testifying to considerable pique against Friedrich; — Ranke says, it was a joint production, all the Ministers gradually contributing each his little pinch of irony to make it spicier, and Louis signing when it was enough; — very considerable pique against Friedrich; and something of the stupid sulkiness as of a fat bad boy, almost glad that the house is on fire, because it will burn his nimble younger brother, whom everybody calls so clever: "Sorry indeed, Sir my Brother, most sorry: — and so you have actually signed that *Hanover Convention* with our worst Enemy? France is far from having done so; France has done, and will do, great things. Our Royal heart grieves much at your situation; but is not alarmed; no, Your Majesty has such invention, vigour and ability, superior to any crisis, our clever younger Brother! And herewith we pray God to have you in his holy keeping." This is the purport of King Louis's Letter; — which Friedrich folds together again, looking up from perusal of it, we may fancy with what a glance of those eyes.*

* Louis's Original, in *Œuvres de Frédéric*, III. 173, 174 (with a much

He is getting instructed, this young King, as to alliances, grand combinations, French and other. His third Note to Villiers intimates, "It being evident that his Polish Majesty will have nothing from us but fighting, we must try to give it him of the best kind we have."* Yes truly; it is the *ultimate* persuasive, that. Here, in condensed form, are the essential details of the course it went, in this instance:

General Grüne, on the road to Berlin, hearing of the rout at Hennersdorf, halted instantly, — hastened back to Saxony, to join Rutowski there, and stand on the defensive. Not now in that Halle Frontier region (Rutowski has quitted that, and all the entrenchments and marshy impregnabilities there); not on that Halle Frontier, but hovering about in the interior, Rutowski and Grüne are in junction; gravitating towards Dresden; — expecting Prince Karl's advent; who ought to emerge from the Saxon Switzerland, in few days, were he sharp; and again enable us to make a formidable figure. Be speedy, Old Dessauer: you must settle the Grüne-Rutowski account before that junction, not after it!

The Old Dessauer has been tolerably successful; and by no means thinks he has been losing time. November 29th, "at three in the morning," he stept over into Saxony with its impregnable camps; drove Rutowski's rearguard, or remnant, out of the quagmires, canals and entrenchments, before daylight; drove it, that same evening, or before dawn of the morrow, out of Leipzig: has seized that Town, — lays heavy contribution on it, nearly 50,000*l.* (such our strait for finance), "and be sure you take only substantial men as sureties!"** — and will, and does after a two-days rest, advance with decent celerity inwards; though "One must first know exactly whither; one must have bread, and preparations and precautions; do all things solidly and in order," thinks the Old

more satirical paraphrase than the above), and Friedrich's Answer adjoined, — after the events had come.

* "Bautzen, 11th December 1745" (*ubi suprà*).

** Orlich, II. 308.

Dessauer. Friedrich well knows the whither; and that Dresden itself is, or may be made, the place for falling in with Rutowski. Friedrich is now himself ready to join, from the Bautzen region; the days and hours precious to him; and spurs the Old Dessauer, with the sharpest remonstrances. "All solidly and in order, your Majesty!" answers the Old Dessauer: solid strong-boned old coach-horse, who has his own modes of trotting, having done many a heavy mile of it in his time; and whose skin, one hopes, is of the due thickness against undue spurring.

Old Dessauer wishes two things: bread to live upon; and a sure Bridge over the Elbe whereby Friedrich may join him. Old Dessauer makes for Torgau, far north, where is both an Elbe Bridge and a Magazine; which he takes; Torgau and pertinents now his. But it is far down the Elbe, far off from Bautzen and Friedrich: "A nearer Bridge and rendezvous, your Highness! Meissen" (where they make the china, only fifty miles from me, and twenty from Dresden), "let that be the Bridge, now that you have got victual. And speedy, for Heaven's sake, speedy!" Friedrich pushes out General Lehwald from Bautzen, with 4,000 men, towards Meissen Bridge; Lehwald does not himself meddle with the Bridge, only fires shot across upon the Saxon party, till the Old Dessauer, on the other bank, come up;—and the Old Dessauer, impatience thinks, will never come. "Three days in Torgau, yes, Your Majesty: I had bread to bake, and the very ovens had to be built." A solid old roadster, with his own modes of trotting; needs thickness of skin.*

At long last, on Sunday, 12th December, about two P.M., the Old Dessauer does appear; or General Gessler, his vanguard, does appear, — Gessler of the sixty-seven standards, —"always about an hour ahead." Gessler has summoned Meissen; has not got it, is haggling with it about terms, when, towards sunset of the short day, Old Dessauer himself arrives. Whereupon the Saxon Commandant quits the Bridge (not much breaking it); and glides off in the dark, clear out of Meissen, towards Dresden, — chased, but successfully defending himself.** "Had he but stood out for two days!"

* Friedrich's Letters to Leopold, in Orlich, II. 431, 435 (6th-10th December 1745).

** See Plan, p. 232.

say the Saxons, — "Prince Karl had then been up, and much might have been different." Well, Friedrich too would have been up, and it had most likely been the same on a larger scale. But the Saxon Commandant did not stand out; he glided off, safe; joined Rutowski and Grüne, who are lying about Wilsdruf, six or seven miles on the hither side of Dresden, and eagerly waiting for Prince Karl. "Bridge and Town of Meissen are your Majesty's," reports the Old Dessauer that night: upon which Friedrich instantly rises, hastening thitherward. Lehwald comes across Meissen Bridge, effects the desired junction; and all Monday the Old Dessauer defiles through Meissen town and territory; continually advances towards Dresden, the Saxons harassing the flanks of him a little, — nay in one defile, being sharp strenuous fellows, they threw his rear into some confusion; cut off certain carts and prisoners, and the life of one brave General, Lieutenant-General Röel, who had charge there. "Spurring one's trot into a gallop! This comes of your fast marching, of your spurring beyond the rules of war!" thinks Old Leopold; and Friedrich, who knows otherwise, is very angry for a moment.

But indeed the crisis is pressing. Prince Karl is across the Metal Mountains, nearing Dresden from the East; Friedrich strikes into march for the same point by Meissen, so soon as the Bridge is his. Old Leopold is advancing thither westward, — steadily hour by hour; Dresden City the fateful goal. There, — in these middle days of December 1745 (Highland Rebellion just whirling back from Derby again, "the London shops shut for one day"), — it is clear there will be a big and bloody game played before we are much older. Very sad indeed: but Count Brühl is not persuadable otherwise. By slumbering and sluggarding, over their money-tills and flesh-pots; trying to take evil for good, and to say, "It will do," when it will not do, respectable Nations come at last to be governed by Brühls; cannot help themselves; — and get their backs broken in consequence. Why not? Would you have a Nation live forever that is content to be governed by Brühls? The gods are wiser! — It is now the 13th; Old Dessauer tramping forward, hour by hour, towards Dresden and some field of Fate.

On Tuesday 14th, by break of day, Old Dessauer gets on

march again; in four columns, in battle order; steady all day, — hard winter weather, ground crisp, and flecked with snow. The Pass at Neustadt, "his cavalry went into it at full gallop;" but found nobody there. That night, he encamps at a place called Röhrsdorf; which may be eight miles west-by-north from Dresden as the crow flies; and ten or more, if you follow the highway round by Wilsdruf on your right. The real direct Highway from Meissen to Dresden is on the other side of the Elbe, and keeps by the River-bank, a fine level road; but on this western side, where Leopold now is, the road is inland, and goes with a bend. Leopold, of course, keeps command of this road; his columns are on both sides of it, River on their left at some miles' distance; and incessantly expect to find Rutowski, drawn out on favourable ground somewhere. The country is of fertile, but very broken character; intersected by many brooks, making obliquely towards the Elbe (obliquely, with a leaning Meissenwards); country always mounting, till here about Röhrsdorf we seem to have almost reached the watershed, and the brooks make for the Elbe, leaning Dresden way. Good posts abound in such broken country, with its villages and brooks, with its thickets, hedges and patches of swamp. But Rutowski has not appeared anywhere, during this Tuesday.

Our four columns, therefore, lie all night, under arms, about Röhrsdorf: and again by morrow's dawn are astir in the old order, crunching far and wide the frozen ground; and advance, charged to the muzzle with potential battle. Slightly upwards always, to the actual watershed of the country; leaving Wilsdruf a little to their right. Wilsdruf is hardly past, when see, from this broad table-land, top of the country: "Yonder is Rutowski, at last; — and this new Wednesday will be a day!" Yonder, sure enough: drawn out three or four miles long; with his right to the Elbe, his left to that intricate Village of Kesselsdorf; bristling with cannon; deep gullet and swampy brook in front of him: the strongest post a man could have chosen in those parts.

The Village of Kesselsdorf itself lies rather in a hollow; in the slight beginning, or uppermost extremity, of a little Valley or Dell, called the Tschonengrund, — which, with its quaggy brook of a Tschone, wends north-eastward into the Elbe, a course of four or five miles: little Valley very deep for its length, and getting altogether chasmy and precipitous towards the Elbe-ward or lower end. Kesselsdorf itself, as we said, is mainly in a kind of hollow: between Old Leopold and Kesselsdorf the ground rather mounts; and there is perceptibly a flat knoll or rise at the head of it, where the Village begins. Some trees there, and abundance of cannon and grenadiers at this moment. It is the south-western or leftmost point of Rutowski's line; impregnable with its cannon-batteries and grenadiers. Rightward Rutowski extends in long lines, with the quaggy dell of Tschonengrund in front of him, parallel to him; Dell ever deepening as it goes. North-eastward, at the extreme right, or Elbe point of it, where Grüne and the Austrians stand, it has grown so chasmy, we judge that Grüne can neither advance nor be advanced upon: so we leave him standing there, — which he did all day, in a purely meditative posture. Rutowski numbers 35,000, now on this ground, with immensity of cannon; 35,000 we, with only the usual field-artillery, and such a Tschonengrund, with its half-frozen quagmires ahead. A ticklish case for the old man, as he grimly reconnoitres it, in the winter morning.

Grim Old Dessauer having reconnoitered, and rapidly considered, decides to try it, — what else? — will range himself on the west side of that Tschonengrund, horse and foot; two lines, wide as Rutowski opposite him; but means to direct his main and prime effort against Kesselsdorf, which is clearly the key of the position, if it can be taken. For which end the Old Dessauer lengthens himself out to rightward, so as to outflank Kesselsdorf; — neglecting Grüne (refusing Grüne, as the soldiers say): — "our horse of the right wing reached "from the Wood called Lerchenbusch (*Larch-Bush*), right-"ward as far as Freyberg road; foot all between that Lerchen-"busch and the big Birch-tree on the road to Wilsdruf; horse "of the left wing, from there to Roitsch." * It was about two P.M. before the old man got all his deployments completed; what corps of his, deploying this way or that, came within wind of Kesselsdorf, were saluted with cannon, thirty pieces or more, which are in battery, in three batteries, on the knoll there; but otherwise no fighting as yet. At two, the Old

* Stille (p. 181), who was present. See Plan, p. 232.

Dessauer is complete; he reverently doffs his hat, as had always been his wont, in prayer to God, before going in. A grim fervour of prayer is in his heart, doubtless; though the words as reported are not very regular or orthodox: "*O Herr Gott*, help me yet this once, let me not be disgraced in my old days! Or if thou wilt not help me, don't help those *Hundsvögte*" (damned Scoundrels, so to speak), "but leave us to try it out ourselves!" That is the Old Scandinavian of a Dessauer's prayer; a kind of *Godur* he too, Priest as well as Captain: Prayer mythically true as given; mythically, not otherwise.* Which done, he waves his hat once, "On, in God's name!" and the storm is loose. Prussian right wing pushing grandly forward, bent in that manner, to take Kesselsdorf and its fire-throats in flank.

The Prussians tramp on with the usual grim-browed resolution, foot in front, horse in rear; but they have a terrible

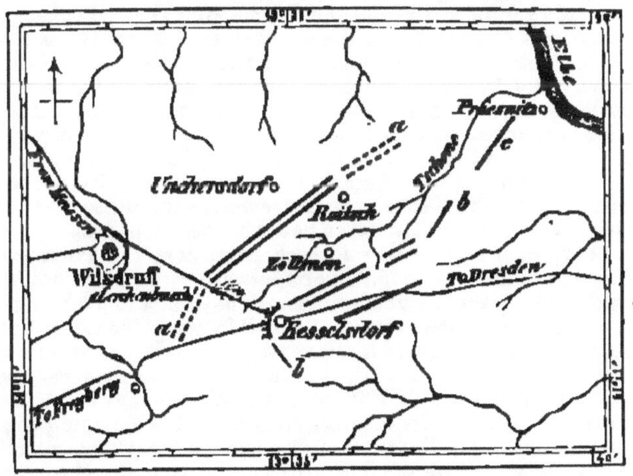

a a. Prussians. b b. Saxons. c. Grüne's Austrians.

* Ranke, III. 334 n.

problem at that Kesselsdorf, with its retrenched batteries, and numerous grenadiers fighting under cover. The very ground is sore against them; uphill, and the trampled snow wearing into a slide, so that you sprawl and stagger sadly. Thirty-one big guns, and about 9,000 small, pouring out mere death on you, from that knoll-head. The Prussians stagger; cannot stand it; bend to rightwards, and get out of shot-range; cannot manage it this bout. Rally, reinforced; try it again. Again, with a will; but again there is not a way. The Prussians are again repulsed; fall back, down this slippery course, in more disorder than the first time. Had the Saxons stood still, steadily handling arms, how, on such terms, could the Prussians ever have managed it?

But at sight of this second repulse, the Saxon grenadiers, and especially one battalion of Austrians who were there (the only Austrians who fought, this day), gave a shout "Victory!" — and in the height of their enthusiasm, rushed out, this Austrian battalion first and the Saxons after them, to charge these Prussians, and sweep the world clear of them. It was the ruin of their battle; a fatal hollahing before you are out of the wood. Old Leopold, quick as thought, noticing the thing, hurls cavalry on these victorious downplunging grenadiers; slashes them asunder, into mere recoiling whirlpools of ruin; so that "few of them got back unwounded;" and the Prussians storming in along with them, — aided by ever new Prussians, from beyond the Tschonengrund even, — the place was at length carried; and the Saxon battle became hopeless.

For, their right being in such hurricane, the Prussians from the centre, as we hint, storm forward withal; will not be held back by the Tschonengrund. They find the Tschonengrund quaggy in the extreme, "brook frozen at the sides, but waist-deep of liquid mud in the centre;" cross it, nevertheless, towards the upper part of it, — young Moritz of Dessau leading the way, to help his old Father in extremity. They climb the opposite side, — quite slippery in places, but "helping one another up;" — no Saxons there till you get fairly atop, which was an oversight on the Saxon part. Fairly atop, Moritz is saluted by the Saxons with diligent musket-volleys; but Moritz also has musket-volleys in him, bayonet-charges in him; eager to help his old Papa at this hard pinch. Old Papa has the Saxons in flank; sends more and ever more other cavalry in on them; and in fact, the right wing altogether storms violently through Kesselsdorf, and sweeps it clean. Whole regiments of the Saxons are made prisoners; Röel's Light Horse we see there, taking standards; cutting violently in to avenge Röel's death, and the affront they had at Meissen lately. Furious Moritz on their front, from across the Tschonengrund; furious Röel (*ghost* of Röel) and others in their flank, through Kesselsdorf: no standing for the Saxons longer.

About nightfall, — their horse having made poorish fight, though the foot had stood to it like men, — they roll universally away. The Prussian left wing of horse are summoned through the Tschonengrund to chase: had there remained another hour of daylight, the Saxon Army had been one wide ruin. Hidden in darkness, the Saxon Army ebbed confusedly towards Dresden; with the loss of 6,000 prisoners and 3,000 killed and wounded: a completely beaten Army. It is the last battle the Saxons fought as a Nation, — or probably will fight. Battle called of Kesselsdorf: Wednesday, 15th December 1745.

Prince Karl had arrived at Dresden the night before; heard all this volleying and cannonading, from the distance; but did not see good to interfere at all. Too wide apart, some say; quartered at unreasonably distant villages, by some irrefragable ignorant War-clerk of Brühl's appointing, — fatal Brühl. Others say, his Highness had himself no mind; and made excuses that his troops were tired, disheartened by the two beatings lately, — what will become of us in case of a third or fourth! It is certain, Prince Karl did nothing. Nor has Grüne's corps, the right wing, done anything except meditate: — it stood there unattacked, unattacking; till deep in the dark night, when Rutowski remembered it, and sent it order to come home. One

Austrian battalion, that of grenadiers on the knoll at Kesselsdorf, did actually fight; — and did begin that fatal outbreak, and quitting of the post there; "which lost the Battle to us!" say the Saxons.

Had those grenadiers stood in their place, there is no Prussian but admits that it would have been a terrible business to take Kesselsdorf and its batteries. But they did not stand; they rushed out, shouting "Victory;" and lost us the battle. And that is the good we have got of the sublime Austrian Alliance; and that is the pass our grand scheme of Partitioning Prussia is come to? Fatal little Brühl of the three hundred and sixty-five clothes-suits; Valet fatally become divine in Valethood, — are not you costing your Country dear!

Old Dessauer, glorious in the last of his fields, lay on his arms, all night, in the posts about; three bullets through his roquelaure, no scratch of wound upon the old man. Young Moritz too "had a bullet through his "coat-skirt, and three horses shot under him; but no "hurt, the Almighty's grace preserving him."* This Moritz is the Third of the Brothers, age now thirty-three; and we shall hear considerably about him in times coming. A lean, tall, austere man; and, "of all the Brothers, most resembled his Father in his ways." Prince Dietrich is in Leipzig at present; looking to that contribution of 50,000*l.*; to that, and to other contributions and necessary matters; — and has done all his fighting (as it chanced), though he survived his Brothers many years. Old Papa will now get his

* *Feldzüge*, i. 434.

discharge before long (quite suddenly, one morning, by paralytic stroke, 7th April 1747); and rest honourably with the Sons of Thor.*

* Young Leopold, the successor, died 16th December 1751, age fifty-two; Dietrich (who had thereupon quitted soldiering, to take charge of his Nephew left minor, and did not resume it), died 2d December 1769; Moritz soldier to the last), 11th April 1760. See *Militair-Lexikon*, i. 43, 84, 58, 47.

CHAPTER XV.

PEACE OF DRESDEN: FRIEDRICH DOES MARCH HOME.

FRIEDRICH himself had got to Meissen, Tuesday 14th; no enemy on his road, or none to speak of: Friedrich was there, or not yet far across, all Wednesday; collecting himself, waiting, on the slip, for a signal from Old Leopold. Sound of cannon, up the Elbe Dresden-ward, is reported there to Friedrich, that afternoon: cannon, sure enough, notes Friedrich; and deep dim-rolling peals, as of volleying small-arms; "the sky all on fire over there," as the hoarfrosty evening fell. Old Leopold busy at it, seemingly. That is the glare of the Old Dessauer's countenance; who is giving voice, in that manner, to the earthly and the heavenly powers; conquering Peace for us, let us hope!

Friedrich, as may be supposed, made his best speed next morning: "All well!" say the messengers; all well, says Old Leopold, whom he meets at Wilsdruf, and welcomes with a joyful embrace; "dismounting from "his horse, at sight of Leopold, and advancing to meet "him, with doffed hat and open arms," — and such words and treatments, that day, as made the old man's face visibly shine. "Your Highness shall conduct me!" And the two made survey together of the actual Field of Kesselsdorf; strewn with the ghastly wrecks of battle, — many citizens of Dresden strolling about, or sorrowfully seeking for their lost ones among the wounded and dead. No hurt to these poor citizens, who dread none; help to them rather: such is Friedrich's mind, — concerning which, in the Anecdote-Books, there are narratives (not worth giving) of a vapidly romantic character, credible though inexact.* Friedrich, who may well be profuse of thanks and praises, charms the Old Dessauer while they walk together; bravo old man with his holed roquelaure. For certain, he has done the work there, — a great deal of work in his time! Joy looks through his old rough face, of gunpowder colour: the Herr Gott has not delivered him to those damned Scoundrels in the end of his days. — On the morrow, Friday, Leopold rolled grandly forward upon Dresden; Rutowski and Prince Karl vanishing into the Metal Mountains, by Pirna for Bohemia, at sound of him, — as he had scarcely hoped they would.

On the Saturday evening, Dresden, capable of not the least defence, has opened all its gates, and Friedrich and the Prussians are in Dresden; Austrians and wrecked Saxons falling back diligently towards the Metal Mountains for Bohemia, diligent to clear the road for him. Queen and Junior Princes are here; to whom, as to all men, Friedrich is courtesy itself; making personal visit to the Royalties, appointing guards of honour, sacred respect to the Royal Houses; himself will lodge at the Princess Lubomirski's, a private mansion.

"That ferocious, false, ambitious King of Prussia" — Well, he is not to be ruined in open fight, on the contrary is ruinous there; nor by the cunningest am-

* For the indisputable part, see Orlich, II. 343, 344; and *Œuvres de Frédéric*, III. 170.

buscades, and secret combinations, in field or cabinet: our overwhelming Winter Invasion of him — see where it has ended! Brühl and Polish Majesty, — the nocturnal sky all on fire in those parts, and loud general doomsday come, — are a much-illuminated pair of gentlemen.

From the time Meissen Bridge was lost, Prince Karl too showing himself so languid, even Brühl had discerned that the case was desperate. On the very day of Kesselsdorf, — not the day *before*, which would have been such a thrift to Brühl and others! — Friedrich had a Note from Villiers, signifying joyfully that his Polish Majesty would accept Peace. Thanks to his Polish Majesty: — and after Kesselsdorf, perhaps the Empress-Queen too will! Friedrich's offers are precisely what they were, what they have always been: "Convention of Hanover; that, in all its parts; old Treaty of Breslau, to be guaranteed, to be actually kept. To me Silesia sure; — from you, Polish Majesty, one million crowns as damages for the trouble and cost this Triple Ambuscade of yours has given me; one million crowns, 150,000 *l.* we will say; and all other requisitions to cease on the day of signature. These are my terms: accept these; then wholly, As you were, Empress-Queen and you, and all surviving creatures: and I march home within a week." Villiers speeds rapidly from Prag, with the due olive-branch; with Count Harrach, experienced Austrian, and full powers. Harrach cannot believe his senses: "Such the terms to be still granted, after all these beatings and re-beatings!" — then at last, does believe, with stiff thankfulness and Austrian bows. The Negotiation need not occupy many hours.

"His Majesty of Prussia was far too hasty with this "Peace," says Valori: "he had taken a threap that he "would have it finished before the Year was done:" — in fact, he knows his own mind, *mon gros Valori*, and that is what few do. You sheer through no end of cobwebs with that fine implement, a wisely fixed resolution of your own. A Peace slow enough for Valori and the French: where could that be looked for! — Valori is at Berlin, in complete disgrace; his Most Christian King having behaved so like a Turk of late. Valori, horror-struck at such Peace, what shall he do to prevent it, to retard it? One effort at least. D'Arget his Secretary, stolen at Jaromirz, is safe back to him; ingenious, ingenuous D'Arget was always a favourite with Friedrich: despatch D'Arget to him. D'Arget is despatched; with reasons, with remonstrances, with considerations. D'Arget's Narrative is given: an ingenuous off-hand Piece; — poor little crevice, through which there is still to be had, singularly clear, and credible in every point, a direct glimpse of Friedrich's own thoughts, in that many-sounding Dresden, — so loud, that week, with dinner-parties, with operas, balls, Prussian war-drums, grand-parades and Peace-negotiations.

The Sieur D'Arget to Excellency Valori (at Berlin).

"Dresden, 1745" (dateless otherwise, must be December, between 18th and 25th).

"Monseigneur, — I arrived yesterday at 7 P.M.; as I had "the honour of forewarning you, by the word I wrote to the "Abbé" (never mind what Abbé; another Valori-Clerk) "from Sonnenwalde" (my halfway house between Berlin and this City). "I went, first of all, to M. de Vaugrenand," our Envoy here; "who had the goodness to open himself to me, "on the Business now on hand. In my opinion, nothing can "be added to the excellent considerations he has been urging, "on the King of Prussia and the Count de Podewils.

"At half-past 8, I went to his Prussian Majesty's; I found "he was engaged with his Concert,"—lodges in the Lubomirski Palace, has his snatch of melody in the evening of such discordant days,—"and I could not see him till after half-"past 9. I announced myself to M. Eichel; he was too over-"whelmed with affairs to give me audience. I asked for "Count Rothenburg; he was at cards with the Princess "Lubomirski. At last, I did get to the King: who received "me in the most agreeable way; but was just going to Supper; "said he must put off answering till tomorrow morning, morn-"ing of this day. M. de Vaugrenand had been so good as "prepare me on the rumours of a Peace with Saxony and the "Queen of Hungary. I went to M. Podewils; who said a "great many kind things to me for you. I could only sketch "out the matter, at that time; and represented to Podewils "the brilliant position of his Master, who had become Arbiter "of the Peace of Europe; that the moment was come for "making this Peace a General one, and that perhaps there "would be room for repentance afterwards if the opportunity "were slighted. He said, his Master's object was that same; "and thus closed the conversation by general questions.

"This morning, I again presented myself at the King of "Prussia's. I had to wait, and wait; in fine, it was not till "half-past 5 in the evening that he returned, or gave me ad-"mittance; and I staid with him till after 7,"—when Concert time was at hand again. Listen to a remarkable Dialogue, of the Conquering Hero with a humble Friend whom he likes. "His Majesty condescended (*a daigné*) to enter with me into "all manner of details; and began by telling me,

"That M. de Valori had done admirably not to come, him-"self, with that Letter from the King" (Most Christian, *our* King; Letter, the sickly Document above spoken of); "that "there could not have been an Answer expected,—the Letter "being almost of ironical strain; his Majesty" (Most Christian) "not giving him the least hope, but merely talking of his "fine genius, and how that would extricate him from the "perilous entanglement, and inspire him with a wise resolu-"tion in the matter! That he had, in effect, taken a resolu-"tion the wisest he could; and was making his Peace with "Saxony and the Queen of Hungary. That he had felt all "the dangers of the difficult situations he had been in," — sheer destruction yawning all round him, in huge imminency, more than once, and no friend heeding; — "that, weary of "playing always double-or-quits, he had determined to end "it, and get into a state of tranquillity, which both himself "and his People had such need of. That France could not, "without difficulty, have remedied his mishaps; and that he "saw by the King's Letter, there was not even the wish to do "it. That his, Friedrich's, military career was completed," — so far as *he* could foresee or decide! "That he would not "again expose his Country to the Caprices of Fortune, whose "past constancy to him was sufficiently astonishing to raise "fears of a reverse (*hear!*). That his ambitions were fulfilled, "in having compelled his Enemies to ask Peace from him in "their own Capital, with the Chancellor of Bohemia" (Harrach, typifying fallen Austrian pride) "obliged to coöperate.

"That he would always be attached to our King's interests, "and set all the value in the world on his friendship; but that "he had not been sufficiently assisted to be content. That, "observing henceforth an exact neutrality, he might be "enabled to do offices of mediation; and to carry, to the one "side and to the other, words of peace. That he offered him-"self for that object, and would be charmed to help in it; but "that he was fixed to stop there. That in regard to the basis "of General Peace, he had Two Ideas" — (which the reader can attend to, and see where they differed from the Event, and where not): — "One was, That France should keep "Ypres, Furnes, Tournay" (which France did not), "giving "up the Netherlands otherwise, with Ostend, to the English" (to the English!), "in exchange for Cape Breton. The other "was, To give up more of our Conquests" (we gave them all up, and got only the glory, and our Codfishery, Cape Breton, back, the English being equally generous), "and bargain for "liberty to reëstablish Dunkirk in its old condition" (not a word of your Dunkirk; there is your Cape Breton, and we also will go home with what glory there is, — not difficult to carry!). "But that it was by England we must make the "overtures, without addressing ourselves to the Court of "Vienna; and put it in his, Friedrich's, power to propose a "receivable Project of Peace. That he well conceived the "great point was the Queen of Spain" (Termagant, and Jenkins's Ear; Termagant's Husband, still living, is a lappet of Termagant's self); "but that she must content herself with "Parma and Piacenza for the Infant, Don Philip" (which the Termagant did); "and give back her hold of Savoy" (partial hold, of no use to her without the Passes) "to the King of "Sardinia." And of the *Jenkins's-Ear* question, generous England will say nothing? Next to nothing; hopes a modicum of putty and diplomatic varnish may close that troublesome question, — which springs, meanwhile, in the centre of the world! —

"These kind condescensions of his Majesty emboldened "me to represent to him the brilliant position he now held; "and how noble it would be, after having been the Hero of "Germany, to become, instead of one's own pacificator, the "Pacificator of Europe. 'I grant you,' said he, '*mon cher* "'D'Arget; but it is too dangerous a part for playing. A re-"'verse brings me to the edge of ruin: I know too well the "'mood of mind I was in, last time I left Berlin' (with that Three-legged Immensity of Atropos, *not* yet mown down at Hennersdorf by a lucky cut), 'ever to expose myself to it "'again! If luck had been against me there, I saw myself a "'Monarch without throne; and my subjects in the cruellest "'oppression. A bad game that: always, mere *Check to your* "'*King;* no other move; — I refer it to you, friend D'Arget: — "'in fine, I wish to be at peace.'

"I represented to him that the House of Austria would "never, with a tranquil eye, see his House in possession of "Silesia. 'Those that come after me,' said he, 'will do as "'they like; the Future is beyond man's reach. Those that "'come after will do as they can. I have acquired; it is theirs "'to preserve. I am not in alarm about the Austrians; — and "'this is my answer to what you have been saying about the "'weakness of my guarantees. They dread my Army; the "'luck that I have. I am sure of their sitting quiet for the "'dozen years or so which may remain to me of life; — quiet "'till I have, most likely, done with it. What! Are we never "'to have any good of our life, then (*Ne dois-je donc jamais* "'*jouir*)? There is more for me in the true greatness of "'labouring for the happiness of my subjects, than in the re- "'pose of Europe. I have put Saxony out of a condition to do "'hurt. She owes 14,775,000 crowns of debt' (two millions and a quarter sterling); 'and by the Defensive Alliance which I "'form with her, I provide myself' (but ask Brühl withal!) 'a "'help against Austria. I would not henceforth attack a cat, "'except to defend myself.' ("These are his very words," adds D'Arget; — and well worth noting.) 'Ambition (*gloire*) "'and my interests, were the occasion of my first Campaigns. "'The late Kaiser's situation, and my zeal for France' (not to mention interests again), "'gave rise to these second: and I "'have been fighting always since for my own hearths, — for "'my very existence, I might say! Once more, I know the "'state I had got into: — if I saw Prince Karl at the gates of "'Paris, I would not stir.' — 'And us at the gates of Vienna,' "answered I promptly, 'with the same indifference?' — 'Yes; "'and I swear it to you, D'Arget. In a word, I want to have "'some good of my life (*veux jouir*). What are we, poor human "'atoms, to get up projects that cost so much blood? Let us "'live, and help to live.'

"The rest of the conversation passed in general talk, "about Literature, Theatres and such objects. My reason- "ings and objectings, on the great matter, I need not farther "detail: by the frank discourse his Prussian Majesty was "kind enough to go into, you may gather perhaps that my "arguments were various, and not ill-chosen; — and it is too "evident they have all been in vain." — Your Excellency's (really in a very faithful way) — D'ARGET.*

D'Arget, about a month after this, was taken into Friedrich's service; Valori consenting, whose occupation was now gone; — and we shall hear of D'Arget again. Take this small Note, as summary of him: "D'Arget (18th January "1746) had some title, 'Secretary at Orders (*Secrétaire des* "*Commandements*),' bit of pension; and continued in the "character of reader, or miscellaneous literary attendant and "agent, very much liked by his Master, for six years coming. "A man much heard of, during those years of office. March "1752, having lost his dear little Prussian Wife, and got into

* Valori, i. 290-294 (no date except "Dresden, 1745," — sleepy Editor feeling no want of any).

"ill health and spirits, he retired on leave to Paris; and next "year, had to give up the thought of returning; — though he "still, and to the end, continued loyally attached to his old "Master, and more or less in correspondence with him. Had "got, before long, through Friedrich's influence at Paris, "some small Appointment in the *Ecole Militaire* there. He is, "of all the Frenchmen Friedrich had about him, with the ex-"ception of D'Argens alone, the most honest-hearted. The "above Letter, lucid, innocent, modest, altogether rational "and practical, is a fair specimen of D'Arget: add to it the "prompt self-sacrifice (and in that fine silent way) at Jaromirz "for Valori, and readers may conceive the man. He lived "at Paris, in meagre but contented fashion, *Rue de l'Ecole* "*Militaire*, till 1778; — and seems, of all the Ex-Prussian "Frenchmen, to have known most about Friedrich; and to "have never spoken any falsity against him. Duvernet, the "'M * *' Biographer of *Voltaire*, frequented him a good "deal; and any true notions, or glimmerings of such, "that he has about Prussia, are probably ascribable to "D'Arget." *

The Treaty of Dresden can be read in Schöll, Flassan, Rousset, Adelung; but, except on compulsion, no creature will now read it, — nor did this Editor, even he, find it pay. Peace is made. Peace of Dresden is signed, Christmas Day 1745: "To me Silesia, without farther treachery or trick; you, wholly as you were." Europe at large, as Friedrich had done, sees 'the sky all on fire about Dresden.' The fierce big battles done against this man have, one and all of them, become big defeats. The strenuous machinations, high-built plans cunningly devised, — the utmost sum-total of what the Imperial and Royal Potencies can, for the life of them, do: behold, it has all tumbled down here, in loud crash; the final peal of it at Kes-

* See *Œuvres de Frédéric*, xx. (p. xii. of *Preface* to the *D'Arget Correspondence* there).

selsdorf; and the consummation is flame and smoke, conspicuous over all the Nations. You will let him keep his own henceforth, then, will you? Silesia, which was *not* yours nor ever shall be? Silesia and no afterthought? The Saxons sign, the high Plenipotentiaries all; in the eyes of Villiers, I am told, were seen sublimely pious tears. Harrach, bowing with stiff, almost incredulous, gratitude, swears and signs; — hurries home to his Sovereign Lady, with Peace, and such a smile on his face; and on her Imperial Majesty's such a smile! — readers shall conceive it.

There are but Two new points in the Treaty of Dresden, — nay properly there is but One point, about which posterity can have the least care or interest; for that other, concerning "The Toll of Schidlo," and settlement of haggles on the Navigation of the Elbe there, was not kept by the Saxons, but continued a haggle still: this One point is the Eleventh Article. Inconceivably small; but liable to turn up on us again, in a memorable manner. That let us translate, — for M. de Voltaire's sake, and time coming! *Steuer* means Land-Tax; *Ober-Steuer-Einnahme* will be something like Royal Exchequer, therefore; and *Steuer-Schein* will be approximately equivalent to Exchequer Bill. Article Eleventh stipulates:

"All subjects and servants of his Majesty the King of "Prussia, who hold Bonds of the Saxon *Ober-Steuer-Einnahme* "shall be paid in full, capital and interest, at the times, and "to the amount, specified in said *Steuer-Scheine* or Bonds." That is Article Eleventh. — "The Saxon Exchequer," says an old Note on it, "thanks to Brühl's extravagance, has been "as good as bankrupt, paying with inconvertible paper, with "*Scheine* (Things to be *Shown*), for some time past; which "paper has accordingly sunk, let us say, 25 per cent below its "nominal amount in gold. All Prussian subjects, who hold "these Bonds, are to be paid in gold; Saxons, and others, "will have to be content with paper till things come round "again, if things ever do." Yes; — and, by ill chance, the matter will attract M. de Voltaire's keen eye in the interim!

Friedrich stayed eight days in Dresden, the loud theme of Gazetteers and rumours; the admired of two classes, in all Countries: of the many who admire success, and also of the few who can understand what it is to deserve success. Among his own Countrymen, this last Winter has kindled all their admirations to the flaming pitch. Saved by him from imminent destruction; their enemies swept home as if by one invincible; nay, sent home in a kind of noble shame, conquered by generosity. These feelings, though not encouraged to speak, run very high. The Dresdeners in private society found him delightful; the high ladies especially: "Could you have thought it; terrific Mars to become radiant Apollo in this manner!" From considerable Collections of Anecdotes illustrating this fact, in a way now fallen vapid to us, — I select only the Introduction:

"Do readers recollect Friedrich's first visit to Dresden" (in 1728), "seventeen years ago; and a certain charming young "Countess Flemming, at that time only fourteen; who, like "a Hebe as she was, contrived beautiful surprises for him, "and among other things presented him, so gracefully, on "the part of August the Strong, with his first flute?" — No reader of this History can recollect it; nor indeed, except in a mythic sense, believe it! A young Countess Flemming (daughter of old Feldmarschall Flemming) doubtless there might be, who presented him a flute; but as to *his first* flute --? — "That same charming young Countess Flemming is "still here, age now thirty-one; charming, more than ever, "though now under a changed name; having wedded a Von "Racknitz (Supreme Gentleman Usher, or some such thing) "a few years ago, and brought him children and the usual fe- "licities. How much is changed: August the Strong, where is "he; and his famous Three hundred and fifty-four, Enchant- "ress Orzelska and the others, where are they! Enchantress "Orzelska wedded, quarrelled, and is in a convent: her "charming destiny concluded. Rutowski is not now in the "Prussian Army: he got beaten, Wednesday last, at Kes- "selsdorf, fighting against that Army. And the Chevalier de "Saxe, he too was beaten there; — clambering now across "the Metal Mountains, ask not of him. And the Maréchal de "Saxe, he takes Cities, fights Battles of Fontenoy, 'mum- "'bling a lead bullet all day;' being dropsical, nearly dead of "debaucheries; the most dissolute (or probably so) of all the "Sons of Adam in his day. August the Physically Strong is "dead. August the Spiritually Weak is fled to Prag with his "Brühl. And we do not come, this time, to get a flute; but "to settle the account of Victories, and give Peace to Nations. "Strange, here as always, to look back, — to look round or "forward, — in the mad huge whirl of that loud-roaring Loom "of Time! — One of Countess Racknitz's Sons happened to "leave *Manuscript Diaries*" (rather feeble, not too exact-looking), "and gives us, from Mamma's reminiscences" * * Not a word more. *

The Peace, we said, was signed on Christmas Day. Next day, Sunday, Friedrich attended Sermon in the Kreuzkirche (Protestant High-Church of Dresden), attended Opera withal; and on Monday morning, had vanished out of Dresden, as all his people had done or were diligently doing. Tuesday, he dined briefly at Wusterhausen (a place we once knew well), with the Prince of Prussia, whose it now is; got into his open carriage again, with the said Prince and his other Brother Ferdinand; and drove swiftly homeward,

* Rödenbeck, *Beyträge*, i. 440 et seq.

Berlin, drunk with joy, was all out on the streets, waiting. On the Heath of Britz, four or five miles hitherward of Berlin, a body of young gentlemen ('Merchants mostly, who had ridden out so far'), saluted him with "*Vivat Friedrich der Grosse* (Long live Friedrich *the Great*)!" thrice over; — as did, in a less articulate manner, Berlin with one voice, on his arrival there; Burgher Companies lining the streets; Population vigorously shouting; Pupils of the Köln Gymnasium, with Clerical and School Functionaries in mass, breaking out into Latin Song:

> *"Vivat, vivat Fridericus Rex;*
> *Vivat Augustus, Magnus, Felix, Pater Patri-æ — —!"*

— — and what not.* On reaching the Portal of the Palace, his Majesty stept down; and, glancing round the Schloss-Platz and the crowded windows and simmering multitudes, saluted, taking off his hat; which produced such a shout, — naturally the loudest of all. And so *exit* King, into his interior. Tuesday, 2-3 P.M., 28th December 1745: a King new-christened in the above manner, so far as people could.

Illuminated Berlin shone like noon, all that night (the beginning of a *Gaudeamus* which lasted miscellaneously for weeks): — but the King stole away to see a friend who was dying; that poor Duhan de Jaudun, his early Schoolmaster, who had suffered much for him, and whom he always much loved. Duhan

* Preuss, i. 220; who cites *Beschreibung* ("Description of his Majesty's Triumphant Entry, on the" &c.) and other Contemporary Pamphlets Rödenbeck i. 124.

died, in a day or two. Poor Jordan, poor Keyserling (the "Cesarion" of young days): them also he has lost; and often laments, in this otherwise bright time.*

* In *Œuvres*, XVII. 268; XVIII. 141; *ib.* 142 (painfully tender Letters to Frau von Camas and others, on these events).

BOOK XVI.

THE TEN YEARS OF PEACE.

1746—1756.

CHAPTER I.

SANS-SOUCI.

FRIEDRICH has now climbed the heights, and sees himself on the upper table-land of Victory and Success; his desperate life-and-death struggles triumphantly ended. What may be ahead, nobody knows; but here is fair outlook that his enemies and Austria itself have had enough of him. No wringing of his Silesia from this "bad Man." Not to be overset, this one, by never such exertions; oversets *us*, on the contrary, plunges us heels overhead into the ditch, so often as we like to apply to him; nothing but heavy beatings, disastrous breaking of crowns, to be had on trying there! "Five Victories!" as Voltaire keeps counting on his fingers, with upturned eyes, — Mollwitz, Chotusitz, Striegau, Sohr, Kesselsdorf (the last done by Anhalt; but omitting Hennersdorf, and that sudden slitting of the big Saxon-Austrian Projects into a cloud of feathers, as fine a feat as any), — "Five Victories!" counts Voltaire; calling on everybody (or everybody but Friedrich himself, who is easily sated with that kind of thing) to admire. In the world are many opinions about Friedrich. In Austria, for instance, what an opinion; sinister, gloomy in the extreme: or in England, which derives from Austria, — only with additional dimness, and with gloomy new provocations of its own before long! Many opinions about Friedrich, all dim enough: but this, that he is a very demon for fighting, and the stoutest King walking the Earth just now, may well be a universal one. A man better not to be meddled with, if he will be at peace, as he professes to wish being.

Friedrich accordingly is not meddled with, or not openly meddled with; and has, for the Ten or Eleven Years coming, a time of perfect external Peace. He himself is decided "not to fight with a cat," if he can get the peace kept; and for about eight years, hopes confidently that this, by good management, will continue possible; — till, in the last three years, electric symptoms did again disclose themselves, and such hope more and more died away. It is well known there lay in the fates a Third Silesian War for him, worse than both the others; which is now the main segment of his History still lying ahead for us, were this Halcyon Period done. Halcyon Period counts from Christmas Day, Dresden, 1745, — "from this day, Peace to the end of my life!" had been Friedrich's fond hope. But on the 9th day of September 1756, Friedrich was again entering Dresden (Saxony some twelve days before); and the Crowning Struggle of his Life was, beyond all expectation, found to be still lying ahead for him, awfully dubious for Seven Years thereafter! —

Friedrich's History during this intervening Halcyon or Peace Period must, in some way, be made known to readers: but for a great many reasons, especially at present, it behoves to be given in compressed form; riddled down, to an immense extent, out of those sad Prussian Repositories, where the grain of perennial, of significant and still memorable, lies overwhelmed under rubbish mountains of the fairly extinct, the poisonously dusty and forgettable; — *Ach Himmel!* Which indispensable preliminary process, how can an English Editor, at this time, do it; no Prussian, at any time, having thought of trying it! From a painful Predecessor of mine, I collect, rummaging among his dismal Paper-masses, the following Three Fragments, worth reading here:

1°. "Friedrich was as busy, in those Years, as in the generality of his life; and his actions, and salutary conquests "over difficulties, were many, profitable to Prussia and to "himself. Very well worth keeping in mind. But not fit for "History; or at least only fit in the summary form; to be delineated in little, with large generic strokes, — if we had "the means; — such details belonging to the Prussian Antiquary, rather than to the English Historian of Friedrich in "our day. A happy Ten Years of time. Perhaps the time "for Montesquieu's aphorism, 'Happy the People whose Annals are blank in History-Books!' The Prussian Antiquary, had he once got any image formed to himself of "Friedrich, and of Friedrich's History in its human lineaments and organic sequences, will glean many memorabilia "in those Years: which his readers then (and not till then) "will be able to intercalate in their places, and get human "good of. But alas, while there is no intelligible human "image, nothing of lineaments or organic sequences, or other "than a jumbled mass of Historical Marine-Stores, presided "over by Dryasdust and Human Stupor (unsorted, unlabelled, "tied up in blind sacks), the very Antiquary will have uphill "work of it, and his readers will often turn round on him with "a gloomy expression of countenance!"

2°. "Friedrich's Life, — little as he expected it, that day "when he started up from his ague-fit at Reinsberg, and "grasped the fiery Opportunity that was shooting past, — is a "Life of War. The chief memory that will remain of him is "that of a King and man who fought consummately well. No

"Peace and the Muses; no, that is denied him, — though he "was so unwilling, always, to think it denied! But his Life-"Task turned out to be a Battle for Silesia. It consists of "Three grand Struggles of War. And not for Silesia only; "— unconsciously, for what far greater things to his Nation "and to him!

"Deeply unconscious of it, they were passing their "'Trials,' his Nation and he, in the great Civil-Service Exa-"mination Hall of this Universe: 'Are you able to defend "'yourselves, then; and to hang together coherent, against "'the whole world and its incoherencies and rages?' A "question which has to be asked of Nations, before they can "be recognised as such, and be baptised into the general "commonwealth; they are mere Hordes or accidental Aggre-"gates, till that Question come. Question which this Nation "had long been getting ready for; which now, under this "King, it answered to the satisfaction of gods and men: "'Yes, Heaven assisting, we can stand on our defence; and "'in the long-run (as with air when you try to annihilate it, or "'crush it to *nothing*) there is even an infinite force in us; and "'the whole world does not succeed in annihilating us!' Upon "which has followed what we term National Baptism; — or "rather this *was* the National Baptism, this furious one in "torrent whirlwinds of fire; done three times over, till in gods "or men there was no doubt left. That was Friedrich's func-"tion in the world; and a great and memorable one; — not to "his own Prussian Nation only, but to Teutschland at large, "forever memorable.

"'Is Teutchland a Nation; is there in Teutschland still a "'Nation?' Austria, not dishonestly, but much sunk in "superstitions and involuntary mendacities, and liable to "sink much further, answers always in gloomy proud tone, "'Yes, I am the Nation of Teutschland!' — but is mistaken, "as turns out. For it is not mendacities, conscious or other, "but veracities, that the Divine Powers will patronise, or "even in the end will put up with at all. Which you ought to "understand better than you do, my friend. For, on the "great scale and on the small, and in all seasons, circum-"stances, scenes and situations where a Son of Adam finds "himself, that is true, and even a sovereign truth. And "whoever does *not* know it, — human charity to him (were "such always possible) would be, that *he* were furnished with "handcuffs as a part of his outfit in this world, and put under "guidance of those who do. Yes; to him, I should say, a "private pair of handcuffs were much usefuller than a ballot-"box, — were the times once settled again, which they are far "from being!" * *

"So that, if there be only Austria for Nation, Teutschland "is in ominous case. Truly so. But there is in Teutschland "withal, very irrecognisable to Teutschland, yet authenti-"cally present, a Man of the properly unconquerable type; "there is also a select Population drilled for him: these two "together will prove to you that there is a Nation. Conquest "of Silesia, Three Silesian Wars; labours and valours as of "Alcides, in vindication of oneself and one's Silesia: — se-"cretly, how unconsciously, that other and higher Question "of Teutschland, and of its having in it a Nation, was Fried-"rich's sore task and his Prussia's at that time. As Teutsch-"land may be perhaps now, in our day, beginning to re-"cognise; with hope, with astonishment, poor Teutsch-"land!" * *

3°. "And in fine, leaving all that, there is one thing un-"deniable: In all human Narrative, it is the battle only, and "not the victory, that can be dwelt upon with advantage. "Friedrich has now, by his Second Silesian War, achieved "Greatness: 'Friedrich the Great;' expressly so deno-"minated, by his People and others. The struggle upwards "is the Romance; your hero once wedded, — to *Glory*, or "whoever the Bride may be, — the Romance ends. Precise "critics do object, That there may still lie difficulties, new "perils and adventures, ahead: — which proves conspicu-"ously true in this case of ours. And accordingly, our Book "not being a Romance but a History, let us, with all fidelity, "look out what these are, and how they modify our Royal "Gentleman who has got his wedding done. With all "fidelity; but with all brevity, no less. For, inasmuch "as" —

Well, brevity in most cases is desirable. And privately, it must be owned there is another consideration of no small weight: That, our Prussian resources falling altogether into bankruptcy during Peace-Periods, Nature herself has so ordered it, in this instance! Partly it is our Books (the Prussian Dryasdust reaching his acme on those occasions), but in part too it is the Events themselves, that are small and want importance: that have fallen dead to us, in the huge new Time and its uproars. Events not of flagrant notability (like battles or war-passages), to bridle Dryasdust, and guide him in some small measure. Events rather which, except as characteristic of one memorable Man and King, are mostly now of no memorability whatever. Crowd all these indiscriminately into sacks, and shake them out pellmell on us: that is Dryasdust's sweet way. As if the largest Marine-stores Establishment in all the world had suddenly, on hest of some Necromancer or maleficent person, taken wing upon you; and were dancing, in boundless mad whirl, round your devoted head; — simmering and dancing, very much at its ease; nowhither; asking *you* cheerfully, "What is your candid opinion, then?" 'Opinion,' Heavens! —

You have to retire many yards, and gaze with a desperate steadiness; assuring yourself: "Well, it does, right indisputably, shadow forth *Some*thing. This was a Thing Alive; and did at one time stick together, as an organic Fact on the Earth, though it now dances in Dryasdust at such a rate!" It is only by self-help of this sort, and long survey, with rigorous selection, and extremely extensive exclusion and oblivion, that you gain the least light in such an element. "Brevity," — little said, when little has been got to be known, — is an evident rule! Courage, reader; by good eyesight, you will still catch some features of Friedrich as we go along. To *say* our little in a not unintelligible manner, and keep the rest well hidden, it is all we can do for you! —

Friedrich declines the Career of Conquering Hero; goes into Law-Reform; and gets ready a Cottage Residence for Himself.

Friedrich's Journey to Pyrmont is the first thing recorded of him by the Newspapers. Gone to take the waters; as he did after his former War. Here is what I had noted of that small Occurrence, and of one or two others contiguous in date, which prove to be of significance in Friedrich's History.

"*May* 12*th*-17*th*, 1746," say the old Books, "his Majesty "sets out for Pyrmont, taking Brunswick by the way; arrives "at Pyrmont, May 17th; stays till June 8th;" three weeks good. "Is busy corresponding with the King of France about "a General Peace, but, owing to the embitterment of both "parties, it was not possible at this time." Taking the waters at least, and amusing himself. From Brunswick, in passing, he had brought with him his Brother-in-law the reigning Duke; Rothenburg was there, and Brother Henri; D'Arget expressly; Flute-player Quanz withal, and various musical people: "in all, a train of above sixty persons." I notice also that Prince Wilhelm of Hessen was in Pyrmont at the time. With whom, one fancies, what speculations there might be: About the late and present War-passages, about the poor Peace Prospects; your Hessian "Siege" so-called "of Blair in Athol" (*Culloden* now comfortably done), and other cognate topics. That is the Pyrmont Journey.

It is no surprise to us to hear, in these months, of new and continual attention to Army matters, to Husbandry matters; and to making good, on all sides, the ruins left by War. Of rebuilding (at the royal expense) "the town of Schmiedeberg, "which had been burnt;" of rebuilding, and repairing from their damage, all Silesian villages and dwellings; and still more satisfactory, How, "in May 1746, there was, in every "Circle of the Country, by exact liquidation of Accounts" (so rapidly got done), "exact payment made to the individuals "concerned, 1°. Of all the hay, straw and corn that had been "delivered to his Majesty's Armies; 2°. of all the horses that "had perished in the King's work; 3°. of all the horses "stolen by the Enemy, and of all the money-contributions "exacted by the Enemy: payment in ready cash, and according to the rules of justice (*baar und billigmässig*), by his Majesty." *

It was from Pyrmont, May 1746, — or more definitely, it was "at Potsdam early in the morning, 15th September" following, — that Friedrich launched, or shot forth from its moorings, after much previous attempting and preparing, a very great Enterprise; which he has never lost sight of since the day he began reigning, nor will till his reign and life end: the actual Reform of Law in Prussia. "May 12th, 1746," Friedrich, on the road to Pyrmont, answers his Chief Law-Minister Cocceji's *Report of Practical Plan* on this matter: "Yes; looks very hopeful!"—and took it with him to consider at Pyrmont, during his leisure. Much considering of it, then and afterwards, there was. And finally, September 15th, early in the morning, Cocceji had an Interview with Friedrich; and the decisive fiat was given: "Yes; start on it, in "God's name! Pommern, which they call the *Provincia litigiosa;* try it there first!" ** And Cocceji, a vigorous old man of sixty-seven, one of the most learned of Lawyers, and a very Hercules in cleaning Law-Stables, has, on Friedrich's urgencies, — which have been repeated on every breathing-time of Peace there has been, and even sometimes in the middle of War (last January, 1745, for example; and again, express Order, January 1746, a fortnight after Peace was signed), — actually got himself girt for this salutary work. "Wash me out that horror of accumulation, let us see the old "Pavements of the place again. Every Lawsuit to be finished "within the Year!"

Cocceji, who had been meditating such matters for a great

* Seyfarth, II. 22, 23.
** Ranke, II. 392.

while,* and was himself eager to proceed, in spite of considerable wigged oppositions and secret reluctances that there were, did now, on that fiat of September 15th, get his Select Commission of Six riddled together and adjoined to him, — the likeliest Six that Prussia, in her different Provinces, could yield; — and got the *Stände* of Pommern, after due committee-ing and deliberating, to consent and promise help. December 31st, 1746, was the day the *Stände* consented: and January 10th, 1747, Cocceji and his Six set out for Pommern. On a longish Enterprise, in that Province and the others; — of which we shall have to take notice, and give at least the dates as they occur.

To sweep out pettifogging Attorneys, cancel improper Advocates, to regulate Fees; to war, in a calm but deadly manner, against pedantries, circumlocutions, and the multiplied forms of stupidity, cupidity, and human owlery in this department; — and, on the whole, to realise from every Court, now and onwards, "A decision to all Lawsuits, within "a Year after their beginning." This latter result, Friedrich thinks, will itself be highly beneficial; and be the sign of all manner of improvements. And Cocceji, scanning it with those potent law-eyes of his, ventures to assure him that it will be possible. As, in fact, it proved, — honour to Cocceji and his King, and King's Father withal. "Samuel von "Cocceji" (says an old Note), "son of a Law-Professor, and "himself once such, — was picked up by Friedrich Wilhelm, "for the Official career, many years ago. A man of whole-"some, by no means weakly aspect, — to judge by his Por-"trait, which is the chief 'Biography' I have of him. Potent "eyes and eyebrows, ditto blunt nose; honest, almost care-"less lips, and deep chin well dewlapped: extensive pene-"trative face, not pincered together, but potently fallen "closed; — comfortable to see, in a wig of such magnitude. "Friedrich, a judge of men, calls him 'a man of sterling cha-"'racter (*caractère intègre et droit*), whose qualities would have "'suited the noble times of the Roman Republic.'"** He has his Herculean battle, his Master and he have, with the Owler-

* "1st March 1738," Friedrich Wilhelm's "Edict" on Law Reform: Cocceji ready, at that time; — but his then Majesty forbore.

** *Œuvres*, IV. 2.

ics and the vulturous Law-Pedantries, — which I always love Friedrich for detesting as he does: — and, during the next five years, the world will hear often of Cocceji, and of this Prussian Law-Reform by Friedrich and him.

His Majesty's exertions to make Peace were not successful; what does lie in his power is, to keep out of the quarrel himself. It appears great hopes were entertained, by some in England, of gaining Friedrich over; of making him Supreme Captain to the Cause of Liberty. And prospects were held out to him, quasi-offers made, of a really magnificent nature, — undeniable, though obscure. Herr Ranke has been among the Archives again; and comes out with fractional snatches of a very strange "Paper from England;" capriciously hiding all details about it, all intelligible explanation: so that you in vain ask, "Where, When, How, By whom?" — and can only guess to yourself that Carteret was somehow at the bottom of the thing; *aut Carteretus aut Diabolus.* "What would your Majesty think to be elected Stadtholder of Holland? Without a Stadtholder, these Dutch are worth nothing; not hoistable, nor of use when hoisted, all palavering and pulling different ways. Must have a Stadtholder; and one that stands firm on some basis of his own. Stadtholder of Holland, King of Prussia, — you then, in such position, take the reins of this poor floundering English-Dutch Germanic Anti-French War, you; and drive it in the style you have. Conquer back the Netherlands to us; French Netherlands as well. French and Austrian Netherlands together, yours in perpetuity; Dutch Stadtholderate as good as ditto: this, with Prussia and its fighting capabilities, will be a pleasant Protestant thing. Austria cares little about the Netherlands, in comparison. Austria, getting back its Lorraine and Alsace, will be content, will be strong on its feet. What if it should even lose Italy? France, Spain, Sardinia, the Italian Petty Principalities and Anarchies: suppose they tug and tussle, and collapse there as they can? But let France try to look across the Rhine again; and to threaten Teutschland, England, and the Cause of Human Liberty temporal or spiritual!"

This is authentically the purport of Herr Ranke's extraordinary Document;* guessable as due to *Carteretus* or *Dia-*

* Ranke, III. 359.

bolus. Here is an outlook; here is a career as Conquering Hero, if that were one's line! A very magnificent ground-plan; hung up to kindle the fancy of a young King, — who is far too prudent to go into it at all. More definite quasi-official offers, it seems, were made him from the same quarter: Subsidies to begin with, such subsidies as nobody ever had before; say 1,000,000*l.* sterling by the Year. To which Friedrich answered, "Subsidies, your Excellency?" (Are We a Hackney-Coachman, then?) — and with much contempt, turned his back on that offer. No fighting to be had, by purchase or seduction, out of this young man. Will not play the Conquering Hero at all, nor the Hackney-Coachman at all; has decided "not to fight a cat" if let alone; but to do and endeavour a quite other set of things, for the rest of his life.

Friedrich, readers can observe, is not uplifted with his greatness. He has been too much beaten and bruised to be anything but modestly thankful, for getting out of such a deadly clash of chaotic swords. Seems to have little pride even in his "Five Victories;" or hides it well. Talks not overmuch about these things; talks of them, so far as we can hear, with his old comrades only, in praise of *their* prowesses; as a simple human being, not as a supreme of captains; and at times acknowledges, in a fine sincere way, the omnipotence of Luck in matters of War.

One of the most characteristic traits, extensively symbolical of Friedrich's intentions and outlooks at this Epoch, is his installing of himself in the little Dwelling-House, which has since become so celebrated under the name of Sans-Souci. The plan of Sans-Souci, — an elegant commodious little "Country Box," quite of modest pretensions, one story high; on the pleasant Hill-top near Potsdam, with other little green Hills, and pleasant views of land and water, all round, — had been sketched in part by Friedrich himself; and the diggings and terracings of the Hill-side were just beginning, when he quitted for the Last War. 'April 14th, 1745,' while he lay in those perilous enigmatic circumstances at Neisse with Pandours and devouring bugbears round him, 'the foundation-stone was laid' (Knobelsdorf being architect, once more, as in the old Reinsberg case): and the work, which had been steadily proceeding while the Master struggled in those dangerous battles and adventures far away from it, was in good forwardness at his return. An object of cheerful interest to him; prophetic of calmer years ahead.

It was not till May 1747, that the formal occupation took place: "Mayday 1747," he had a grand House-heating, or "First Dinner, of 200 covers: and May 19th-20th was the first "night of his sleeping there." For the next Forty Years, especially as years advanced, he spent the most of his days and nights in this little Mansion; which became more and more his favourite retreat, whenever the noises and scenic etiquettes were not inexorable. "*Sans-Souci;*" which we may translate "No-Bother." A busy place this too, but of the quiet kind; and more a home to him than any of the Three fine Palaces (ultimately Four), which lay always waiting for him in the neighbourhood. Berlin and Charlottenburg are about twenty miles off; Potsdam, which, like the other two, is rather consummate among Palaces, lies leftwise in front of him within a short mile. And at length, to *right* hand, in a similar distance and direction, came the "*Neue Schloss*" (New Palace of Potsdam), called also the "*Palace* of Sans-Souci," in distinction from the Dwelling-House, or as it were Garden-House, which made that name so famous.

Certainly it is a significant feature of Friedrich; and discloses the inborn proclivity he had to retirement, to study and reflection, as the chosen element of human life. Why he fell upon so ambitious a title for his Royal Cottage? "*No*-Bother" was not practically a thing he, of all men, could consider possible in this world: at the utmost perhaps, by good care, "*Less*-Bother!" The name, it appears, came by accident. He had prepared his Tomb, and various Tombs, in the skirts of this new Cottage: looking at these, as the building of them went on, he was heard to say, one day (Spring, 1746), D'Argens strolling beside him: "*Quì, alors je serai sans souci* (Once *there*, one will be out of bother)!" A saying which was rumoured of, and repeated in society, being by such a man. Out of which rumour in society, and the evident aim of the Cottage Royal, there was gradually born, as Venus from the froth of the sea, this name: "Sans-Souci;"—which Friedrich adopted; and, before the Year was out, had put upon his lintel in gold letters. So that, by 'Mayday 1747,' the name was in all men's memories; and has continued ever since.* Tourists know this Cottage Royal: Friedrich's "Three Rooms in it; one of them a "Library; in another, a little Alcove with an iron Bed" (iron, without curtains; old softened *hat* the usual royal nightcap)— altogether a soldier's lodging: — all this still stands as it did. Cheerfully looking down on its garden-terraces, stairs, Greek statues, and against the free sky: — perhaps we may visit it in time coming, and take a more special view. In the Years now on hand, Friedrich, I think, did not much practically live there, only shifted thither now and then. His chief residence is still Potsdam Palace; and in Carnival time, that of Berlin; with Charlottenburg for occasional festivities, especially in summer, the gardens there being fine.

This of Sans-Souci is but portion of a wider Tendency, wider set of endeavours on Friedrich's part, which returns upon him now that Peace has returned: That of improving his own Domesticities, while he labours at so many public improvements. Gazing long on that simmering "Typhoon of Marine-stores" above mentioned, we do trace Three great Heads of Endeavour in this Peace Period. *First*, the Reform of Law; which, as above hinted, is now earnestly pushed forward again, and was brought to what was thought completion before long. With much rumour of applause from contemporary mankind. Concerning which we are to give some indications, were it only dates in their order: though, as the affair turned out not to be completed, but had to be taken up again long after, and is an affair lying wide of British ken, — there need not, and indeed cannot, be much said of it just now. *Secondly*, there is eager Furthering of the Husbandries, the Commerces, Practical Arts, — especially at present, that of Foreign Commerce, and Shipping

* Preuss, I. 268, &c.; Nicolai, III. 1200.

from the Port of Embden. Which shall have due notice. And *thirdly*, what must be our main topic here, there is that of Improving the Domesticities, the Household Enjoyments such as they were; — specially definable as Renewal of the old Reinsberg Program; attempt more strenuous than ever to realise that beautiful ideal. Which, and the total failure of which, and the consequent quasi-abandonment of it for time coming, are still, intrinsically and by accident, of considerable interest to modern readers.

Curious, and in some sort touching, to observe how that old original Life-Program still reëmerges on this King: "Something of melodious possible in one's poor life, is not there? A Life to the Practical Duties, yes; but to the Muses as well!" — Of Friedrich's success in his Law-Reforms, in his Husbandries, Commerces and Furtherances, conspicuously great as it was there is no possibility of making careless readers cognisant at this day. Only by the great results, — a "Prussia *quadrupled*" in his time, and the like, — can studious readers convince themselves, in a cold and merely statistic way. But in respect of Life to the Muses, we have happily the means of showing that in actual vitality; in practical struggle towards fulfilment, — and how extremely disappointing the result was. In a word, Voltaire pays his Fifth and final Visit in this Period; the Voltaire matter comes to its consummation. To that, as to one of the few things which are perfectly knowable in this Period of *Ten-Years Peace*, and in which mankind still take interest, we purpose mostly to devote ourselves here.

Ten years of a great King's life, ten busy years

too; and nothing visible in them, of main significance, but a crash of Author's Quarrels, and the Crowning Visit of Voltaire? Truly yes, reader; so it has been ordered. Innumerable high-dressed gentlemen, gods of this lower world, are gone all to inorganic powder, no comfortable or profitable memory to be held of them more, and this poor Voltaire, without implement except the tongue and brain of him, — he is still a shining object to all the populations; and they say and symbol to me, "Tell us of him! He is the man!" Very strange indeed. Changed times since, for dogs barking at the heels of him, and lions roaring ahead, — for Asses of Mirepoix, for foul creatures in high dizenment, and foul creatures who were hungry valets of the same, — this man could hardly get the highways walked! And indeed had to keep his eyes well open, and always have covert within reach, — under pain of being torn to pieces, while he went about in the flesh, or rather in the bones, poor lean being. Changed times; within the Century last past! For indeed there was in that man what far transcends all dizenment, and temporary potency over valets, over legions, treasure-vaults, and dim millions mostly blockhead: a spark of Heaven's own lucency, a gleam from the Eternities (in small measure); — which becomes extremely noticeable when the Dance is over, when your tallow-dips and wax-lights are burnt out, and the brawl of the night is gone to bed.

CHAPTER II.

PEEP AT VOLTAIRE AND HIS DIVINE EMILIE (BY CANDLE-LIGHT) IN THE TIDE OF EVENTS.

PUBLIC European affairs require little remembrance; the War burning well to leeward of us henceforth. A huge world of smoky chaos; the special fires of it, if there be anything of fire, are all the more clear far in the distance. Of which sort, and of which only, the reader is to have notice. Maréchal de Saxe, — King Louis oftenest personally there, to give his name and countenance to things done, — is very glorious in the Netherlands; captures, sometimes by surprisal, place after place (beautiful surprisal of Brussels last winter); with sieges of Antwerp, Mons, Charleroi, victoriously following upon Brussels: and, before the end of 1746, he is close upon Holland itself; intent on having Namur and Maestricht; for which the poor Sea-Powers, with a handful of Austrians, fight two Battles, and are again beaten both times.* A glorious, ever-victorious Maréchal; and has an Army very "high-toned," in more than one sense: indeed, I think, one of the loudest-toned Armies ever on the field before. Loud not with

* 1°. Battle of Roucoux, 11th October 1746; Prince Karl commanding, English taking mainly the stress of fight, — Saxe having already outwitted poor Karl, and *got* Namur. 2°. Battle of Lawfelt, or Lauffeld, called also of *Val*, 2d July 1747; Royal Highness of Cumberland commanding (and taking most of the stress; Ligonier made prisoner, &c.), — Dutch fighting ill, and Bathyani and his Austrians hardly in the fire at all.

well-served Artillery alone, but with playactor Thunderbarrels (always an itinerant Theatre attends), with gasconading talk, with orgies, debaucheries, — busy service of the Devil, *and* pleasant consciousness that we are Heaven's masterpiece, and are in perfect readiness to die at any moment; — our *elasticity* and agility ("*élan*" as we call it) well kept up, in that manner, for the time being.

Hungarian Majesty, contrary to hope, neglects the Netherlands, "Holland and England, for their own sake, will manage there!" — and directs all her resources, and her lately Anti-Prussian Armies (General Browne leading them) upon Italy, as upon the grand interest now. Little to the comfort of the Sea-Powers. But Hungarian Majesty is decided to cut in upon the French and Spaniards, in that fine Country, — who had been triumphing too much of late; Maillebois and Señor de Gages doing their mutual exploits (though given to quarrel); Don Philip wintering in Milan even (1745—1746); and the King of Sardinia getting into French courses again.

Strong cuts her Hungarian Majesty does inflict, on the Italian side; tumbles Infant Philip out of Milan and his Carnival gaieties, in plenty of hurry; besieges Genoa, Marquis Botta d'Adorno (our old acquaintance Botta) her siege-captain, a native of this region; brings back the wavering Sardinian Majesty; captures Genoa, and much else. Captures Genoa, we say, — had not Botta been too rigorous on his countrymen, and provoked a revolt again, Revolt of Genoa, which proved difficult to settle. In fine, Hungarian Majesty has, in the course of this year 1746, with aid of the reconfirmed Sardinian Majesty, satisfactorily beaten the French and

Spaniards. Has, — after two murderous Battles gained over the Maillebois-Gages people, — driven both French and Spaniards into corners, Maillebois altogether home again across the Var; — nay has descended in actual Invasion upon France itself. And, before New-year's day 1747, General Browne is busy besieging Antibes, aided by English Seventy-fours; so that "sixty French Battalions" have to hurry home, from winter-quarters, towards those Provençal Countries; and Maréchal de Belleisle, who commands there, has his hands full. Triumphant enough her Hungarian Majesty, in Italy; while in the Netherlands, the poor Sea-Powers have met with no encouragement from the Fates or her.* All which the reader may keep imagining at his convenience; — but will be glad rather, for the present, to go with us for an actual look at M. de Voltaire and the divine Emilie, whom we have not seen for a long time. Not much has happened in the interim; one or two things only which it can concern us to know; — scattered fragments of memorial, on the way thus far:

1°. *M. de Voltaire has, in 1745, made way at Court.* Divine Emilie picked up her Voltaire from that fine Diplomatic

* "Battle of Placenza" (Prince Lichtenstein, with whom is Browne, *versus* Gages and Maillebois), 16th June 1746 (*Adelung*, v. 427); "Battle of Rottofreddo" (Botta chief Austrian there, and our old friend Bärenklau getting killed there), 12th August 1746 (*ib.* 462): whereupon, 7th *September*, Genoa (which had declared itself Anti-Austrian latterly, not without cause, and brought the tug of War into those parts) is coerced by Botta to open its gates, on grievous terms (*ib.* 484-489); so that, *November 30th*, Browne, no Bourbon Army now on the field, enters Provence (crosses the Var, that day), and tries Antibes: *5th-11th December*, Popular Revolt in Genoa, and Expulsion of proud Botta and his Austrians (*ib.* 518-523); upon which surprising event (which could not be mended during the remainder of the War), Browne's enterprise became impossible. See Buonamici, *Histoire de la dernière Révolution de Gênes*; Adelung, v. 516; vi. 31; &c. &c.

course, and went home with him out of our sight, in the end of 1743; the Diplomatic career gradually declaring itself barred to him thenceforth. Since which, nevertheless, he has had his successes otherwise, especially in his old Literary course: on the whole, brighter sunshine than usual, though never without tempestuous clouds attending. Goes about, with his divine Emilie, now wearing browner and leaner, both of them, and takes the good and evil of life, mostly in a quiet manner; sensible that afternoon is come.

The thrice-famous Pompadour, who had been known to him in the Chrysalis state, did not forget him on becoming Head-Butterfly of the Universe. By her help, one long wish of his soul was gratified, and did not hunger or thirst any more. Some uncertain footing at Court, namely, was at length vouchsafed him: — uncertain; for the Most Christian Majesty always rather shuddered under those carbuncle eyes, under that voice "sombre and majestious," with such turns lying in it: — some uncertain footing at Court; and from the beginning of 1745, his luck, in the Court spheres, began to mount in a wonderful and world-evident manner. On grounds tragically silly, as he thought them. On the Dauphin's Wedding, — a Termagant's Infanta coming hither as Dauphiness. at this time, — there needed to be Court-shows, Dramaticules, Transparencies, Feasts of Lanterns, or I know not what. Voltaire was the chosen man; Voltaire and Rameau (readers have heard of *Rameau's Nephew*, and musical readers still esteem Rameau) did their feat; we may think with what perfection, with what splendour of reward. Alas, and the feat done was, to one of the parties, so unspeakably contemptible. Voltaire pensively surveying Life, brushes the sounding strings; and hums to himself, the carbuncle eyes carrying in them almost something of wet:

"*Mon* Henri Quatre *et ma* Zaïre,
"*Et mon Américain* Alzire,
"*Ne m'ont jamais valu un seul regard du Roi;*
"*J'avais mille ennemis et très peu de gloire:*
"*Les honneurs et les biens pleuvent enfin sur moi*
"*Pour une Farce de la Foire.*" *

* "My *Henri Quatre*, my *Zaïre*, my *Alzire*' (high works very many), "could never purchase me a single glance of the King; I had multitudes

Yes, my friend; it is a considerable ass, this world; by no means the Perfectly Wise put at the top of it (as one could wish), and the Perfectly Foolish at the bottom. Witness — nay, witness Psyche Pompadour herself, is not she an emblem! Take your luck without criticism; luck good and bad visits all.

2°. *And got into the Academy next Year, in consequence.* In 1746, the Academy itself, Pompadour favouring, is made willing; Voltaire sees himself among the Forty: soul, on that side too, be at ease, and hunger not nor thirst any more.* This highest of felicities could not be achieved without an ugly accompaniment from the surrounding Populace. Desfontaines is dead, safe down in Sodom; but wants not for a whole successor, for a Doggery of such. Who are all awake, and giving tongue on this occasion. There is M. Roi the "Poet," as he was then reckoned; jingling Roi, who concocts satirical calumnies; who collects old ones, reprints the same, — and sends Travenol, an Opera-Fiddler, to vend them. From which sprang a Lawsuit, *Procès Travenol*, of famous melancholy sort. As Voltaire had rather the habit of such sad melancholy Lawsuits, we will pause on this of Travenol for a moment:

3°. *Summary of Travenol Lawsuit.* "Monday, 9th May 1746, "was the Day of reception at the Academy; reception and "fruition, thrice savoury to Voltaire. But what an explosion "of the Doggeries, before, during, and after that event! "Voltaire had tried to be prudent, too. He had been corre-"sponding with Popes, with Cardinals; and, in a fine frank-"looking way, capturing their suffrages: — not by lying,

"of enemies, and very little fame: — honours and riches rain on me, at "last, for a Farce of the Fair" (*Œuvres*, II. 151).

The "Farce" (which by no means *called* itself such) was *Princesse de Navarre* (*Œuvres*, LXXIII. 251): first acted, 23d February 1745, Day of the Wedding. Gentlemanship of the Chamber thereupon (which Voltaire, by permission, sold, shortly after, for 2,500*l.*, with titles retained), and appointment as Historiographer Royal. Poor Dauphiness did not live long; Louis XVI.'s Mother was a *second* Wife, Saxon-Polish Majesty's Daughter.

* "May 9th, 1746, Voltaire is received at the Academy; and makes a "very fine Discourse" (*Barbier*, II. 488). *Œuvres de Voltaire*, LXXIII, 355, 395, and I. 97.

"which in general he wishes to avoid, but by speaking half the "truth; in short, by advancing, in a dexterous, diplomatic "way, the *un*cloven foot, in those Vatican precincts. And had "got the Holy Father's own suffrage for *Mahomet* (think of "that, you Ass of Mirepoix!), among other cases that might "rise. When this seat among the Forty fell vacant, his very "first measure, — mark it, Orthodox reader, — was a Letter "to the Chief Jesuit, Father Latour, Head of one's old College "of Louis le Grand. A Letter of fine filial tenor: 'My ex-"'cellent old Schoolmasters, to whom I owe everything; the "'representatives of learning, of decorum, of frugality and "'modest human virtue: — in what contrast to the obscure "'Doggeries poaching about in the street-gutters, and flying "'at the peaceable passenger!'* Which captivated Father "Latour; and made matters smooth on that side; so that "even the *Ancien de Mirepoix* said nothing, this time: What "could he say? No cloven foot visible, and the Authorities "strong.

"Voltaire had started as Candidate with these judicious "preliminaries. Voltaire was elected, as we saw; fine Dis-"course, 9th May; and on the Official side all things comfort-"able. But, in the mean while, the Doggeries, as natural, "seeing the thing now likely, had risen to a never-imagined "pitch; and had filled Paris, and, to Voltaire's excruciated "sense, the Universe, with their howlings and their hyæna-"laughter, with their pasquils, satires, old and new. So that "Voltaire could not stand it; and, in evil hour, rushed down "stairs upon them; seized one poor dog, Travenol, unknown "to him as Fiddler or otherwise; pinioned Dog Travenol, with "pincers, by the ears, him for one; — proper Police-pincers, "for we are now well at Court; — and had a momentary joy! "And, alas, this was not the right dog; this, we say, was "Travenol a Fiddler at the Opera, who, except the street "noises, knew nothing of Voltaire; much less had the least "pique at him; but had taken to hawking certain Pasquils "(Jingler Roi's *Collection*, it appears), to turn a desirable penny "by them.

* In *Voltairiana, ou Eloges Amphigouriques, &c.* (Paris, 1748), I. 150-160, the *Letter* itself, "Paris, 7th February 1746;" omitted (without need, or real cause on any side) in the common Collections of *Œuvres de Voltaire.*

"And mistakes were made in the Affair Travenol, — old "*Father* Travenol haled to prison, instead of Son, — by the "Lieutenant of Police and his people. And Voltaire took "the high-hand method (being well at Court): — and there-"upon hungry Advocates took up Dog Travenol and his "pincered ears: 'Serene Judges of the Châtelet, Most Christian "'Populace of Paris, did you ever see a Dog so pincered by an "'Academical Gentleman before, merely for being hungry?' "And Voltaire, getting madder and madder, appealed to the "Academy (which would not interfere); filed Criminal Infor-"mations; appealed to the Châtelet, to the Courts above and "to the Courts below; and, for almost a year, there went on "the '*Procès-Travenol*:'* Olympian Jove in distressed circum-"stances, *versus* a hungry Dog who had eaten dirty puddings. "Paris, in all its Saloons and Literary Coffeehouses (figure "the *Antre de Procope*, on Publication nights!), had, monthly "or so, the exquisite malign banquet; and grinned over the "Law Pleadings: what Magazine Serial of our day can be so "interesting to the emptiest mind!

"Lasted, I find, for above a year. From Spring 1746 till "towards Autumn 1747: Voltaire's feelings being — Haha, so "exquisite, all the while! — Well, reader, I can judge how "amusing it was to high and low. And yet Phœbus Apollo "going about as mere Cowherd of Admetus, and exposed to "amuse the populace by his duels with dogs that have bitten "him? It is certain Voltaire was a fool, not to be more "cautious of getting into gutter quarrels; not to have a "thicker skin, in fact."

Procès-Travenol escorting one's Triumphal Entry; what an adjunct! Always so: always in your utmost radiance of sunshine a shadow; and in your softest outburst of Lydian or Spheral symphonies, something of eating Care! Then too, in the Court circle itself, "is Trajan pleased," or are all things well? Readers have heard of that "*Trajan est-il con-*

* About Mayday 1746, Seizure of Travenol; Pleadings are in vigour, August 1746; not done, April 1747. In *Voltairiana*, II. 141-200, Pleadings &c. copiously given; and most of the original Libels, in different parts of that sad Book (compiled by Travenol's Advocate, a very sad fellow himself): see also *Œuvres de Voltaire*, LXXIII. 355 n., 385 n.; *ib.* I. 97; *Barbier*, II. 487. All in a very jumbled, dateless, vague and incorrect condition.

tent?" It occurred, Winter 1745 (27th November 1745, a date worth marking), while things were still in the flush of early hope. That evening, our *Temple de la Gloire* (Temple of Glory) had just been acted for the first time, in honour of him we may call "Trajan," returning from a "Fontenoy and Seven Cities captured:" *

"*Reviens, divin Trajan, vainqueur* "*doux et terrible;*	"Return, divine Trajan, conqueror "sweet and terrible;
"*Le monde est mon rival, tous les* "*cœurs sont à toi;*	"The world is my rival, all hearts "are thine;
"*Mais est-il un cœur plus sensible,*	"But is there a heart more loving,
"*Et qui t'adore plus que moi?*" **	"Or that adores thee more than I?"

An allegoric Dramatic Piece; naturally very admirable at Versailles. Issuing radiant from Fall of the Curtain, Voltaire had the farther honour to see his Majesty pass out; Majesty escorted by Richelieu, one's old friend in a sense: "Is Trajan pleased?" whispered Voltaire to his Richelieu; overheard by Trajan, — who answered in words nothing, but in a visible glance of the eyes, did answer, "Impertinent Lackey!" — Trajan being a man unready with speech; and disliking trouble with the people whom he paid for keeping his boots in polish. Oh my winged Voltaire, to what dunghill Bubbly-Jocks *(Coqs d'Inde)* you do stoop with homage, constrained by their appearance of mere size! —

Evidently no perfect footing at Court, after all. And then the Pompadour, could she, Head Butterfly of the Universe, be an anchor that would hold, if gales rose? Rather she is herself somewhat of a gale, of a continual liability to gales; unstable as the wind! Voltaire did his best to be useful, as Court Poet, as director of Private Theatricals; — above all, to soothe, to flatter Pompadour; and never neglected this evident duty. But, by degrees, the envious Lackey-people made cabals; turned the Divine Butterfly into comparative indifference for Voltaire; into preference of a Crébillon's poor faded Pieces: "Suitabler, these, Madame, for the Private Theatricals of a Most Christian Majesty." Think

* Seven of them; or even eight, of a kind: Tournay, Ghent, Bruges, Nieuport, Dendermond, Ath, Ostend; and nothing lost but Cape Breton and one's Codfishery.

** *Temple de la Gloire*, Acte IV. (*Œuvres*, XII. 328).

what a stab; crueller than daggers through one's heart: "Crébillon?" M. de Voltaire said nothing; looked nothing, in those sacred circles; and never ceased outwardly his worship, and assiduous tuning, of the Pompadour: but he felt — as only Phœbus Apollo, in the like case, can! "Away!" growled he to himself, when this atrocity had culminated. And, in effect, is, since the end of 1746 or so, pretty much withdrawn from the Versailles Olympus; and has set, privately in the distance (now at Cirey, now at Paris, in our *petit palais* there), with his whole will and fire, to do Crébillon's dead Dramas into living ones of his own. Dead *Catilina* of Crébillon into *Rome Sauvée* of Voltaire, and the other samples of dead into living, — that stupid old Crébillon himself and the whole Universe may judge, and even Pompadour feel a remorse! — Readers shall fancy these things; and that the world is coming back to its old poor drab colour, with M. de Voltaire; his divine Emilie and he rubbing along on the old confused terms. One face-to-face peep of them, readers shall now have; and that is to be enough, or more than enough:

Voltaire and the divine Emilie appear suddenly, one Night, at Sceaux.

About the middle of August 1747, King Friedrich, I find, was at home; — not in his new *Sans-Souci* by any means, but running to and fro; busy with his Musterings, "grand review, and mimic attack on Börnstadt, near Berlin;" *Invaliden-Haus* (Military Hospital) getting built; Silesian Reviews just ahead; and, for the present, much festivity and moving about, to Charlottenburg, to Berlin and the different Palaces; Wilhelmina, "August 15th," having come to see him; of which fine visit, especially of Wilhelmina's thoughts on it, — why have the envious Fates left us nothing!

While all this is astir in Berlin and neighbourhood, there is, among the innumerable other visits in this world, one going on near Paris, in the Mansion or Palace of Sceaux, which has by chance become memorable. A visit by Voltaire and his divine Emilie, direct from Paris, I suppose, and rather on the sudden. Which has had the luck to have a *Letter* written on it, by one of those rare creatures, a seeing Witness, who can make others see and believe. The seeing Witness is little Madame de Staal (by no means Necker's Daughter, but a much cleverer), known as one of the sharpest female heads; she from the spot reports it to Madame du Deffand, who also is known to readers. There is such a glimpse afforded here, into the actuality of old things and remarkable human creatures, that Friedrich himself would be happy to read the Letter.

Duchesse du Maine, Lady of Sceaux, is a sublime old personage, with whom and with whose high ways and magnificent hospitalities at Sceaux, at Anet and elsewhere, Voltaire had been familiar for long years past.* This Duchess, granddaughter of the great Condé, now a dowager for ten years, and herself turned of seventy, has been a notable figure in French History, this great while: a living fragment of Louis le Grand, as it were. Was wedded to Louis's "Legitimated" Illegitimate, the Duc du Maine; was in trouble with the Regent d'Orléans about Alberoni-Cellamare conspiracies (1718), Regent having stript her Husband of his high legitimatures and dignities, with little ceremony; which led her to conspire a good deal, at one time.** She was never very beautiful; but had a world of grace and witty intelligence; and knew a Voltaire when she saw him. Was the soul of courtesy and benignity, though proud enough, and carrying her head at its due height; and was always very charming, in her lofty gracious way, to mankind. Interesting to all, were it only as a living fragment of the Grand Epoch, — kind of French Fulness of Time, when the world was at length

* In *Œuvres de Voltaire*, LXXIII. 434 n., X. 8, &c., 'Clog.' and others represent *this* Visit as having been to Anet, — though the record otherwise is express.

** *Duc du Maine* with *Comte de Toulouse* were products of Louis XIV. and Madame de Montespan: — "legitimated" by Papa's fiat, in 1673, while still only young children; dislegitimated again by Regent d'Orléans, autumn 1718; grand scene, "guards drawn out" and the like, on this occasion (*Barbier*, I. 8-11, II. 161); futile Conspiracies with Alberoni thereupon; arrest of Duchess and Duke (29th December 1718), and closure of that poor business. Duc du Maine died, 1736; Toulouse next year; ages, each about sixty-five. "Duc de Penthièvre," Egalité's father-in-law, was Toulouse's son; Maine has left a famous Dowager, whom we see. Nothing more of notable about the one or the other.

blessed with a Louis Quatorze, and Ne-plus-ultra of a Gentleman determined to do the handsome thing in this world. She is much frequented by high people, especially if of a Literary or Historical turn. President Hénault (of the *Abrégé Chronologique*, the well-frilled, accurately powdered, most correct old legal gentleman) is one of her adherents; Voltaire is another, that may stand for many: there is an old Marquis de St. Aulaire, whom she calls "*mon vieux berger* (my old shepherd," that is to say, sweetheart or flame of love);* there is a most learned President de Mesmes, and others we have heard of, but do not wish to know. Little De Staal was at one time this fine Duchess's maid; but has far outgrown all that, a favourite guest of the Duchess's instead; holds now mainly by Madame du Deffand (not yet fallen blind), — and is well turned of fifty, and known for one of the shrewdest little souls in the world, at the time she writes. Her Letter is addressed "*To Madame du Deffand*, at Paris;" most free-flowing female Letter; of many pages, runs on, day after day, for a fortnight or so; — only Excerpts of it introducible here:

"*Sceaux, Tuesday, 15th August* 1747. * * Madame du "Châtelet and Voltaire, who had announced themselves as "for to-day, and whom nobody had heard of otherwise, made "their appearance yesternight, near midnight; like two "Spectres, with an odour of embalmment about them, as if "just out of their tombs. We were rising from table; the "Spectres, however, were hungry ones: they needed supper; "and what is more, beds, which were not ready. The House-"keeper *(Concierge)*, who had gone to bed, rose in great "haste. Gaya" (amiable gentleman, conceivable, not known), "who had offered his apartment for pressing cases, "was obliged to yield it in this emergency: he flitted with as "much precipitation and displeasure as an army surprised in "its camp; leaving a part of his baggage in the enemy's "hands. Voltaire thought the lodging excellent, but that did "not at all console Gaya.

"As to the Lady, her bed turns out not to have been well "made; they have had to put her in a new place today.

* *Barbier*, II. 87; see ib. (I. 8-11; II. 181, 436; &c.) for many notices of her affairs and her.

"Observe, she made that bed herself, no servants being up, "and had found a blemish or *défaut* of" — word wanting: who knows what? — "in the mattresses; which I believe "hurt her exact mind, more than her not very delicate body. "She has got, in the interim, an apartment promised to some-"body else; and she will have to leave it again on Friday or "Saturday, and go into that of Maréchal de Maillebois, who "leaves at that time.

— Yes; Maillebois in the body, O reader. This is he, with the old ape-face renewed by paint, whom we once saw marching with an "Army of Redemption," haggling in the Passes about Eger, unable to redeem Belleisle; marching and haggling, more lately, with a "Middle-Rhine Army," and the like non-effect; since which, fighting his best in Italy, — pushed home last winter, with Browne's bayonets in his back; Belleisle succeeding him in dealing with Browne. Belleisle, and the "Revolt of Genoa" (fatal to Browne's Invasion of us), and the Defence of Genoa and the mutual worryings thereabout, are going on at a great rate, — and there is terrible news out of those Savoy Passes, while Maillebois is here. Concerning which by and by. He is grandson of the renowned Colbert, this Maillebois. A Field-Marshal evidently extant, you perceive, in those vanished times: is to make room for Madame on Friday, says our little De Staal; and take leave of us, — if for good, so much the better!

"He came at the time we did, with his daughter and "grand-daughter: the one is pretty, the other ugly and "dreary" — (*l'une*, *l'autre;* no saying which, in such important case! Madame la Maréchale, the mother and grandmother, I think must be dead. Not beautiful she, nor very benignant, "*une très-méchante femme,* very cat-witted woman," says Barbier; "shrieked like a devil, at Court, upon the "Cardinal," about that old *Army-of-Redemption* business; but all her noise did nothing).* — "M. le Maréchal has "hunted here with his dogs, in these fine autumn woods and "glades; chased a bit of a stag, and caught a poor doe's "fawn: that was all that could be got there.

"Our new Guests will make better sport: they are going "to have their Comedy acted again" (Comedy of *The Exchange,* much an entertainment with them): "Vanture" (conceivable,

* Barbier, II. 339 ("November 1742").

not known) "is to do the Count de Boursoufle *(de Blister* or *de* "*Windbag)*; you will not say this is a hit, any more than "Madame du Châtelet's doing the Hon. Miss Piggery *(La* "*Cochonnière)*, who ought to be fat and short."* — Little De Staal then abruptly breaks off, to ask about her Correspondent's health, and her Correspondent's friend old President Hénault's health; touches on those "grumblings and discords in the Army *(tracasseries de l'Armée)*," which are making such a stir; how M. d'Argenson, our fine War-Minister, man of talent amid blockheads, will manage them; and suddenly exclaims: "O my queen, what curious animals "men and women are! I laugh at their manœuvres, the days "when I have slept well; if I have missed sleep, I could kill "them. These changes of temper prove that I do not break "off kind. Let us mock other people, and let other people "mock us; it is well done on both sides." — (Poor little De Staal: to what a posture have things come with you, in that fast-rotting Epoch, of Hypocrisies becoming all insolvent!)

"*Wednesday, 16th.* Our Ghosts do not show themselves "by daylight. They appeared yesterday at ten in the "evening; I do not think we shall see them sooner today: "the one is engaged in writing high feats" *(Siècle de Louis XV*, or what at last became such); "the other in commenting "Newton. They will neither play nor walk: they are, in "fact, equivalent to *zeros* in a society where their learned "writings are of no significance." — (Pauses, without notice given, for some hours, perhaps days; then resuming): — "Nay, worse still: their apparition tonight has produced a "vehement declamation on one of our little social diversions "here, the game of *Cavagnole:*** it was continued and main-"tained," on the part of Madame du Châtelet, you guess, "in a tone which is altogether unheard of in this place; "and was endured," on the part of Serene Highness, "with a "moderation not less surprising. But what is unendurable "is my babble" — And herewith our nimble little woman hops off again into the general field of things; and gossips largely, How you are, my queen, Whither you are going,

* *L'Echange*, The Exchange, *or When shall I get married!* Farce in three acts: *Œuvres*, x. 167-222; used to be played at Cirey and elsewhere (see plenty of details upon it, exact or not quite so, *ib.* 7-9).

** "Kind of *Biribi*," it would appear; in the height of fashion then.

Whither we; That the Maillebois people are away, and also the Villeneuves, if anybody knew them now; then how the Estillacs, to the number of four, are coming tomorrow; and Cousin Soquence, for all his hunting, can catch nothing; and it is a continual coming and going; and how Boursoufle is to be played, and a Dame Dufour is just come, who will do a character. Rubrics, vanished Shadows, nearly all those high Dames and Gentlemen; *la pauvre* Saint-Pierre, "eaten with gout," who is she? "Still drags herself about, as well as she "can; but not with me, for I never go by land, and she "seems to have the hydrophobia, when I take to the water." (Thread of date is gone! I almost think we must have got to Saturday by this time: — or perhaps it is only Thursday, and Maillebois off prematurely, to be out of the way of the Farce? Little De Staal takes no notice; but continues gossiping rapidly):

"Yesterday Madame du Châtelet got into her third lodg-"ing: she could not any longer endure the one she had "chosen. There was noise in it, smoke without fire: — pri-"vately meseems, a little the emblem of herself! As to noise, "it was not by night that it incommoded her, she told me, but "by day, when she was in the thick of her work: it deranges "her ideas. She is busy reviewing her *Principles*" — *Newton's Principia*, no doubt, but De Staal will understand it only as *Principes*, Principles in general: — "it is an exercise she "repeats every year, without which the Principles might get "away, and perhaps go so far she would never find them "again" (You satirical little gipsy!). "Her head, like "enough, is a kind of lock-up for them, rather than a birth-"place, or natural home: and that is a case for watching care-"fully lest they get away. She prefers the high air of this "occupation to every kind of amusement, and persists in not "showing herself till after dark. Voltaire has produced some "gallant verses" (unknown to Editors), "which help off, a "little, the bad effect of such unusual behaviour.

"*Sunday, 27th.* I told you on Thursday" (no, you didn't; you only meant to tell) "that our Spectres were going on the "morrow, and that the Piece was to be played that evening: "all this has been done. I cannot give you much of Bour-"soufle" (done by one Vanture). "Mademoiselle Piggery" (*de la Cochonnière*, Madame Du Châtelet herself) "executed "so perfectly the extravagance of her part, that I own it gave "me real pleasure. But Vanture only put his own fatuity into "the character of Boursoufle, which wanted more: he played "naturally in a Piece where all requires to be forced, like the "subject of it." — What a pity none of us has read this fine "Farce! "One Pâris did the part of *Muscadin* (Little Cox-"comb), which name represents his character: in short, it can "be said the Farce was well given. The Author ennobled it "by a Prologue for the Occasion; which he acted very well, "along with Madame Dufour as *Barbe* (Governess Barbara), "— who, but for this brilliant action, could not have put up "with merely being Governess to Piggery. And, in fact, she "disdained the simplicity of dress which her part required; — "as did the chief Actress," Du Châtelet herself (age now forty-one); "who, in playing *Piggery*, preferred the interests "of her own face to those of the Piece, and made her entry in "all the splendour and elegant equipments of a Court Lady," — her "*Principles*," though the key is turned upon them, not unlike jumping out of window, one would say! "She had a "crow to pluck" (*maille à partir*, "clasp to open," which is better) "with Voltaire on this point: but she is sovereign, and "he is slave. I am very sorry at their going, though I was "worn out with doing her multifarious errands all the time she "was here.

Wednesday, 30th. "M. le President" (Hénault) "has been "asked hither; and he is to bring you, my Queen! Tried all "I could to hinder; but they would not be put off. If your "health and disposition do suit, it will be charming. In any "case, I have got you a good apartment: 'it is the one that "'Madame du Châtelet had seized upon, after an exact review "'of all the Mansion. There will be a little less furniture than "'she had put in it; Madame had pillaged all her previous "'apartments to equip this one. We found about seven "'tables in it, for one item: she needs them of all sizes; im-"'mense, to spread out her papers upon; solid, to support her "'*nécessaire;* slighter, for her nicknacks (*pompons*), for her "'jewels. And this fine arrangement did not save her from an "'accident like that of Philip II., when, after spending all "'the night in writing, he got his despatches drowned by the "'oversetting of an inkbottle. The Lady did not pretend to "'imitate the moderation of that Prince; at any rate, he was "'only writing on affairs of state; and the thing they blotted, "'on this occasion, was Algebra, much more difficult to clean "'up again.

"'This subject ought to be exhausted: one word more, "'and then it does end. The day after their departure, I "'receive a Letter of four pages, and a Note enclosed, which "'announces dreadful hurly-burly: M. de Voltaire has mis-"'laid his Farce, forgotten to get back the parts, and lost his "'Prologue: I am to find all that again'" (excessively tremulous about his Manuscripts, M. de Voltaire; of such value are they, of such danger to him; there is *La Pucelle*, for example, — enough to hang a man, were it surreptitiously launched forth in print!) — "'I am to send him the Prologue instantly, "'not by post, because they would copy it; to keep the parts "'for fear of the same accident, and to lock up the Piece "'"under a hundred keys." I should have thought one pad-"'lock sufficient for this treasure! I have duly executed his "'orders.'" *

And herewith *explicit de Staal.* Scene closes: *exeunt omnes;* are off to Paris or Versailles again; to Lunéville and the Court of Stanislaus again, — where also adventures await them, which will be heard of!

"Figure to yourself," says some other Eyewitness, "a lean Lady, with big arms and long legs; small head, "and countenance losing itself in a cloudery of head-"dress; cocked nose" (*retroussé*, say you? Very slightly, then; quite an unobjectionable nose!) "and pair of "small greenish eyes; complexion tawny, and mouth "too big: this was the divine Emilie, whom Voltaire "celebrates to the stars. Loaded to extravagance with "ribbons, laces, face-patches, jewels and female orna-"ments; determined to be sumptuous in spite of Eco-"nomics, and pretty in spite of Nature:" Pooh, it is an enemy's hand that paints! "And then by her side," continues he, "the thin long figure of Voltaire, that

* *Madame de Graffigny* (Paris, 1820), pp. 283-291.

"Anatomy of an Apollo, affecting worship of her,"* — yes; that thin long Gentleman, with high red-heeled shoes, and the daintiest polite attitudes and paces; in superfine coat, laced hat under arm; nose and underlip ever more like coalescing (owing to decay of teeth), but two eyes shining on you like carbuncles; and in the ringing voice, such touches of speech when you apply for it! Thus they at Sceaux and elsewhere; walking their Life-minuet, making their entrances and exits.

One thing is lamentable: the relation with Madame is not now a flourishing one, or capable again of being: "Does not love me as he did, the wretch!" thinks Madame always; — yet sticks by him, were it but in the form of blister. They had been to Lunéville, Spring 1747; happy dull place, within reach of Cirey; far from Versailles and its cabals. They went again, 1748, in a kind of permanent way; Titular Stanislaus, an opulent dawdling creature, much liking to have them; and Father Menou, his Jesuit, — who is always in quarrel with the Titular Mistress, — thinking to displace *her* (as you gradually discover), and promote the Du Châtelet to that improper dignity! In which he had not the least success, says Voltaire; but got "two women on his ears instead of one." It was not to be Stanislaus's mistress; nor a *titular* one at all, but a real, that Madame was fated in this dull happy place! Idle readers know the story only too well; — concerning which, admit this other Fraction and no more:

* From Bödenbeck (quoting somebody, whom I have surely seen in French; whom Bödenbeck tries to name, as he could have done, but curiously without success), i. 179.

"Stanislaus, as a Titular King, cannot do without some "kind of Titular Army, — were it only to blare about as "Lifeguard, and beat kettledrums on occasion. A certain tall "high-sniffing M. de St. Lambert, a young Lorrainer of long "pedigree and light purse, had just taken refuge in this Life-"guard" (Summer 1748, or so), "I know not whether as Cap-"tain or Lieutenant, just come from the Netherlands Wars: "of grave stiff manners; for the rest, a good-looking young "fellow; thought to have some poetic genius, even; — who is "precious, surely, in such an out-of-the-way place. Welcome "to Voltaire, to Madame still more. Alas, readers know the "History, — on which we must not dwell. Madame, a brown "geometric Lady, age now forty-two, with a Great Man who "has scandalously ceased to love her, casts her eye upon St. "Lambert: 'Yes, you would be the shoeing-horn, Monsieur, "'if one had time, you fine florid fellow, hardly yet into your "'thirties —' And tries him with a little coquetry; I always "think, perhaps in this view chiefly? And then, at any rate, "as he responded, the thing itself became so interesting: "'Our Ulysses-bow, we can still bend it, then, aha!' And is "not that a pretty stag withal, worth bringing down; florid, "just entering his thirties, and with the susceptibilities of "genius! Voltaire was not blind, could he have helped it, — "had he been tremulously alive to help it. 'Your Verses to "'her, my St. Lambert, — ah, Tibullus never did the like of "'them. Yes, to you are the roses, my fine young friend, to "'me are the thorns:' thus sings Voltaire in response; * per-"haps not thinking it would go so far. And it went, — alas, "it went to all lengths, mentionable, and not mentionable: "and M. le Marquis had to be coaxed home in the Spring of "1749, — still earlier it had been suitabler; — and in Septem-"ber ensuing, M. de St. Lambert looking his demurest, there "is an important lying-in to be transacted! Newton's *Prin-"cipia* is, by that time, drawing diligently to its close; — "complicated by such far abstruser Problems, not of the "geometric sort! Poor little lean brown woman, what a Life, "after all; what an End of a Life!" —

* *Œuvres*, XVII. 323 ("*Epître à M. de St. Lambert*, 1749"); &c. &c. In *Memoires sur Voltaire par Longchamp et Wagnière* (Paris, 1826), II. 229 et seq., details enough and more.

War-Passages in 1747.

The War, since Friedrich got out of it, does not abate in animosity, nor want for bloodshed, battle and sieging; but offers little now memorable. March 18th, 1747, a ghastly Phantasm of a Congress, "Congress of Breda," which had for some months been attempting Peace, and was never able to get into conference, or sit in its chairs except for moments, flew away altogether;* and left the War perhaps angrier than ever, more hopelessly stupid than ever. Except, indeed, that resources are failing; money running low in France, Parliaments beginning to murmur, and among the Population generally a feeling that glory is excellent, but will not make the national pot boil. Perhaps all this will be more effective than Congresses of Breda? Here are the few Notes worth giving:

April 23d-30th, 1747, *The French invade Holland; whereupon, suddenly, a Stadtholder there.* "After Fontenoy, there "has been much sieging and capturing in that Netherlands "Country, a series of successes gloriously delightful to "Maréchal de Saxe and the French Nation: likewise (in bar "of said sieging, in futile attempt to bar it) a Battle of "Roucoux, October 1746; with victory, or quasi-victory, to "Saxe, at least with prostration to the opposite part. And "farther on, there is a Battle of Lauffeld coming, 2d July "1747; with similar results; frustration evident, retreat evi"dent, victory not much to speak of. And in this gloriously "delightful manner, Saxe and the French Nation have "proceeded, till in fact the Netherlands Territory with all

* In September 1746, had got together; but would not take life, on trying and again trying, and fell forgotten: February 1747, again gleams up into hope: March 18th and the following days, vanishes for good (*Adelung*, v. 50; vi. 6, 62).

"strongholds, except Maestricht alone, was theirs, — and "they decided on attacking the Dutch Republic itself. And "(17th April 1747) actually broke in upon the frontier Fortress-"es of Zealand; found the same dry-rotten every where; "and took them, Fortress after Fortress, at the rate of a "cannon salvo each: 'Ye magnanimous Dutch; see what you "'have got by not sitting still, as recommended!' To the "horror and terror of the poor Zealanders, and general Dutch "Population. Who shrieked to England for help; — and "were, on the very instant, furnished with a modicum of "Seventy-fours (Dutch Courier returning by the same); which "landed the Courier, April 23d, and put Walcheren in a state "of security. *

"Whereupon the Dutch Population turned round on its "Governors, with a growl of indignation, spreading ever "wider, waxing ever higher: 'Scandalous laggards, is this "'your mode of governing a free Republic? Freedom to let "'the State go to dry-rot, and become the laughing-stock of "'mankind. To provide for your own paltry kindred in the "'State-employments; to palaver grandly with all comers; "'and publish melodious Despatches of Van Hoey? Had not "'Britannic Majesty, for his dear Daughter's sake, come to "'the rescue in this crisis, where had we been? We demand a "'Stadtholder again; our glorious Nassau Orange, to keep "'some bridle on you!' And actually, in this way, Populus "and Plebs, by general turning out into the streets, in a "gloomily indignant manner, which threatens to become "vociferous and dangerous, — cowed the Heads of the Re-"public into choosing the said Prince, with Princess and "Family, as Stadtholder, High Admiral, High-Everything "and Supreme of the Republic. Hereditary, no less, and "punctually perpetual; Princess and Family to share in it. "In which happy state (ripened into Kingship latterly) they "continue to this day. A result painfully surprising to Most "Christian Majesty; gratifying to Britannic proportionately, "or more; — and indeed beneficial towards abating dry-rot "and melodious palaver in that poor Land of the Free. Con-"summated, by popular outbreak of vociferation, in the dif-"ferent Provinces, in about a week from April 23d, when "those helpful Seventy-fours hove in sight. Stadtholdership

* Adelung, vi. 105, 125-134.

"had been in abeyance for forty-five years. * The new Stadt-"holder did his best; could not, in the short life granted him, "do nearly enough. — Next year there was a *second* Dutch "outbreak, or general turning into the streets; of much more "violent character; in regard to glaringly unjust Excises and "Taxations, and to 'instant dismissal of your Excise-Farmers,' "as the special first item. ** Which salutary object being ac-"complished (new Stadtholder well aiding, in a valiant and "judicious manner), there has no third dose of that dangerous "remedy been needed since.

"*July 19th, Fate of Chevalier de Belleisle.* At the Fortress of "Exilles, in one of those Passes of the Savoy Alps, — Pass of "Col di Sieta, memorable to the French soldier ever since, — "there occurred a lamentable thing;" doubtless much talked of at Sceaux while Voltaire was there. "The Revolt of Genoa "(popular outburst, and expulsion of our poor friend Botta "and his Austrians, then a famous thing, and a rarer than "now) having suddenly recalled the victorious General "Browne from his Siege of Antibes and Invasion of Provence, "— Maréchal Duc de Belleisle, well reinforced and now be-"come 'Army of Italy' in general, followed stedfastly for "'Defence of Genoa' against indignant Botta, Browne and "Company. For defence of Genoa; nay for attack on Turin, "which would have been 'defence' in Genoa and everywhere, "— had the captious Spaniard consented to coöperate. Cap-"tious Spaniard would not; Couriers to Madrid, to Paris "thereupon, and much time lost; — till, at the eleventh hour, "came consent from Paris, 'Try it by yourself, then!' Belle-"isle tries it; at least his Brother does. His Brother, the "Chevalier, is to force that Pass of Exilles; a terrible fiery "business, but the back-bone of the whole adventure: in "which, if the Chevalier can succeed, he too is to be Maréchal "de France. Forward, therefore, climb the Alpine stairs "again; snatch me that Fort of Exilles.

"And so, July 19th, 1747, the Chevalier comes in sight of "the Place; scans a little the frowning buttresses, bristly

* Since our Dutch William's death, 1702.

** *Adelung*, vi. 364 et seq.; *Raumer*, 182-193 ("March—September 1748"); or, in *Chesterfield's Works*, Dayrolles's Letters to Chesterfield: somewhat unintelligent and unintelligible, both Raumer and he.

"with guns; the dumb Alps, to right and left, looking down "on him and it. Chevalier de Belleisle judges that, however "difficult, it can and must be possible to French valour; and "storms in upon it, huge and furious (20,000, or if needful "30,000); — but is torn into mere wreck, and hideous recoil; "rallies, snatches a standard, 'We must take it or die,' — and "dies, does not take it; falls shot on the rampart, 'pulling at "'the palisades with his own hands,' nay some say 'with his "'teeth,' when the last moments came. Within one hour, he "has lost 4,000 men; and himself and his Brother's Enterprise "lie ended there.* Fancy his poor Brother's feelings, who "much loved him! The discords about War-matters (*tracas-* "*series de l'Armée*) were a topic at Sceaux lately, as De Staal "intimated. 'Why starve our Italian Enterprises; heaping "'every resource upon the Netherlands and Saxe?' Diligent "Defence of Genoa (chiefly by flourishing of swords on the "part of France, for the Austrians were not yet ready) is "henceforth all the Italian War there is; and this explosion "at Exilles may fitly be finis to it here. Let us only say that "Infant Philip did, when the Peace came, get a bit of Apan- "age (Parma and Piacenza or some such thing, contemptibly "small to the Maternal heart), and that all things else lapsed "to their pristine state, *minus* only the waste and ruin there "had been.

July 12th — September 18th: Siege of the chief Dutch Fortress. "Unexpected Siege of Bergen-op-Zoom; two months of in- "tense excitement to the Dutch Patriots and Cause-of-Liberty "Gazetteers, as indifferent and totally dead as it has now "become. Maréchal de Saxe, after his victory at Lauffeld, "2d July, did not besiege Maestricht, as had been the universal "expectation; but shot off an efficient lieutenant of his, one "Löwendahl, in due force, privately ready, to overwhelm "Bergen-op-Zoom with sudden Siege, while he himself lay "between the beaten enemy and it. Bergen is the heart of "Holland, key of the Scheld, and quite otherwise important "than Maestricht. 'Coehorn's masterpiece!' exclaimed the "Gazetteers: 'Impregnable, you may depend!' 'We shall "'see,' answered Saxe, answered Löwendahl the Dane (who

* Voltaire, xxv. 221 et seq. (*Siècle de Louis Quinze*, c. 22); Adelung, vi. 174.

"also became Maréchal by this business); and after a great "deal of furious assaulting and battering, took the Place, "September 18th, before daylight," by a kind of surprisal or quasi-storm; — "the Commandant, one Cronström, a brave "old Swede, age towards ninety, not being of very wakeful "nature! 'Did as well as could be expected of him,' said the "Court Martial sitting on his case, and forbore to shoot the "poor old man.* A sore stroke, this of Bergen, to Britannic "Majesty and the Friends of Liberty; who nevertheless refuse "to be discouraged.

December 25th, Russians in behalf of Human Liberty. March "of 36,000 Russians from the City of Moscow, this day; on a "very long journey, in the hoary Christmas weather! Most "Christian Majesty is ruinously short of money; Britannic "Majesty has still credit, and a voting Parliament, but owing "to French influence on the Continent, can get no recruits to "hire. Gradually driven upon Russia, in such stress, Britannic Majesty has this year hired for himself a 35,000 Russians; "30,000 regular foot; 4,000 ditto horse, and 1,000 Cossacks; "— uncommonly cheap, only 150,000*l.* the lot, not 4*l.* per "head by the year. And, in spite of many difficulties and "hagglings, they actually get on march, from Moscow, 25th "December 1747; and creep on, all Winter, through the "frozen peaty wildernesses, through Lithuania, Poland, towards Böhmen, Mähren: are to appear in the Rhine Countries, joined by certain Austrians; and astonish mankind "next Spring. Their Captain is one Repnin, Prince Repnin, "afterwards famous enough in those Polish Countries;" — which is now the one point interesting to us in the thing. "Their Captain *was*, first, to be Lacy, old Marshal Lacy; "then, failing Lacy, 'Why not General Keith?' — but proves "to be Repnin, after much hustling and intriguing:" Repnin, not Keith, that is the interesting point.

"Such march of the Russians, on behalf of Human Liberty, "in pay of Britannic Majesty, is a surprising fact; and considerably discomposes the French. Who bestir themselves "in Sweden and elsewhere against Russia and it: with no "result, — except perhaps the incidental one, of getting our

* *Adelung,* VI. 184, 206; — "for Cronström," if anyone is curious, "see Schlötzer, *Schwedische Biographie,* II. 252 (*in voce*)."

"esteemed old friend Guy Dickens, now Sir Guy, dismissed "from Stockholm, and we hope put on half-pay on his return "home."*

Marshal Keith comes to Prussia (Sept. 1747).

"Much hustling and intriguing," it appears, in regard to the Captaincy of these Russians. Concerning which there is no word worthy to be said, — except for one reason only, That it finished off the connexion of General Keith with Russia. That this of seeing Repnin, his junior and inferior, preferred to him, was, of many disgusts, the last drop which made the cup run over; — and led the said General to fling it from him, and seek new fields of employment. From Hamburg, having got so far, he addresses himself, 1st September 1747, to Friedrich, with offer of service; who grasps eagerly at the offer: "Feldmarschall your rank; income, 1,200 *l.* a year; income, welcome, all suitable:" — and October 28th, Feldmarschall Keith finishes, at Potsdam, a long Letter to his Brother Lord Marischal, in these words, worth giving, as those of a very clear-eyed sound observer of men and things:

"I have now the honour, and which is still more, the "pleasure, of being with the King at Potsdam; where he "ordered me to come," 17th current, "two days after he de-"clared me Fieldmarshal; where I have the honour to dine "and sup with him almost every day. He has more wit than "I have wit to tell you; speaks solidly and knowingly on all "kinds of subjects; and I am much mistaken if, with the ex-"perience of Four Campaigns, he is not the best Officer of "his Army. He has several persons," Rothenburg, Winter-

* *Adelung*, vi. 250, 302: — Sir Guy, not yet invalided, "went to Russia," and other errands.

feld, Swedish Rudenskjöld (just about departing), not to speak of D'Argens and the French, "with whom he lives in "almost the familiarity of a friend, — but has no favourite; — "and shows a natural politeness for everybody who is about "him. For one who has been four days about his person, "you will say I pretend to know a great deal of his character: "but what I tell you, you may depend upon. With more "time, I shall know as much of him as he will let me know; — "and all his Ministry knows no more."*

A notable acquisition to Friedrich; — and to the two Keiths withal; for Friedrich attached both of them to his Court and service, after their unlucky wanderings; and took to them both, in no common degree. As will abundantly appear.

While that Russian Corps was marching out of Moscow, Cocceji and his Commissions report from Pommern, that the Pomeranian Law-stables are completely clear; that the New Courts have, for many months back, been in work, and are now, at the end of the Year, fairly abreast with it, according to program; — have "decided of Old-Pending Lawsuits 2,400, all that there "were (one of them 200 years old, and filling seventy "Volumes); and of the 994 New ones, 772; not one "Lawsuit remaining over from the previous Year." A highly gratifying bit of news to his Majesty; who answers emphatically, *Engel* and directs that the Law Hercules proceed now to the other Provinces, — to the Kur-Mark, now, and Berlin itself, — with his salutary industries. Naming him "Grand Chancellor," moreover; that is to say, under a new title, Head of

* Varnhagen von Ense, *Leben des Feldmarschalls Jakob Keith* (Berlin, 1844), p 100; Adelung, vi. 244.

Prussian Law, — old Arnim, "Minister of Justice," having shown himself disaffected to Law-Reform, and got rebuked in consequence, and sulkily gone into private life.*

In February of this Year, 1747, Friedrich had something like a stroke of apoplexy; "sank suddenly motionless, one day," and sat insensible, perhaps for half an hour: to the terror and horror of those about him. Hemiplegia, he calls it; rush of blood to the head; — probably indigestion, or gouty humours, exasperated by overfatigue. Which occasioned great rumour in the world; and at Paris, to Voltaire's horror, reports of his death. He himself made light of the matter:** and it did not prove to have been important; was never followed by anything similar through his long life; and produced no change in his often-wavering health, or in his habits, which were always steady. He is writing *Memoirs;* settling "Colonies" (on his waste moors); improving Harbours. Waiting when this European War will end; politely deaf to the offers of Britannic Majesty as to taking the least personal share in it.

* Stenzel, IV. 321; Ranke, III. 389.

** To Voltaire, 22d February 1747 (*Œuvres de Frédéric*, XXII. 164): see *ib.* 164 n.

CHAPTER III.

EUROPEAN WAR FALLS DONE: TREATY OF AIX-LA-CHAPELLE.

The preparations for Campaign 1748 were on a larger scale than ever. Britannic Subsidies, a New Parliament being of willing mind, are opulent to a degree; 192,000 men, 60,000 Austrians for one item, shall be in the Netherlands; — coupled with this remarkable new clause, "And they are to be there in "fact, and not on paper only," and with a tare-and-tret of 30 or 40 per cent, as too often heretofore! Holland, under its New Stadtholder, is stanch of purpose, if of nothing else. The 35,000 Russians, tramping along, are actually dawning over the horizon, towards Teutschland, — King Friedrich standing to arms along his Silesian Border, vigilant "Cordon of Troops all the way," in watch of such questionable transit.* Britannic Majesty and Parliament seem resolute to try, once more, to the utmost, the power of the breeches-pocket in defending this sacred Cause of Liberty so-called.

Breeches-pocket *minus* most other requisites: alas, with such methods as you have, what can come of it? Royal Highness of Cumberland is a valiant man, knowing of War little more than the White Horse of Hano-

* In *Adelung*, vi. 110, 143, 167, 399 ("April 1747 — August 1748"), account of the more and more visible ill-will of the Czarina: "jealousy" about Sweden, about Dantzig, Poland, &c. &c.

ver does; — certain of ruin again, at the hands of Maréchal de Saxe. So think many, and have their dismal misgivings. "Saxe having eaten Bergen-op-Zoom before our eyes, what can withstand the teeth of Saxe?" In fact, there remains only Maestricht, of considerable; and then Holland is as good as his! As for King Louis, glory, with funds running out, and the pot ceasing to boil, has lost its charm to an afflicted France and him. King Louis's wishes are known, this long while; — and Ligonier, generously dismissed by him after Lauffeld, has brought express word to that effect, and outline of the modest terms proposed in one's hour of victory, with pot ceasing to boil.

On a sudden, too, "March 18th," — wintry blasts and hailstorms still raging, — Maréchal de Saxe, regardless of Domestic Hunger, took the field, stronger than ever. Manœuvered about; bewildering the mind of Royal Highness and the Stadtholder ("Will he besiege Breda? Will he do this, will he do that?") — poor Highness and poor Stadtholder; who "did not agree well together," and had not the half of their forces come in, not to speak of handling them when come! Bewilderment of those two once completed, Maréchal de Saxe made "a beautiful march upon Maestricht;" and, April 15th, opened trenches, a very Vesuvius of artillery, before that place; Royal Highness gazing into it, in a doleful manner, from the adjacent steeple-tops. Royal Highness, valour's self, has to admit; "Such an outlook; not half of us got together! The 60,000 Austrians are but 30,000; the — In fact, you will have to make Peace, what else?"*

* His Letters, in Coxe's *Pelham* ("March 29th — April 2d, 1748"), i. 405-410.

Nothing else, as has been evident to practical Official People (especially to frugal Pelham, Chesterfield, and other leading heads) for these two months last past.

In a word, those 35,000 Russians are still far away under the horizon, when thoughts of a new Congress, "Congress of Aix-la-Chapelle," are busying the public mind: "Mere moonshine again?" "Something real this time?" — And on and from March 17th (Lord Sandwich first on the ground, and Robinson from Vienna coming to help), the actual Congress begins assembling there. April 24th, the Congress gets actually to business; very intent on doing it; at least the three main parties, France, England, Holland, are supremely so. Who, finding, for five diligent days, nothing but haggle and objection on the part of the others, did by themselves meet under cloud of night, "night of April 29th-30th;" and — bring the Preliminaries to perfection. And have them signed before daybreak; which is, in effect, signing, or at least fixing as certain, the Treaty itself; so that Armistice can ensue straightway, and the War essentially end.

A fixed thing; the Purseholders having signed. On the safe rear of which, your recipient Subsidiary Parties can argue and protest (as the Empress-Queen and her Kaunitz vehemently did, to great lengths), and gradually come in and finish. Which, in the course of the next six months, they all did, Empress-Queen and Excellency Kaunitz not excepted. And so, October 18th, 1748, all details being, in the interim, either got settled, or got flung into corners as unsettleable (mostly the latter), — Treaty itself was signed by everybody; and there was "Peace of Aix-la-Chapelle." Upon which, except to remark transiently how inconclusive a conclusion it was, mere end of war because your powder is run out, mere truce till you gather breath and gunpowder again, we will spend no word in this place.*

"The Treaty of Aix-la-Chapelle was done in a hurry and "a huddle; greatly to Maria Theresa's disgust. 'Why not "'go on with your expenditures, ye Sea-Powers? Can money "'and life be spent better? I have yet conquered next to "'nothing for the Cause of Liberty and myself!' But the "Sea-Powers were tired of it; the Dutch especially, who had "been hoisted with such difficulty, tended strongly, New "Stadtholder notwithstanding, to plump down again into "stable equilibrium on the broad-bottom principle. Huddle "up the matter; end it, well if you can; any way end it. The "Treaty contained many Articles, now become forgettable to "mankind. There is only One Article, and the Want of One, "which shall concern us in this place. The One Article is: "guarantee by all the European Powers to Friedrich's Treaty "of Dresden. Punctually got as bargained for, — French "especially willing; Britannic Majesty perhaps a little languid, "but his Ministers positive on the point; so that Friedrich's "Envoy had not much difficulty at Aix. And now, Friedrich's "Ownership of Silesia recognised by all the Powers to be "final and unquestionable, surely nothing more is wanted? "Nothing, — except keeping of this solemn stipulation by all "the Powers. How it was kept by some of them; in what "sense some of them are keeping it even now, we shall see by "and by.

"The Want of an Article was, on the part of England, "concerning *Jenkins's Ear*. There is not the least conclusion "arrived at on that important Spanish-English Question;

* Complete details in *Adelung*, vi. 225-409: "October 1747," Ligonier returning, and first rumour of new Congress (226), "17th March 1748," Sandwich come (323); "April 29-30th," meet under cloud of night (326); Kaunitz protesting (339): "2d August," Russians to halt and turn (397); "are over into the Oberpfalz, magazines ahead at Nürnberg;" in September, get to Böhmen again, and winter there: "18th October 1748," Treaty finished (398, 409); Treaty itself given (*ib.*, Beylage, 44). See *Gentleman's Magazine*, and *Old Newspapers* of 1748; Coxe's *Pelham*, ii. 7-41, i. 366-416.

"blind beginning of all these conflagrations; and which, in "its meaning to the somnambulant Nation, is so immense. "No notice taken of it; huddled together, some hasty shovel-"ful or two of diplomatic ashes cast on it, 'As good as extinct, "'you see!' Left smoking, when all the rest is quenched. "Considerable feeling there was, on this point, in the heart "of the poor somnambulant English Nation; much dumb or "semi-articulate growling on such a Peace-Treaty: 'We "'have arrived nowhere, then, by all this fighting, and squan-"'dering, and perilous stumbling among the chimney-pots? "'Spain (on its own showing) owed us 95,000*l.* Spain's debt "'to Hanover; yes, you take care of that; some old sixpenny "'matter, which nobody ever heard of before: and of Spain's "'huge debt to England you drop no hint; of the 95,000*l.*, "'clear money, due by Spain; or of one's liberty to navigate "'the High Seas, none!'* A Peace the reverse of applauded "in England; though the wiser Somnambulants, much more "Pitt and Friends, who are broad awake on these German "points, may well be thankful to see such a War end on any "terms."

— Well, surely this old admitted 95,000*l.* should have been paid! And, to a moral certainty, Robinson and Sandwich must have made demand of it from the Spaniard. But there is no getting old Debts in, especially from that quarter. "King Friedrich" (let me interrupt, for a moment, with this poor composite Note) "is trying in Spain even now, — ever since 1746, "when Termagant's Husband died, and a new King "came, — for payment of old debt: Two old Debts; "quite tolerably just, both of them. King Friedrich "keeps trying till 1749, three years in all: and in the "end, gets nothing whatever. Nothing, — except some "Merino Rams in the interim," gift from the new King of Spain, I can suppose, which proved extremely useful

* *Protest of English Merchants against &c.* ("May 1748"), given in *Adelung*, vi. 353-356.

in our Wool Industries; "and, from the same polite "Ferdinand VI., a Porcelain Vase filled with Spanish "Snuff." That was all! —

King Friedrich, let me note farther, is getting decidedly deep into snuff; holds by *Spaniol* (a dry yellow pungency, analogous to Lundy-Foot or Irish-Blackguard, known to snuffy readers); always by Spaniol, we say; and more specially "the kind used by her Majesty of Spain," the now Dowager Termagant:* which, also, is to be remembered. Dryasdust adds, in his sweetly consecutive way: "Friedrich was very expensive about "his snuff-boxes; wore two big rich boxes in his pockets; "five or six stood on tables about; and more than a "hundred in store, coming out by turns for variety. "The cheapest of them cost 300 *l.* (2,000 thalers); "he had them as high as 1,500 *l.* At his death, there "were found 130 of various values: they were the "substance of all the jewelry he had; besides these "snuff-boxes, two gold watches only, and a very small "modicum of rings. Had yearly for personal Expen-"diture 1,200,000 thalers" (180,000 *l.* of Civil List, as we should say); "*spent* 33,300 *l.* of it, and yearly gave "the rest away in Royal beneficences, aid of burnt

* Orders this kind, from his Ambassador in Paris, "30th September 1743:" the earliest extant trace of his snuffing habits (Preuss, i. 409). — *Note farther* (if interesting): "The Termagant still lasted as Dowager, con-"suming *Spaniol* at least, for near twenty years (died, 11th July 1766); — "the new King, Ferdinand VI., was her *stepson*, not her son; he went "mad, poor soul, and died (10th August 1759): upon which, Carlos of "Naples, our own 'Baby Carlos' that once was, succeeded in Spain, 'King "Carlos III. of Spain;' leaving his Son, a young boy under tutelage, as "King of the Two Sicilies (King 'Ferdinand IV.,' who did not die, but had "his difficulties, till 1825). Don Philip, who had fought so in those Savoy "Passes, and got the bit of Parmesan Country, died 1765, the year before "Mamma."

"Villages, inundated Provinces, and multifarious *Pater-* "*Patriæ* objects." * — In regard to *Jenkins's Ear*, my Constitutional Friend continues:

"*Silesia* and *Jenkins's Ear*, we often say, were the two bits "of realities in this enormous hurlyburly of imaginations, in- "sane ambitions, and zeros and negative quantities. Negative "Belleisle goes home, not with Germany cut in Four and put "under guidance of the First Nation of the Universe (so ex- "tremely fit for guiding self and neighbours), but with the "First Nation itself reduced almost to wallet and staff; bank- "rupt, beggared — 'Yes,' it answers, 'in all but glory! Have "'not we gained Fontenoy, Roucoux, Lauffeld; and strong- "'places innumerable' (mostly in a state of dry-rot)? 'Did "'men ever fight as we Frenchmen; combining it with theatri- "'cal entertainments, too! Sublime France, First Nation of "'the Universe, will try another flight (*essor*), were she "'breathed a little!'

"Yes, a new *essor* ere long, and perhaps surprise herself "and mankind! The losses of men, money and resource "under this mad empty Enterprise of Belleisle's were enorm- "ous, palpable to France and all mortals: but perhaps these "were trifling to the replacement of them by such *gloire* as "there had been. A *gloire* of plunging into War on no cause "at all; and with an issue consisting only of foul gases of ex- "treme levity. Messieurs are of confessed promptitude to "fight; and their talent for it, in some kinds, is very great "indeed. But this treating of battle and slaughter, of "death, judgment and eternity, as light playhouse matters; "this of rising into such transcendency of valour, as to snap "your fingers in the face of the Almighty Maker; this, Mes- "sieurs, give me leave to say so, is a thing that will conduct "you and your *Première Nation* to the Devil, if you do not "alter it. Inevitable, I tell you! Your road lies that way, "then? Good morning, Messieurs! let me still hope, Not!"

Diplomatist Kaunitz gained his first glories in this Congress of Aix; which are still great in the eyes of

* Preuss, i. 409, 410.

some. Age now thirty-seven; a native of these Western parts; but henceforth, by degrees ever more, the shining star and guide of Austrian Policies down almost to our own New Epoch. As, unluckily, he will concern us not a little, in time coming, let us read this Note, as foreshadow of the man and his doings:

"The glory of Count, ultimately Prince, von Kaunitz-"Rietberg, is great in Diplomatic Circles of the past Century. "'The greatest of Diplomatists,' they all say; — and surely "it is reckoned something to become the greatest in your line. "Farther than this, to the readers of these times, Kaunitz-"Rietberg's glory does not go. A great character, great "wisdom, lasting great results to his Country, readers do not "trace in Kaunitz's diplomacies, — only temporary great re-"sults, or what he and the bystanders thought such, to "Kaunitz himself. He was the Supreme Jove, we perceive, "in that extinct Olympus; and regards with sublime pity, "not unallied to contempt, all other diplomatic beings. A "man sparing of words, sparing even of looks; will hardly "lift his eyelids for your sake, — will lift perhaps his chin, in "slight monosyllabic fashion, and stalk superlatively through "the other door. King of the vanished Shadows. A de-"termined hater of Fresh Air; rode under glass cover, on the "finest day; made the very Empress shut her windows, when "he came to audience; fed, cautiously daring, on boiled "capons: more I remember not, — except also that he would "suffer no mention of the word *Death* by any mortal.* A "most high-sniffing, fantastic, slightly insolent shadow-king; "— ruled, in his time, the now-vanished Olympus; and had "the difficult glory (defective only in result) of uniting France "and Austria *against* the poor old Sea-Power milk-cows, for "the purpose of recovering Silesia from Friedrich, a few "years hence!" — These are wondrous results; hidden under the horizon, not very far either; and will astonish Britannic Majesty and all readers, in a few years.

* Hormayr, *Oesterreichischer Plutarch*, IV. (Sites), 231-233.

Maréchal de Saxe pays Friedrich a Visit.

In Summer 1749, Maréchal de Saxe, the other shiny figure of this mad Business of the Netherlands, paid Friedrich a visit; had the honour to be entertained by him three days (July 13th-16th, 1749), in his Royal Cottage of Sans-Souci seemingly, in his choicest manner. Curiosity, which is now nothing like so vivid as it then was, would be glad to listen a little, in this meeting of two Suns, or of one Sun and one immense Tar-Barrel, or Atmospheric Meteor really of shining nature, and taken for a Sun. But the Books are silent; not the least detail, or hint, or feature granted us. Only Fancy; — and this of Smelfungus, by way of long farewell to one of the parties:

* * "It was at Tongres, or in headquarters near it, "10th October 1746, — Battle expected on the morrow" (Battle of *Roucoux*, over towards Herstal, which we used to know), — "that M. Favart, Saxe's Playwright and Theatre-"Director, gave out in cheerful doggerel on fall of the Cur-"tain, the announcement:

"*Demain nous donnerons relâche,*
"*Quoique le Directeur s'en fâche,*
"*Vous voir combleroit nos desirs:*

"*On doit céder tout à la gloire;*
"*Vous ne songez qu'à la victoire,*
"*Nous ne songeons qu'à vos plaisirs.*"*

"Tomorrow is no Play,
"To the Manager's regret,
"Whose sole study is to keep you
"happy:

"But, you being bent upon victory,
"What can he do? —
"Day after tomorrow, —

"'Day after tomorrow,' added he, taking the official tone, 'in "'honour of your laurels' (gained already, since you resolve "'on gaining them), we will have the honour of presenting' — "such and such a gay Farce, to as many of you as remain "alive! Which was received with gay clapping of hands: "admirable to the Universe, at least to the Parisian *Univers*

* Biographie Universelle, xiv. 209, § *Favart*; Espagnac, ii. 162.

"and oneself. Such a prodigality of light daring is in these "French gentlemen, skilfully tickled by the Maréchal; who "uses this Playwright, among other implements, for keeping "them at the proper pitch. Was there ever seen such radiancy "of valour? Very radiant indeed; — yet it seems to me, "gone somewhat into the phosphorescent kind; shining in "the dark, as fish will do when rotten! War has actually its "serious character; nor is Death a farcical transaction, how-"ever high your genius may go. But what then; it is the "Maréchal's trade to keep these poor people at the cutting "pitch, on any terms that will hold for the moment.

"I know not which was the most dissolute Army ever seen "in the world: but this of Saxe's was very dissolute. Play-"wright Favart had withal a beautiful clever Wife, — upon "whom the courtships, munificent blandishments, threaten-"ings and utmost endeavours of Maréchal de Saxe (in his "character of goatfooted Satyr) could not produce the least "impression. For a whole year, not the least. Whereupon "the Goatfooted had to get *Lettre de Cachet* for her; had to — "in fact, produce the brutallest Adventure that is known of "him, even in this brutal kind. Poor Favart, rushing about "in despair, not permitted to run him through the belly, and "die with his Wife undishonoured, had to console himself, he "and she; and do agreeable theatricalities for a living as "heretofore. Let us not speak of it!

"Of Saxe's Generalship, which is now a thing fallen pretty "much into oblivion, I have no authority to speak. He had "much wild natural ingenuity in him; cunning rapid whirls "of contrivance; and gained Three Battles and very many "Sieges, amid the loudest clapping of hands that could well "be. He had perfect intrepidity; not to be flurried by any "amount of peril or confusion; looked on that English Co-"lumn, advancing at Fontenoy with its *feu infernal*, steadily "through his perspective; chewing his leaden bullet: 'Going "'to beat me, then? Well — !' Nobody needed to be braver. "He had great good nature too, though of hot temper and so "full of multifarious voracities; a substratum of inarticulate "good sense withal, and much magnanimity run wild, or run "to seed. A big-limbed, swashing, perpendicular kind of "fellow; haughty of face, but jolly too; with a big, not ugly "strut; — captivating to the French Nation, and fit God of

"War (fitter than 'Dalhousie,' I am sure!) for that susceptive "People. Understood their Army also, what it was then and "there, and how, by theatricals and otherwise, to get a great "deal of fire out of it. Great deal of fire; — whether by "gradual conflagration or not, on the road to ruin or not; "how, he did not care. In respect of military 'fame' so-"called, he had the great advantage of fighting always "against bad Generals, sometimes against the very worst. "To his fame an advantage; to himself and his real worth, "far the reverse. Had he fallen in with a Friedrich, even "with a Browne or a Traun, there might have been different "news got. Friedrich (who was never stingy in such matters, "except to his own Generals, where it might do hurt) is pro-"fuse in his eulogies, in his admirations of Saxe; amiable to "see, and not insincere; but which, perhaps, practically do "not mean very much.

"It is certain the French Army reaped no profit from its "experience of Maréchal de Saxe, and the high theatricalities, "ornamental blackguardisms, and ridicule of death and life. "In the long-run a graver face would have been of better "augury. King Friedrich's soldiers, one observes, on the "eve of battle, settle their bits of worldly business; and wind "up, many of them, with a hoarse whisper of prayer. Oliver "Cromwell's soldiers did so, Gustaf Adolf's; in fact, I think "all good soldiers. Roucoux with a Prince Karl, Lauffeld "with a Duke of Cumberland; you gain your Roucoux, your "Lauffeld, Human Stupidity permitting: but one day you "fall in with Human Intelligence, in an extremely grave "form; — and your '*élan*,' elastic outburst, the quickest in "Nature, what becomes of it? Wait but another decade; "we shall see what an Army this has grown. Cupidity, dis-"honesty, floundering stupidity, indiscipline, mistrust; and "an elastic outspurt (*élan*) turned often enough into the form "of *Sauve-qui-peut!*

"M. le Maréchal survived Aix-la-Chapelle little more "than two years. Lived at Chambord, on the Loire, an Ex-"Royal Palace; in such splendour as never was. Went down "in a rosepink cloud, as if of perfect felicity; of glory that "would last forever, — which it has by no means done. He "made despatch; escaped, in this world, the Nemesis, which "often waits on what they call 'fame.' By diligent service of "the Devil, in ways not worth specifying, he saw himself, "November 21st, 1750, flung prostrate suddenly: 'Putrid "'fever!' gloom the Doctors ominously to one another: and, "November 30th, the Devil (I am afraid it was he, though "clad in roseate effulgence, and melodious exceedingly) "carried him home on those kind terms, as from a Universe "all of Opera. 'Wait till 1759, — till 1789!' murmured the "Devil to himself."

Tragic News that concern us, of Voltaire and Others.

About two months after those Saxe-Friedrich hospitalities at Sans-Souci, Voltaire, writing, late at night, from the hospitable Palace of Titular Stanislaus, has these words, to his trusted D'Argental:

Lunéville, 4th September 1749. * * "Madame du Châtelet, this night, while scribbling over her *Newton*, felt a little "twinge; she called a waiting-maid, who had only time to "hold out her apron, and catch a little Girl, whom they carried "to its cradle. The Mother arranged her papers, went to "bed; and the whole of that *(tout cela)* is sleeping like a "dormouse, at the hour I write to you. My guardian angels, "poor I shan't have so easy a delivery of my *Catilina*" (my *Rome Saved*, for the confusion of old Crébillon and the cabals)!† * *

And then, six days later, hear another Witness present there:

Lunéville Palace, 10th September. "For the first three or "four days, the health of the Mother appeared excellent; "denoting nothing but the weakness inseparable from her "situation. The weather was very warm. Milk-fever came, "which made the heat worse. In spite of remonstrances, she "would have some iced barley-water; drank a big glass of it;

† *Œuvres*, LXXIV. 57 (Voltaire to d'Argental).

"— and some instants after, had great pain in her head; "followed by other bad symptoms." Which brought the Doctor in again, several Doctors, hastily summoned; who, after difficulties, thought again that all was coming right. And so, on the sixth night, 10th September, inquiring friends had left the sick-room hopefully, and gone down to supper, "the rather as Madame seemed inclined to sleep. There re-"mained none with her but M. de St. Lambert, one of her "maids and I. M. de St. Lambert, as soon as the strangers "were gone, went forward and spoke some moments to her; "but seeing her sleepy, drew back, and sat chatting with us "two. Eight or ten minutes after, we heard a kind of rattle "in the throat, intermixed with hiccoughs: we ran to the bed; "found her senseless; raised her to a sitting posture, tried "vinaigrettes, rubbed her feet, knocked into the palms of her "hands; — all in vain; she was dead!

"Of course the supper-party burst up, into her room; "M. le Marquis du Châtelet, M. de Voltaire, and the others. "Profound consternation: to tears, to cries succeeded a "mournful silence. Voltaire and St. Lambert remained the "last about her bed. At length Voltaire quitted the room; "got out by the Grand Entrance, hardly knowing which way "he went. At the foot of the Outer Stairs, near a sentry's "box, he fell full length on the pavement. His lackey, who "was a step or two behind, rushed forward to raise him. At "that moment came M. de St. Lambert; who had taken the "same road, and who now hastened to help. M. de Voltaire, "once on his feet again, and recognising who it was, said, "through his tears and with the most pathetic accent, '*Ah,* "'*mon ami,* it is you that have killed her to me!' — and then "suddenly, as if starting awake, with the tone of reproach "and despair, '*Eh, mon Dieu, Monsieur, de quoi vous avisiez-*"'*vous de lui faire un enfant* (Good God, Sir, what put it into "'your head to — to —)!'"* —

Poor M. de Voltaire; suddenly become widower, and flung out upon his shifts again, at his time of life! May now wander, Ishmael-like, whither he will, in this

* Longchamp et Wagnière, *Mémoires sur Voltaire,* II. 250, 251; — Longchamp *loquitur.*

hard lonesome world. His grief is overwhelming, mixed with other sharp feelings due on the matter; but does not last very long, in that poignant form. He will turn up on us, in his new capacity of single-man, again brilliant enough, within year and day.

Last Autumn, September 1748, Wilhelmina's one Daughter, one child, was wedded; to that young Durchlaucht of Würtemberg, whom we saw gallanting the little girl, to Wilhelmina's amusement, some years ago. About the wedding, nothing; nor about the wedded life, what would have been more curious: — no Wilhelmina now to tell us anything; not even whether Mamma the Improper Duchess was there. From Berlin, the Two youngest Princes, Henri and Ferdinand, attended at Baireuth; — Mannstein, our old Russian friend, now Prussian again, escorting them.* The King, too busy, I suppose, with Silesian Reviews and the like, sends his best wishes, — for indeed the Match was of his sanctioning and advising; — though his wishes proved mere disappointment in the sequel. Friedrich got no "furtherance in the Swabian Franconian Circles," or favour anywhere, by means of this Durchlaucht; in the end, far the reverse! — In a word, the happy couple rolled away to Würtemberg (September 26th, 1748); he twenty, she sixteen, poor young creatures; and in years following, became unhappy to a degree.

There was but one child, and it soon died. The young Serene Lady was of airy high spirit; graceful, clever, good too, they said; perhaps a thought too proud: — but as for her Reigning Duke, there was

* Seyfarth, II. 76.

seldom seen so lurid a Serenity; and it was difficult to live beside him. A most arbitrary Herr, with glooms and whims; dim-eyed, ambitious, voracious, and the temper of an angry mule, — very fit to have been haltered, in a judicious manner, instead of being set to halter others! Enough, in six or seven years' time, the bright Pair found itself grown thunderous, opaque beyond description; and (in 1759) had to split asunder for good. "Owing to the reigning Duke's behaviour," said everybody. "Has behaved so, I would run him through the body, if we met!" said his own Brother once: — Brother Friedrich Eugen, a Prussian General by that time, whom we shall hear of.* What thoughts for our dear Wilhelmina, in her latter weak years; — lapped in eternal silence, as so much else is.

* Preuss, IV. 149; Michaelis, III. 451.

CHAPTER IV.

COCCEJI FINISHES THE LAW REFORM; FRIEDRICH IS PRINTING HIS POESIES.

In these years, Friedrich goes on victoriously with his Law-Reform; Herculean Cocceji with Assistants, backed by Friedrich, beneficently conquering Province after Province to him; — Kur-Mark, Neu-Mark, Cleve (all easy, in comparison, after Pommern), and finally Preussen itself; — to the joy and profit of the same. Cocceji's method, so far as the Foreign onlooker can discern across much haze, seems to be threefold:

1°. Extirpation (painless, were it possible) of the Pettifogger Species; indeed, of the Attorney Species altogether: "Seek other employments; disappear, all of you, from these precincts, under penalty!" The Advocate himself takes charge of the suit, from first birth of it; and sees it ended, — he knows within what limit of time.

2°. Sifting out of all incompetent Advocates, "Follow that Attorney-Company, you; away!" — sifting out all these, and retaining in each Court, with fees accurately settled, with character stamped sound, or at least *soundest*, the number actually needed. In a milder way, but still more strictly, Judges stupid or otherwise incompetent are riddled out; able Judges appointed, and their salaries raised.

3°. What seems to be Friedrich's own invention, what in outcome he thinks will be the summary of all good Law-Procedure: A final Sentence (three "instances" you can have, but the third ends it for you) within the Year. Good, surely. A justice that intends to be exact, must front the complicacies in a resolute piercing manner, and will not be tedious. Nay a justice that is not moderately swift, — human hearts waiting for it, the while, in a cancerous state, instead of hopefully following their work, — what, comparatively, is the use of its being never so exact! —

Simple enough methods; rough and ready. Needing, in the execution, clear human eyesight, clear human honesty, — which happen to be present here, and without which, no "method" whatever can be executed that will really profit.

In the course of 1748, Friedrich, judging by Pommern and the other symptoms that his enterprise was safe, struck a victorious Medal upon it: "*Fridericus Borussorum Rex*," pressing with his sceptre the oblique Balance to a level posture; with Epigraph, "*Emendato Jure*."* And by Newyears-day, 1750, the matter was in effect completed; and "justice cheap, expeditious, certain," a fact in all Prussian Lands.

Nay, in 1749-1751, to complete the matter, Cocceji's "Project of a general Law-Code," *Projekt des Corporis Juris Fridericiani*, came forth in print:** to the admiration of mankind, at home and abroad; "the First

* Letter to Cocceji, accompanying Copy of the medal in Gold, "24th June 1748" (Seyfarth, II. 67 n.).

** Halle, 2 voll., folio (Preuss, I. 316; see *ib.* 315 n., as to the *Law Procedure* &c. now settled by Cocceji).

Code attempted since Justinian's time," say they. *Project* translated into all languages, and read in all countries. A poor mildewed copy of this *Codex Fridericianus*, — done at Edinburgh, 1761, not said by whom; evidently bought at least *twice*, and mostly never yet read (nor like being read), — is known to me, for years past, in a ghastly manner! Without the least profit to this present, or to any other Enterprise; — though persons of name in Jurisprudence call it meritorious in their Science; the first real attempt at a Code in Modern times. But the truth is, this Cocceji *Codex* remained a *Project* merely, never enacted anywhere. It was not till 1773, that Friedrich made actual attempt to build a Law-Code; and did build one (the foundation-story of one, for his share, completed since), in which this of Cocceji had little part. In 1773, the thing must again be mentioned; the "Second Law-Reform," as they call it. What we practically know from this time is, That Prussian Lawsuits, through Friedrich's Reign, do all terminate, or push at their utmost for terminating, within one year from birth; and that Friedrich's fame, as a beneficent Justinian, rose high in all Countries (strange in Countries that had thought him a War-scourge and Conquering Hero); strange, but undeniable;* and that his own People, if more silently, yet in practice very gladly indeed, welcomed his Law-Reform; and, from day to day, enjoyed the same, — no doubt with occasional remembrance who the Donor was.

* See *Gentleman's Magazine*, xx. 215-218 ("May 1750"): eloquent, enthusiastic *Letter*, given there, "of Baron de Spon to Chancellor D'Aguesseau," on these inimitable Law Achievements.

Of Friedrich's Literary works, nobody, not even Friedrich himself, will think it necessary that we say much. But the fact is, he is doing a great many things that way! in Prose, the *Memoirs of Brandenburg*, coming out as Papers in the Academy from time to time:* in Verse, very secret as yet, the *Palladion* ("exquisite Burlesque," think some), the *Art of War* (reckoned truly his best Piece in verse): — and wishes sometimes he had Voltaire here to perfect him a little. This too would be one of the practical charms of Voltaire.** For though King Friedrich knows and remembers always, that these things, especially the Verse part, are mere amusements in comparison, he has the creditable wish to do these well; one would not fantasy *ill* even on the Flute, if one could help it. "Why doesn't Voltaire come; as Quantz of the Flute has done?" Friedrich, now that Voltaire has fallen widower, renews his pressings, "Why don't you come?" Patience, your Majesty; Voltaire will come.

Nobody can wish details in this Department: but there is one thing necessary to be mentioned, That Friedrich in these years, 1749-1752, has Printers out at Potsdam, and is Printing, "in beautiful quarto form, with copperplates," to the extent of twelve copies, the *Œuvres* (Poetical, that is) *du Philosophe de Sans-Souci*. Only twelve Copies, I have heard; gift of a single copy indicating that you are among the choicest of the chosen. Copies have now fallen extremely rare (and

* From 1746 and onward: first published complete (after slight revision by Voltaire), Berlin, 1751.

** Friedrich's Letter to Algarotti (*Œuvres*, xviii. 66), "12th September 1749."

are not in request at all, with my readers or me): but there was one Copy which, or the Mis-title of which, as *Œuvre de "Poéshie" du Roi mon Maître*, became miraculously famous in a year or two; — and is still memorable to us all! On Voltaire's arrival, we shall hear more of these things. Enough to say at present that the *Œuvres du Philosophe de Sans-Souci: Au Donjon du Château: Avec Privilège d'Apollon*, — "three thinnish "quarto volumes, all the Poetry then on hand," — was finished early in 1750, before Voltaire came. That, when Voltaire came, a revisal was undertaken, a new Edition, with Voltaire's corrections and other changes (total suppression of the *Palladion*, for one creditable change): that this Edition was to have been in Two Volumes; that One, accordingly, rather thicker than the former sort, was got finished in 1752 (same *Title*, only the new Date, and "no *Donjon du Château* this time"), One Volume in 1752; after which, owing to the explosions that ensued, no Second came, nor ever will; — and that the actual contents of that far-famed *Œuvre de "Poéshie"* (number of volumes even) are points of mystery to me, at this day.*

Friedrich's other employments are multifarious as those of a Land's Husband (not inferior to his Father in that respect); and, like the benefits of the diurnal

* Herr Preuss, — in the *Chronological List* of Friedrich's Writings (a useful accurate Piece otherwise), and in two other places where he tries, — is very indistinct on this of *Donjon du Château*; and it is all but impossible to ascertain from him, *what*, in an indisputable manner, the *Œuvre de 'Poéshie'* may have been. Here are the places for groping, if another should be induced to try: *Œuvres de Frédéric*, x. (Preface, p. IX.); *ib.* XI. (Preface, p. IX.); ib. *Table Chronologique* (in *what* Volume this is, you cannot yet say; seems preliminary to a *General Index*, which is infinitely wanted, but has not yet appeared to this Editor's aid), p. 14.

Sun, are to be considered incessant, innumerable and, — in result to usward, — *silent* also, impossible to speak of in this place. From the highest pitch of State-craft (Russian Czarina now fallen plainly hostile, and needing lynx-eyed diplomacy ever and anon), down to that of Dredging and Fascine-work (as at Stettin and elsewhere), of Oder-canals, of Soap-boiler Companies, and Mulberry-and-Silk Companies; nay of ordaining Where, and where not, the Crows are to be shot, and (owing to cattle murrain) No *veal* to be killed:* daily comes the tide of great and of small, and daily the punctual Friedrich keeps abreast of it, — and Dryasdust has noted the details, and stuffed them into blind sacks, — for forty years.

The Review seasons, I notice, go somewhat as follows. For Berlin and neighbourhood, May, or perhaps end of April (weather now bright, and ground firm); sometimes with considerable pomp ("both Queens out," and beautiful Female Nobilities, in "twenty-four green tents"), and often with great complicacy of manœuvre. In June, to Magdeburg, round by Cleve; and home again for some days. July, is Pommern: onward thence to Schlesien, oftenest in August; Schlesien the last place, and generally not done with till well on in September. But we will speak of these things, more specially, another time. Such "Reviews," for strictness of inspection civil and military, as probably were not seen in the world since, — or before, except in the case of this King's Father only.

* Seyfarth, II. 71, 83, 61; Preuss, *Buch für Jedermann*. I. 101-109; &c.

CHAPTER V.

STRANGERS OF NOTE COME TO BERLIN, IN 1750.

BRITISH Diplomacies, next to the Russian, cause some difficulties in those Years: of which more by and by. Early in 1748, while Aix-la-Chapelle was starting, Ex-Exchequer Legge came to Berlin; on some obscure object of a small Patch of Principality, hanging loose during those Negotiations: "Could not we secure it for his Royal Highness of Cumberland, thinks your Majesty?" Ex-Exchequer Legge was here;* got handsome assurances of a general nature; but no furtherance towards his obscure, completely impracticable object; and went home in November following, to a new Parliamentary Career.

And the second year after, early in 1750, came Sir Hanbury Williams, famed London-Wit of Walpole's circle, on objects which, in the main, were equally chimerical: "King of the Romans, much wanted;" "No Damage to your Majesty's Shipping from our British Privateers;" and the like; — about which some notice, and not very much, will be due farther on. Here, in his own words, is Hanbury's Account of his First Audience:

* * "On Thursday," 16th July 1750, "I went to Court "by appointment, at 11 A.M. The King of Prussia arrived

* Coxe's *Pelham*, I. 431, &c.; Rödenbeck, pp. 155, 160 (first audience, 1st May 1748); — recalled, 22d November, Aix being over.

"about 12" (at Berlin; King in from Potsdam, for one day); "and Count Podewils immediately introduced me into the "Royal closet; when I delivered his Britannic Majesty's "Letters into the King of Prussia's hands, and made the "usual compliments to him in the best manner I was able. "To which his Prussian Majesty replied, to the best of my "remembrance, as follows:

"'I have the truest esteem for the King of Britain's person; "'and I set the highest value on his friendship. I have at "'different times received essential proofs of it; and I desire "'you would acquaint the King your Master that I will (*sic*) "'never forget them.' His Prussian Majesty afterwards said "something with respect to myself, and then asked me "several questions about indifferent things and persons. He "seemed to express a great deal of esteem for my Lord "Chesterfield, and a great deal of kindness for Mr. Villiers," useful in the Peace-of-Dresden time; "but did not once "mention Lord Hyndford or Mr. Legge," — how singular!

"I was in the closet with his Majesty exactly five minutes "and a half. My audience done, Prussian Majesty came out "into the general room, where Foreign Ministers were wait-"ing. He said, on stepping in, just one word" to the Austrian Excellency; not even one to the Russian Excellency, nor to me the Britannic; "conversed with the French, "Swedish, Danish;" — happy to be off, which I do not wonder at; to dine with Mamma at Monbijou, among faces pleasant to him; and return to his Businesses and Books next day.*

Witty Excellency Hanbury did not succeed at Berlin on the "Romish-King Question," or otherwise; and indeed went off rather in a hurry. But for the next six or seven years, he puddles about, at a great rate, in those Northern Courts; giving away a great deal of money, hatching many futile expensive intrigues at Petersburg, Warsaw (not much at Berlin, after the first trial there); and will not be altogether avoidable

* Walpole, *George the Second*, I. 440; Rödenbeck, I. 204.

to us in time coming, as one could have wished. Besides, he is Horace Walpole's friend and select London Wit: he contributed a good deal to the English notions about Friedrich; and has left considerable bits of acrid testimony on Friedrich, "clear words of an Eye-witness," men call them, — which are still read by everybody; the said Walpole, and others, having since printed them, in very dark condition.* Brevity is much due to Hanbury and his testimonies, since silence in the circumstances is not allowable. Here is one Excerpt, with the necessary light for reading it:

* * It is on this Romish-King, and other the like chimerical errands, that witty Hanbury, then a much more admirable man than we now find him, is prowling about in the German Courts, off and on, for some ten years in all, six of them still to come. A sharp-eyed man, of shrewish quality; given to intriguing, to spying, to bribing; anxious to win his Diplomatic game by every method, though the stake (as here) is oftenest zero; with fatal proclivity to Scandal, and what in London circles he has heard called Wit. Little or nothing of real laughter in the soul of him, at any time; only a laboured continual grin, always of malicious nature, and much trouble and jerking about, to keep that up. Had evidently some modicum of real intellect, of capacity for being wise; but now has fatally devoted it nearly all to being witty, on those poor terms! A perverse, barren, spiteful little wretch; the grin of him generally an affliction, at this date. His Diplomatic Correspondence I do not know.** He

* In Walpole, *George the Second* (i. 448-461), the Pieces which regard Friedrich. In *Sir Charles Hanbury Williams's Works* (edited by a diligent, reverential, but ignorant gentleman, whom I could guess to be Bookseller Jeffery in person: London, 1822, 3 vols. small 8vo), are witty Verses, and considerable sections of Prose, relating to other persons and objects now rather of an obsolete nature.

** Nothing of him is discoverable in the State-Paper Office. Many of his Papers, it would seem, are in the Earl of Essex's hands; — and might be of some Historical use, not of very much, could the British Museum get did a great deal of Diplomatic business, issuing in zero, — of which I have sometimes longed to know the exact dates; seldom anything farther. His "History of Poland," transmitted to the Right Hon. Henry Fox, by instalments from Dresden, in 1748, is* — Well, I should be obliged to call it worthier of Goody Two-Shoes than of that Right Hon. Henry, who was a man of parts, but evidently quite a vacuum on the Polish side!

Of Hanbury's News-Letters from Foreign Courts, four or five, incidentally printed, are like the contents of a slop-pail; uncomfortable to the delicate mind. Not lies on the part of Hanbury, but foolish scandal poured into him; a man more filled with credulous incredible scandal, evil rumours, of malfeasances by Kings and magnates, than most people known. His rumoured mysteries between poor Polish Majesty and pretty Daughter-in-law (the latter a clever and graceful creature, Daughter of the late unfortunate Kaiser, and a distinguished Correspondent of Friedrich's), are to be regarded as mere poisoned wind.** That "Polish Majesty gets "into his dressing-gown at two in the afternoon" (inaccessible thenceforth, poor lazy creature), one most readily believes; but there, or pretty much there, one's belief has to stop. The stories, in *Walpole*, on the King of Prussia, have a grain of fact in them, twisted into huge irrecognisable caricature in the Williams optic-machinery. Much else one can discern to be, in essence, false altogether. Friedrich, who could not stand that intriguing, spying, shrewish unfriendly kind of fellow at his Court, applied to England in not many months hence, and got Williams sent away:*** on to Russia, or I forget whither; — which did not mend the Hanbury optical-machinery on that side.

The dull, tobacco-smoking Saxon-Polish Majesty, about whom he idly retails so many scandals, had never done him any offence. — On the whole, if anybody wanted a swim in

possession of them. Abundance of *Back-stairs* History, on those Northern Courts, especially on Petersburg, and Warsaw-Dresden, — authentic Court-gossip, generally malicious, often not true, but never mendacious on the part of Williams, — is one likely item.

* See *Hanbury's Works*, vol. III.

** In *Hanbury's Works*, II. 209-240.

*** "22d January 1751" (Ms. *List* in State-Paper Office).

the slop-pails of that extinct generation, Hanbury, could he find an Editor to make him legible, might be printed. For he really was deep in that slop-pail or extinct-scandal department, and had heard a great many things. Apart from that, in almost any other department, — except in so far as he seems to *date* rather carefully, — I could not recommend him. The Letters and Excerpts given in Walpole are definable as one pennyworth of bread, — much ruined by such immersion, but very harmless otherwise, could you pick it out and clean it, — to twenty gallons of Hanbury sherris-sack, or chamber-slop. I have found nothing that seems to be, in all points, true or probable, but this; worth cutting out, and rendering legible, on other accounts. Hanbury *loquitur* (in condensed form):

"In the summer of last year, 1749, there was, somewhere "in Mähren, a great Austrian Muster or Review;" all the more interesting, as it was believed, or known, that the Prussian methods and manœuvres were now to be the rule for Austria. Not much of a Review otherwise, this of 1749; Empress-Queen and Husband not personally there, as in coming Years they are wont to be; that high Lady being ardent to reform her Army, root and branch, according to the Prussian model, — more praise to her.* "At this Muster "in Mähren, Three Prussian Officers happened to make their "appearance, — for several imaginable reasons, of little "significance: 'For the purpose of inveigling people to "'desert, and enlist with them!' said the Austrian Autho-"rities; and ordered the Three Prussian Officers uncere-"moniously off the ground. Which Friedrich, when he "heard of it, thought an unhandsome pipeclay procedure, "and kept in mind against the Austrian Authorities.

"Next Summer," next Spring, 1750, "an Austrian Captain "being in Mecklenburg, travelling about, met there an old "acquaintance, one Chapeau" (*Hat!* can it be possible?) "who is in great favour with the King of Prussia:" — very well, Excellency Hanbury; but who, in the name of wonder, can this *Hat*, or Chapeau, have been? After study, one perceives that Hanbury wrote Chazeau, meaning *Chasot*, an

* *Maria Theresiens Leben*, p. 160 (what she did that way, *Anno* 1749); p. 162 (*present* at the Reviews, *Anno* 1750).

old acquaintance of our own! Brilliant, sabring, melodying Chasot, Lieutenant-Colonel of the Baireuth Dragoons; who lies at Treptow, close on Mecklenburg, and is a declared favourite of the Duchess, often running over to the *Residenz* there. Often enough; but *Honi soit*, O reader; the clever Lady is towards sixty, childless, musical; and her Husband, — do readers recollect him at all? — is that collapsed *tailoring* Duke whom Friedrich once visited, — and whose Niece, Half-Niece, is Charlotte, wise little hard-favoured creature now of six, in clean bib and tucker, Ancestress of England that is to be; whose Papa will succeed, if the Serene Tailor die first, — which he did not quite. To this Duchess, musical gallant Chasot may well be a resource, and she to him. Naturally the Austrian Captain, having come to Mecklenburg, dined with Serene Highness, he and Chasot together, with concert following, and what not, at the Schloss of Neu-Strelitz: — And now we will drop the "Chapeau," and say Chasot, with comfort, and a shade of new interest.

"The grand May Review at Berlin just ahead, won't you "look in; it is straight on your road home?" suggests Chasot to his travelling friend. "One would like it, of all things," answered the other: "but the King?" "Tush," said Chasot; "I will make that all straight!" And applies to the King, accordingly: "Permission to an Austrian Officer, a good "acquaintance of mine." "Austrian Officer?" Friedrich's eyes lighten; and he readily gives the permission. This was at Berlin, on the very eve of the Review; and Chasot and his Austrian are made happy in that small matter. "And on the "morrow" (end of May 1750), "the Austrian attends accord-"ingly; but to his astonishment, has hardly begun to taste "the manœuvres, when — one of Friedrich's Aides-de-Camp "gallops up: 'By the King's command, Mein Herr, you "'retire on the instant!'

"Next day, the Austrian is for challenging Chasot. 'As "'you like, that way,' answers Chasot; 'but learn first, that "'on your affront I rode up to the King; and asked, publicly, "'Did not your Majesty grant me permission?' 'Unquestion-"'ably, Monsieur Chasot; — and if he had not come, how "'could I have paid back the Moravian business of last "'year!'"* — This is much in Friedrich's way; not the

* Walpole, *George the Second*, i. 437, 438.

unwelcomer that it includes a satirical twitch on Chasot, whom he truly likes withal, or did like, though now a little dissatisfied with those too frequent Mecklenburg excursions and extra-military cares. Of this, merely squeezing the Hanbury venom out of it, I can believe every particular.

"Did you ever hear of anything so shocking?" is Hanbury's meaning here and elsewhere. "I must tell you a "story of the King of Prussia's regard for the Law of "Nations," continues he to Walpole.* Which proves to be a story, turned topsyturvy, of one Hofmann, Brunswick Envoy, who (quite *beyond* commission, and a thing that must not be thought of at all!) had been detected in dangerous intriguings with the ever-busy Russian Excellency, or another; and got flung into Spandau,**—seemingly pretty much his due in the matter. And so of other Hanbury things. "What a Prussia; for rigour of command, one huge prison, in a manner!" King intent on punctuality, and all his business upon the square. Society, official and unofficial, kept rather strictly to their tackle; their mode of movement not that of loose oxen at all! "Such a detestable Tyrant,"—who has ordered *me*, Hanbury, elsewhither with my exquisite talents and admired wit! —

Candidatus Linsenbarth (quasi "Lentil-beard") *likewise visits Berlin.*

By far the notablest arrival in Berlin is M. de Voltaire's, July 10th; a few days before Hanbury got his First Audience, "five minutes long." But that arrival will require a Chapter to itself; — most important arrival, that of all! The least important, again, is probably that of Candidatus Linsenbarth, in these same weeks; — a rugged poverty-stricken old Licentiate of Theology; important to no mortal in Berlin or elsewhere: — upon whom, however, and upon his proce-

* Walpole, *George the Second*, I. 458.
** Adelung, V. 564; VII. 133-144.

dures in that City, we propose, for our own objects, to bestow a few glances; rugged Narrative of the thing, in singular exotic dialect, but true every word, having fortunately come to us from Linsenbarth's own hand.*

Berlin, it must be admitted, after all one's reading in poor Dryasdust, remains a dim empty object; Teutschland is dim and empty: and out of the forty blind sacks, or out of four hundred such, what picture can any human head form to itself of Friedrich as King or Man? A trifling Adventure of that poor individual, called Linsenbarth *Candidatus Theologiæ*, one of the poorest of mortals, but true and credible in every particular, comes gliding by chance athwart all that; and like the glimmer of a poor rushlight, or kindled straw, shows it us for moments, a thing visible, palpable; as it worked and lived. In the great dearth, Linsenbarth, if I can faithfully interpret him for the modern reader, will be worth attending to.

Date of Linsenbarth's Adventure is June — August 1750. "Schloss of Beichlingen" and "Village of Hemmleben" are in the Thüringen Hill Country (Weimar not far off to eastward): the Hero himself, a tall awkward raw-boned creature, is, for perhaps near forty years past, a *Candidatus*, say Licentiate, or Curate without Cure. Subsists, I should guess, by schoolmastering, — cheapest schoolmaster conceivable, wages mere nothing, — in the Villages about; in the Village of Hemmleben latterly; age, as I discover, grown to be sixty-one, in those straitened but by no means forlorn circumstances. And so, here is veteran Linsenbarth of Hemmleben, a kind of Thuringian Dominie Sampson; whose Interview with such a brother mortal

* Through Rödenbeck, *Beyträge*, i. 462 et seq.

as Friedrich King of Prussia may be worth looking at, — if I can abridge it properly.

Well, it appears, in the year 1750, at this thrice-obscure Village of Hemmleben, the worthy old Pastor Cannabich died; — worthy old man, how he had lived there, modestly studious, frugal, chiefly on farm-produce, with tobacco and Dutch theology; a modest blessing to his fellow creatures! And now he is dead, and the place vacant. Twenty pounds a Year certain; let us guess it twenty, with glebeland, piggeries, poultry-hutches: who is now to get all that? Linsenbarth starts with his Narrative, in earnest.

Linsenbarth, who I guess may have been Assistant to the deceased Cannabich, and was now out of work, says: "I had "not the least thought of profiting by this vacancy; but what "happened? The Herr Graf von Werthern, at Schloss Beich-"lingen, sent his Steward" *(Lehnsdirector, Fief-director* is the title of this Steward, which gives rise to obsolete thought of mill-dues, road-labour, payments *in natura)*, "his Lehns-"director, Herr Kettenbeil, over to my *logis*" (cheap boarding quarters); "who brought a gracious salutation from his Lord; "saying farther, That I knew too well" (excellent Cannabich gone from us, alas!) "the Pastorate of Hemmleben was "vacant; that there had various competitors announced them-"selves, *supplicando*, for the place; the Herr Graf, however, "had yet given none of them the *fiat*, but waited always till "I should apply. As I had not done so, he (the Lord Graf) "would now of his own motion give me the preference, and "hereby confer the Pastorate upon me!" —

"Without all controversy, here was a *vocatio divina*, to be "received with the most submissive thanks! But the lame "*second* messenger came hitching in" *(halting messenger*, German proverb) "very soon. Kettenbeil began again: 'He must "'mention to me *sub rosâ*, Her Ladyship the Frau Gräfin "'wanted to have her Lady's-maid provided for by this pro-"'motion, too; I must marry her, and take the living at the "'same time.'"

Whew! And this is the noble Lady's way of thinking, up in her fine Schloss yonder? Linsenbarth will none of it. "For my notion fell at once," says he, "when I heard it was

"*Do ut facias*, *Facio ut facias* (I give that thou mayest do, I do "that thou mayst do; Wilt have the kirk, then take the irk, "*Willst du die Pfarre, so nimm die Quarre)*; on those terms, "my reply was: 'Most respectful thanks, Herr Fief-judge, "'and No, for such a vocation! And why? The vocation must "'have *libertatem*, there must be no *vitium essentiale* in it; it "'must be right *in essentiali*, otherwise no honest man can "'accept it with a good conscience. This were a marriage on "'constraint; out of which a thousand *inconvenientiæ* might "'spring!'" Hear Linsenbarth, in the piebald dialect, with the sound heart, and preference of starvation itself to some other things! Kettenbeil (*Chain-axe*) went home; and there was found another Candidatus willing for the marriage on constraint, "out of which *inconvenientiæ* might spring," in Linsenbarth's opinion.

"And so did the sneakish courtly gentleman" (*Hofmann*, courtier as Linsenbarth has it), "who grasped with both "hands at my rejected offer, experience before long," continues Linsenbarth. "For the loose thing of court-tatters led "him such a life that, within three years, age yet only thirty, "he had to bite the dust" (*bite at the grass*, says Linsenbarth, proverbially), which was an *inconvenientia* including all others. "And I had *legitimam causam* to refuse the vocation *cum tali* "*conditione*.

"However, it was very ill taken of me. All over that "Thuringian region, I was cried out upon as a headstrong "foolish person: The Herr Graf von Werthern, so ran the "story, had of his own kindness, without request of mine, "offered me a living; *rara avis*, singular instance; and I, "rash and without head, flung away such gracious offer. In "short, I was told to my face" (by good-natured friends), "Nobody would ever think of me for promotion again;" — universal suffrage giving it clear against poor Linsenbarth, in this way.

"To get out of people's sight at least," continues he, "I "decided to leave my native place, and go to Berlin," 250 miles away or more. "And so it was that, on June the 20th, "1750, I landed at Berlin for the first time: and here straightway at the *Packhof* (or Customhouse), in searching of my "things, 400 *thalers* (some 60*l*.), all in Nürnberg *batzen*, were "seized from me;" — *batzen*, quarter groats we may say;

7½ batzen go to a shilling; what a sack there must have been of them, 9,000 in all, about the size of herring-scales, in bad silver; fruit of Linsenbarth's stern thrift from birth upwards: —all snatched from him at one swoop. "And why?" says he, quite historically: Yes, Why? The reader, to understand it wholly, would need to read in Mylius's *Edicten-Sammlung*, in *Seyfarth* and elsewhere;* and to know the scandalous condition of German coinage at this time and long after; every needy little Potentate mixing his coin with copper at discretion, and swindling mankind with it for a season; needing to be peremptorily forbidden, confiscated, or ordered home, by the like of Friedrich. Linsenbarth answers his own "And why?" with historical calmness:

"The King had, some (six) years ago, had the batzen "utterly cried down (*ganz undgar*); they were not to circulate "at all in his Countries; and I was so bold, I had brought "batzen hither into the King's Capital, *Königliche Residenz* "itself! At the Packhof, there was but one answer, 'Contra-"'band, Contraband!'" — Here was a welcome for a man. "I made my excuses: Did not the least know; came straight "from Thüringen, many miles of road; could not guess there "What His Majesty the King had been pleased to forbid in "His (*Theiro*) Countries. 'You should have informed yourself,' "said the Packhof people; and were deaf to such considera-"tions. 'A man coming into such a Residenz Town as Berlin, "'with intent to abide there, should have inquired a little "'what was what, especially what coins were cried down, "'and what allowed,' said they of the Packhof." Poor Linsenbarth! "'But what am I to do now? How am I to live, if "'you take my very money from me?' 'That is your outlook,' "said they; — and added, He must even find stowage for his "sack of herring-scales or batzen, so soon as it was sealed up; "'we have no room for it in the Packhof!' Here is a roughish welcome for a man: "I must leave all my money here; and "find stowage for it, in a day or two.

"There was, accordingly, a truck-porter called in; he "loaded my effects on his barrow, and rolled away. He "brought me to the *White Swan* in the *Judenstrasse*" (none of the grandest of streets, that Berlin *Jewry*), "threw my things "out, and demanded four groschen. Two of my batzen,"

* Mylius, *Edict* XLI., January 1744; &c. &c.

2½ exact, "would have done; but I had no money at all. The "landlord came out: seeing that I had a stuffed featherbed" (note the luggage of Linsenbarth: "*Feder-bett*," of extreme tenuity), "a trunk full of linens, a bag of Books and other "trifles, he paid the man; and sent me to a small room in the "courtyard" (Inn forms a Court, perhaps four stories high): "'I could stay there,' he said; 'he would give me food and "'drink in the mean while.' And so I lived in this Inn eight "weeks long, without one red farthing, in mere fear and "anxiety." June 20th *plus* eight weeks brings us to August 15th; Voltaire in *height* of feather; and very great things just ahead! * — of which soon.

The White Swan was a place where Carriers lodged: some limb of the Law, of subaltern sort, whom Linsenbarth calls "*der Advocat B.*" (one of the Ousted of Cocceji, shall we fancy!), had to do with Carriers and their pie-powder law-suits. Advocat B. had noticed the gray dreary *Candidatus*, sitting sparrow-like in remote corners; had spoken to him; — undertook for a *Louis d'or*, no purchase no pay, to get back his batzen for him. They went accordingly, one morning, to "a grand House;" it was a Minister's (name not given), very grand Official Man: he heard the Advocat B.'s short statement; and made answer: "Monsieur, and is it you that will "pick holes in the King's Law? I have understood you were "rather aiming at the *Hausvogtei*" (Common Jail of Berlin): "Go on in that way, and you are sure of your promotion!" — Advocat B. rushed out with Linsenbarth, into the street; and there was neither pay nor purchase in that quarter.

Poor Linsenbarth was next advised, by simple neighbours, to go direct to the King; as every poor man can, at certain hours of the day. "Write out your Case (Memorial) with "extreme brevity," said they; "nothing but the essential "points, and those clear." Linsenbarth, steam at the high pressure, composed *(conzipirte)* a Memorial of that right laconic sort; wrote it fair *(mundirte es)*; — and went off therewith "at opening of the Gates" (middle time of August 1750, no date farther) ** — "without one farthing in my pocket, in "God's name, to Potsdam." He continues:

* "Grand Carrousel, 25th August;" &c.

** August 21st? (See Rödenbeck, *Diary*, which we often quote, i. 205.)

"And at Potsdam I was lucky enough to see the King; my "first sight of him. He was on the Palace Esplanade there, "drilling his troops" (fine trim sanded Expanse, with the Palace to rear, and Garden-walks and River to front; where Friedrich Wilhelm sat, the last day he was out, and ordered Jockey Philips's house to be actually set about; where the troops do evolutions every morning; — there is Friedrich with cocked hat and blue coat; say about 11 A.M.).

"When the drill was over, his Majesty went into the "Garden, and the soldiers dispersed; only four Officers re-"mained lounging upon the Esplanade, and walked up and "down. For fright I knew not what to do; I pulled the Papers "out of my pocket, — these were my Memorial, two Certi-"ficates of character, and a Thüringen Pass" (poor soul). "The Officers noticed this; came straight to me, and said, "'What Letters has He there, then?' I thankfully and "gladly imparted the whole; and when the Officers had read "them, they said, 'We will give you' (Him, not even *Thee*) "'a good advice. The King is extra-gracious today, and is "'gone alone into the Garden. Follow him straight. Thou "'wilt have luck.'

"This I would not do; my awe was too great. They there-"upon laid hands on me" (the mischievous dogs, not ill-humoured either): "one took me by the right arm, another "by the left, 'Off, off; to the Garden!' Having got me "thither, they looked out for the King. He was among the "gardeners, examining some rare plant; stooping over it, "and had his back to us. Here I had to halt; and the Officers "began, in underhand tone" (the dogs!), "to put me through "my drill: 'Hat under left arm! — Right foot foremost! — "'Breast well forward! — Head up! — Papers from Pouch! — "'Papers aloft in right hand! — Steady! Steady!' — And "went their ways, looking always round, to see if I kept my "posture. I perceived well enough they were pleased to "make game of me; but I stood, all the same, like a wall, "being full of fear. The Officers were hardly out of the "Garden, when the King turned round, and saw this extra-"ordinary machine," — telegraph figure or whatever we may call it, with papers pointing to the sky. "He gave such a "look at me, like a flash of sunbeams glancing through you; "and sent one of the gardeners to bring my papers. Which "having got, he struck into another walk with them, and "was out of sight. In few minutes he appeared again at the "place where the rare plant was, with my Papers open in his "left hand; and gave me a wave with them To come nearer. "I plucked up a heart, and went straight towards him. Oh, "how thrice and four-times graciously this great Monarch "deigned to speak to me! —

King. "My good Thuringian *(lieber Thüringer)*, you came "to Berlin, seeking to earn your bread by industrious teach-"ing of children; and here, at the Packhof, in searching "your things, they have taken your Thüringen hoard from "you. True, the batzen are not legal here; but the people "should have said to you: You are a stranger, and didn't "know the prohibition; — well then, we will seal up the Bag "of Batzen; you send it back to Thüringen, get it changed "for other sorts; we will not take it from you! —

"Be of heart, however, you shall have your money again, "and interest too. — But, my poor man, Berlin pavement is "bare, they don't give anything gratis: you are a stranger; "before you are known and get teaching, your bit of money "is done; what then?"

"I understood the speech right well; but my awe was too "great to say: 'Your Majesty will have the all-highest grace "'to allow me something!' But as I was so simple and asked "for nothing, he did not offer anything. And so he turned "away; but had scarcely gone six or eight steps, when he "looked round, and gave me a sign I was to walk by him; "and then began catechising:

King. "Where did you *(Er)* study?"

Linsenbarth. "Your Majesty, in Jena."

King. "What years?"

Linsenbarth. "From 1716 to 1720." *

King. "Under what Pro-rector were you inscribed?"

Linsenbarth. "Under the *Professor Theologiæ* Dr. Förtsch."

King. "Who were your other Professors in the Theological Faculty?"

Linsenbarth — names famed men; sunk now, mostly, in the bottomless waste-basket: "Buddäus" (who did a *Dictionary* of the *Bayle* sort, weighing four stone troy, out of which I have learned many a thing), "Buddæus," "Danz," "Weis-

* Born 1689 (p. 474); twenty-five when he went.

senborn," "Wolf" (now back at Halle after his tribulations, — poor man, his immortal System of Philosophy, where is it!)

King. "Did you study *Biblica* diligently?"

Linsenbarth. "With Buddæus (*beym Buddäo*)."

King. "That is he who had such quarrelling with Wolf?"

Linsenbarth. "Yea, your Majesty! He was —"

King (does not want to know what he was). "What other "useful Courses of Lectures (*Collegia*) did you attend?"

Linsenbarth. "Thetics and Exegetics with Förtsch" (How the deuce did Förtsch teach these things?); "Hermeneutics "and Polemics with Walch" (editor of *Luther's Works*, I suppose); "Hebraics with Dr. Danz; Homiletics with Dr. Weissen-"born; *Pastorale* (not Pastoral Poetry, but the Art of Pastor-"ship) and *Morale* with Dr. Buddæus." (There, your Majesty! — what a glimpse, as into infinite extinct Continents, filled with ponderous thorny inanities, invincible nasal drawling of didactic Titans, and the awful attempt to spin, on all manner of wheels, road-harness out of split cobwebs: Hoom! Hoom-m-m! Harness not to be had on those terms. Let the dreary Limbus close again, till the general Day of Judgment for all this.)

King (glad to get out of the Limbus). "Were things "as wild then at Jena, in your time, as of old, when the "Students were forever scuffling and ruffling, and the Coup-"let went:

> "*Wer kommt von Jena ungeschlagen,*
> "*Der had von grossem Glück zu sagen.*
>
> "He that comes from Jena *sine bello*,
> "He may think himself a lucky fellow?"

Linsenbarth. "That sort of folly is gone quite out of "fashion; and a man can lead a silent and quiet life there, "just as at other Universities, if he will attend to the *Dic, cur* "*hic?*" (or know what his real errand is). "In my time their "Serene Highnesses, the Nursing-fathers of the University "(*Nutritores Academiæ*), — of the Ernestine Line" (Weimar-Gotha Highnesses, that is), "were in the habit of having the "Rufflers (*Renomisten*), Renowners as they are called, who "made so much disturbance, sent to Eisenach to lie in the "Wartburg a while; there they learned to be quiet." (Clock strikes Twelve, — dinner-time of Majesty.)

King. "Now I must go: they are waiting for their soup" (and so ends Dialogue for the present). Did the King bid me wait?

"When we got out of the Garden," says Linsenbarth, silent on this point, "the four Officers were still there upon "the Esplanade" (Captains of Guard belike); "they went "into the Palace with the King," — clearly meaning to dine with his Majesty.

"I remained standing on the Esplanade. For twenty-"seven hours I had not tasted food: not a farthing *in bonis*" (of principal or interest) "to get bread with; I had waded "twenty miles hither, in a sultry morning, through the sand. "Not a difficult thing to keep down laughter in such circum-"stances!" — Poor soul; but the Royal mind is human too. — "In this tremor of my heart, there came a *Kammer-hussar*" (Soldier-Valet, Valet reduced to his simplest expression) "out of the Palace, and asked, 'Where is the man that was "'with my King' (*meinem König*, — *thy* King particularly?) "'in the Garden?' I answered. 'Here!' And he led me "into the Schloss, to a large Room, where pages, lakeys, and "Kammer-hussars were about. My Kammer-hussar took me "to a little table, excellently furnished; with soup, beef; "likewise carp dressed with garden-salad, likewise game "with cucumber-salad: bread, knife, fork, spoon, and salt "were all there" (and I with an appetite of twenty-seven hours; I too was there). "My hussar set me a chair, said: "'This that is on the table, the King has ordered to be served "'for you (*Ihm*): you are to eat your fill, and mind nobody; "'and I am to serve. Sharp, then, fall to!' — I was greatly "astonished, and knew not what to do; least of all could it "come into my head that the King's Kammer-hussar, who "waited on his Majesty, should wait on me. I pressed him to "sit by me; but as he refused, I did as bidden; sat down, "took my spoon, and went at it with a will (*frisch*)!

"The hussar took the beef from the table, set it on the "charcoal dish (to keep it hot till wanted); he did the like "with the fish, and roast game; and poured me out wine and "beer" — (was ever such a lucky Barmecide)? "I ate and "drank till I had abundantly enough. Dessert, confectionery, "what I could, — a plateful of big black cherries, and a "plateful of pears, my waiting man wrapped in paper, and "stuffed them into my pockets, to be a refreshment on the "way home. And so I rose from the Royal table; and "thanked God and the King in my heart, that I had so "gloriously dined," — *herrlich* "gloriously" at last. Poor excellent downtrodden Linsenbarth, one's heart opens to him, not one's larder only.

"The hussar took away. At that moment a Secretary "came; brought me a sealed Order (Rescript) to the Packhof "at Berlin, with my Certificates (*Testimonia*), and the Pass; "told down on the table five Tail-ducats (*Schwanz-dukaten*), "and a Gold Friedrich under them" (about 3*l.* 10*s.*, I think; better than 10*l.* of our day to a common man, and better than 100*l.* to a Linsenbarth), — "saying, The King sent me this to "take me home to Berlin again.

"And if the hussar took me into the Palace, it was now "the Secretary that took me out again. And there, yoked "with six horses, stood a royal Proviant-wagon; which having "led me to, the Secretary said: 'You people, the King has "'given order you are to take this stranger to Berlin, and "'also to accept no drink-money from him.' I again, through "the *Herrn Secretarium*, testified my most submissive thank-"fulness for all Royal graciousnesses; took my place, and "rolled away.

"On reaching Berlin, I went at once to the Packhof, "straight to the office-room," — standing more erect this time, — "and handed them my Royal Rescript. The Head "man opened the seal; in reading, he changed colour, went "from pale to red; said nothing, and gave it to the second "man to read. The second put on his spectacles; read, and "gave it to the third. However, he" (the Head man) "rallied "himself at last: I was to come forward, and be so good as "write a quittance (receipt), 'That I had received, for my "'400 thalers all in batzen, the same sum in Brandenburg coin, "'ready down, without the least deduction.' My cash was at "once accurately paid. And thereupon the Steward was "ordered, To go with me to the White Swan in the Jūden-"strasse, and pay what I owed there, whatever my score was. "For which end they gave him twenty-four thalers; and if "that were not enough, he was to come and get more." On these high terms Linsenbarth marched out of the Packhof for the second time; the sublime head of him (not turned either) sweeping the very stars.

"That was what the King had meant when he said, 'You "'shall have your money back and interest too;' *videlicet* "that the Packhof was to pay my expenses at the White "Swan. The score, however, was only 10 thaler, 4 groschen, "6 pfennigs" (30 shillings, 5 pence, and 2 or perhaps 3 quarter-farthings), "for what I had run up in eight weeks," — an uncommonly frugal rate of board, for a man skilled in Hermeneutics, Hebraics, Polemics, Thetics, Exegetics, Pastorale, Morale (and Practical Christianity and the Philosophy of Zeno, carried to perfection, or nearly so)! "And herewith "this troubled History had its desired finish." And our gray-whiskered, raw-boned, great-hearted Candidatus lay down to sleep, at the White Swan; probably the happiest man in all Berlin, for the time being.

Linsenbarth dived now into Private-teaching, "*Information*," as he calls it; *forming*, and kneading into his own likeness, such of the young Berliners as he could get hold of: — surely not without some good effect on them, the model having, besides Hermeneutics in abundance, so much natural worth about it. He himself found the mine of Informing a very barren one, as to money: continued poor in a high degree, without honour, without emolument to speak of; and had a straitened, laborious, and what we might think very dark Life-pilgrimage. But the darkness was nothing to him, he carried such an inextinguishable frugal rushlight within. Meat, clothes, and fire, he did not again lack, in Berlin, for the time he needed them, — some twenty-seven years still. And if he got no printed praise in the Reviews, from baddish judges writing by the sheet, — here and there brother mortals, who knew him by their own eyes and experiences, looked, or transiently spoke, and even did, a most real praise upon him now and then. And, on the whole, he can do without praise; and will stand strokes even, without wincing or kicking, where there is no chance.

A certain Berlin Druggist ("Herr Medicinal-Assessor Rose," whom we may call Druggist First, for there were Two that had to do with Linsenbarth) was good and human to him. In Rose's House, where he had come to teach the children, and which continued, always thenceforth, a home to him when needful, he wrote this *Narrative* (Anno 1774); and died there, three years afterwards, — "24th August 1777, of apoplexy, "age 88," say the Burial Registers.* Druggist Second, on succeeding the humane Predecessor, found Linsenbarth's papers in the drug-stores of the place: Druggist Second chanced to be one Klaproth, famed among the Scientific of the world; and by him the Linsenbarth Narrative was forwarded to publication, and such fame as is requisite.

Sir Jonas Hanway stalks across the Scene, too; in a pondering and observing Manner.

Of the then very famous "Berlin Carrousel of 1750" we propose to say little; the now chief interesting point in it being that M. de Voltaire is curiously visible to us there. But the truth is, they were very great days at Berlin, those of Autumn 1750; distinguished strangers come or coming; the King giving himself up to entertainment of them, to enjoyment of them; with such a hearty outburst of magnificence, this Carrousel the apex of it, as was rare in his reign. There were his Sisters of Schwedt and Baireuth, with suite, his dear Wilhelmina* queen of the scene;** there were — It would be tedious to count what other high Herrschaften and Durchlauchtig Persons. And to crown the whole, and entertain Wilhelmina as a Queen should be, there had come M. de Voltaire; conquered at length to us, as we hope, and the Dream of our Youth realised. Voltaire's reception, July 10th and ever since, has

* In Rödenbeck, *Beyträge*, i. 472-475, these latter Details (with others, in confused form); *ib.* 462-471, the *Narrative* itself.

** "Came, 8th August" (Rödenbeck, 205.)

been more splendour and kindness; really extraordinary, as we shall find farther on. Reception perfect in all points, except that of the Pompadour's Compliments alone. "That sublime creature's compliments to your Majesty; such her express command!" said Voltaire. "*Je ne la connais pas*," answered Friedrich, with his clear-ringing voice, "I don't know her;"* — sufficient intimation to Voltaire, but painful and surprising. For which some diplomatic persons blame Friedrich to this day; but not I, or any reader of mine. A very proud young King; in his silent way, always the prouder! and stands in no awe of the Divine Butterflies and Crowned Infatuations never so potent, as more prudent people do.

In a Berlin of such stir and splendour, the arrivals of Sir Jonas Hanway, of the "young Lord Malton" (famed Earl or Marquis of Rockingham that will be), or of the witty Excellency Hanbury, are as nothing; — Sir Jonas's as less than nothing. A Sir Jonas noticed by nobody; but himself taking note, dull worthy man; and mentionable now on that account. Here is a Scrap regarding him, not quite to be thrown away:

"Sir Jonas Hanway was not always so extinct as he has "now become. Readers might do worse than turn to his now "old Book of *Travels* again, and the strange old London it "awakens for us: A 'Russian Trading Company,' full of hope "to the then mercantile mind; a Mr. Hanway despatched,

* Voltaire to Madame Denis, "Potsdam, 11th August 1750" (*Œuvres*, LXXIV. 184).

"years ago, as Chief Clerk, inexpressibly interested to "manage well; — and managing, as you may read at large. "Has done his best and utmost, all this while; and had such "travellings through the Naphtha Countries, sailings on the "Caspian; such difficulties, successes, — ultimately, failure. "Owing to Mr. Elton and Thamas Kouli Khan mainly. "Thamas Kouli Khan, — otherwise called Nadir Shah (and a "very hard-headed fellow, by all appearance), — wiled and "seduced Mr. Elton, an Ex-Naval gentleman, away from his "Ledgers, to build him Ships; having set his heart on getting "a Navy. And Mr. Elton did build him (spite of all I could "say) a Bark or two on the Caspian; — most hopeful to the "said Nadir Shah: but did it come to anything? It disgusted, "it alarmed the Russians; and ruined Sir Jonas, — who is re-"turning at this period, prepared to render account of him-"self at London, in a loftily resigned frame of mind.*

"The remarks of Sir Jonas upon Berlin, — for he exercises "everywhere a sapient observation, on men and things, — "are of dim tumidly insignificant character, reminding us of "an extinct Minerva's Owl; and reduce themselves mainly to "this bit of ocular testimony, That his Prussian Majesty rides "much about, often at a rapid rate; with a pleasant business "aspect, humane though imperative; handsome to look upon, "though with face perceptibly reddish" (and perhaps snuff on it, were you near). "His age now thirty-eight gone; a set "appearance, as if already got into his forties. Complexion "florid, figure muscular, almost tending to be plump.

"Listen well through Hanway, you will find King Fried-"rich is an object of great interest, personal as well as official, "and much the theme in Berlin society; admiration of him, "pride in him, not now the audiblest tone, though it lies at "the bottom too: 'Our Friedrich the Great' after all" (so Hanway intimates, though not express as to epithets or words used.) "The King did a beautiful thing to Lieutenant-"Colonel Keith the other day" (as some readers may re-

* Jonas Hanway, *An Account of &c.* (or in brief, *Travels*: London, 8 voll. 4to, 1753), ii. 183. "Arrived in Berlin from the Caspian and Petersburg side, "August 15th, 1750."

member): "to Lieutenant-Colonel Keith; that poor Keith "who was nailed to the gallows for him (in effigy), at Wesel "long ago; and got far less than he had expected. The other "day, there had been a grand Review, part of it extending "into Madame Knyphausen's ground, who is Keith's Mother-"in-law. 'Monsieur Keith,' said the King to him, 'I am sorry "'we had to spoil Madame's fine Shrubbery by our ma-"'nœuvres: have the goodness to give her that, with my "'apologies,' — and handed him a pretty Casket with key to "it, and in the interior 10,000 crowns. Not a shrub of Ma-"dame's had been cut or injured; but the King, you see, "would count it 1,500*l*. of damage done, and here is acknow-"ledgment for it, which please accept. Is not that a gracious "little touch?

"This King is doing something at Embden, Sir Jonas "fears, or trying to do, in the Trade-and-Navigation way: "scandalous that English capitalists will lend money in "furtherance of such destructive schemes by the Foreigner! "For the rest, Sir Jonas went to call on Lord Malton (Mar-"quis of Rockingham that will be): an amiable and sober "young Nobleman, come thus far on his Grand Tour," and in time for the Carrousel. "His Lordship's reception at Court "here, one regretted to hear, was nothing distinguished; quite "indifferent, indeed, had not the Queen-Mother stept in with "amendments. The Courts are not well together; pity for "it. My Lord and his Tutor did me the honour to return my "visit; the rather as we all quartered in the same Inn. "Amiable young Nobleman," — so distinguished since, for having had unconsciously an Edmund Burke, and such torrents of Parliamentary Eloquence, in his breeches-pocket (*breeches-pocket* literally; how unknown to Hanway!) — "Amiable young Nobleman, is not it one's duty to salute, in "passing such a one? Though I would by no means have it "over-done, and am a calmly independent man.

"Sir Jonas also saw the Carrousel" (of which presently); "and admired the great men of Berlin. Great men, all ob-"solete now, though then admired to infinitude, some of them: "'You may abuse me,' said the King to some stranger arrived "in Berlin; 'you may abuse me, and perhaps here and there "'get praise by doing it: but I advise you not to doubt of

"'Lieberkühn' (the fashionable Doctor) 'in any company in "'Berlin.'"* — How fashionable are men!

One Collini, a young Italian, quite new in Berlin, chanced also to be at the Carrousel, or at the latter half of it, — though by no means in quest of such objects just at present, poor young fellow! As he came afterwards to be Secretary or Amanuensis of Voltaire, and will turn up in that capacity, let us read this Note upon him:

"Signor Como Alessandro Collini, a young Venetian gen-"tleman of some family and education, but of no employment "or resource, had in late years been asking zealously all "round among his home circle, What am I to do with myself? "mere echo answering, What, — till a Signora Sister of "Barberina the Dancer's answered: 'Try Berlin, and King "'*Friderico il Grande* there? I could give you a letter to my "'Sister!' At which Collini grasps; gets under way for "Berlin, — through wild Alpine sceneries, foreign guttural "populations; and with what thoughts, poor young fellow. "It is a common course to take, and sometimes answers, "sometimes not. The cynosure of vague creatures, with a "sense of faculty without direction. What clouds of winged "migratory people gathering in to Berlin, all through this "Reign! Not since Noah's Ark a stranger menagerie of "creatures, mostly wild. Of whom Voltaire alone is, in our "time, worth mention.

"Collini gazed upon the Alpine chasms, and shaggy ice-"palaces, with tender memory of the Adriatic; courageously "steered his way through the inoffensive guttural popula-"tions; had got to Berlin, just in this time; been had to "dinner daily by the hospitable Barberinas, young Cocceji "always his fellow-guest, — 'Privately, my poor Signorina's "Husband!' whispered old Mamma. Both the Barberinas "were very kind to Collini; cheering him with good auguries, "and offers of help. Collini does not date with any punc-

* *Hanway*, II. 190, 202, &c.

"tuality; but the German Books will do it for him. August "25th-27th, was Carrousel; and Collini had arrived few days "before."*

And now it is time we were at the Carrousel ourselves, — in a brief transient way.

* Collini, *Mon Séjour auprès de Voltaire* (Paris, 1807), pp. 1-21.

END OF VOL. VIII.

PRINTING OFFICE OF THE PUBLISHERS.

www.ingramcontent.com/pod-product-compliance
Lightning Source LLC
Chambersburg PA
CBHW021115270326
41929CB00009B/898

* 9 7 8 3 7 4 1 1 6 1 4 2 1 *